The Common European Framework of Reference

MIX
Paper from responsible sources
FSC
www.fsc.org
FSC® C018575

LANGUAGES FOR INTERCULTURAL COMMUNICATION AND EDUCATION

Series Editors: Michael Byram, *University of Durham, UK* and Alison Phipps, *University of Glasgow, UK*

The overall aim of this series is to publish books which will ultimately inform learning and teaching, but whose primary focus is on the analysis of intercultural relationships, whether in textual form or in people's experience. There will also be books which deal directly with pedagogy, with the relationships between language learning and cultural learning, between processes inside the classroom and beyond. They will all have in common a concern with the relationship between language and culture, and the development of intercultural communicative competence.

Full details of all the books in this series and of all our other publications can be found on http://www.multilingual-matters.com, or by writing to Multilingual Matters, St Nicholas House, 31-34 High Street, Bristol BS1 2AW, UK.

The Common European Framework of Reference

The Globalisation of Language Education Policy

Edited by

Michael Byram and Lynne Parmenter

MULTILINGUAL MATTERS
Bristol • Buffalo • Toronto

Library of Congress Cataloging in Publication Data
A catalog record for this book is available from the Library of Congress.
The Common European Framework of Reference: The Globalisation of Language Education Policy/Edited by Michael Byram and Lynne Parmenter.
Includes bibliographical references.
1. Language policy--Europe. 2. Language and languages--Study and teaching.
3. Language and languages--Globalization. I. Byram, Michael. II. Parmenter, Lynne.
P119.32.E85C66 2012
306.44'94–dc23 2012009129

British Library Cataloguing in Publication Data
A catalogue entry for this book is available from the British Library.

ISBN-13: 978-1-84769-730-1 (hbk)
ISBN-13: 978-1-84769-729-5 (pbk)

Multilingual Matters
UK: St Nicholas House, 31-34 High Street, Bristol BS1 2AW, UK.
USA: UTP, 2250 Military Road, Tonawanda, NY 14150, USA.
Canada: UTP, 5201 Dufferin Street, North York, Ontario M3H 5T8, Canada.

The policy of Multilingual Matters/Channel View Publications is to use papers that are natural, renewable and recyclable products, made from wood grown in sustainable forests. In the manufacturing process of our books, and to further support our policy, preference is given to printers that have FSC and PEFC Chain of Custody certification. The FSC and/or PEFC logos will appear on those books where full certification has been granted to the printer concerned.

Typeset by The Charlesworth Group.
Printed and bound in Great Britain by the MPG Books Group.

Contents

Series Editor's Preface ix

Introduction
Michael Byram and Lynne Parmenter 1

The Common European Framework of Reference: Learning, Teaching, Assessment
The author 13

1 The Common European Framework of Reference for Languages and its Background: A Case Study of Cultural Politics and Educational Influences
John L.M. Trim 14

Part 1: The *CEFR* in Europe

France
The authors 36

2 Policy Perspectives from France
Francis Goullier 37

3 Academic Perspectives from France
Véronique Castellotti 45

Germany
The authors 53

4 Policy Perspectives from Germany
Henny Rönneper 54

5 Academic Perspectives from Germany
Adelheid Hu 66

Bulgaria
The authors 76

6 Policy Perspectives from Bulgaria
Maria Stoicheva 77

7 Academic Perspectives from Bulgaria
Maria Stoicheva and Pavlina Stefanova 86

Poland
The authors 96

8 Policy Perspectives from Poland
Pawel Poszytek 97

9 Academic Perspectives from Poland
Hanna Komorowska 104

Commentary on the European Cases
Michael Byram and Lynne Parmenter 114

Part 2: The *CEFR* beyond Europe

America

Argentina
The authors 118

10 Policy Perspectives from Argentina
Melina Porto and Silvana Barboni 119

11 Academic Perspectives from Argentina
Melina Porto 129

Colombia
The authors 139

12 Policy Perspectives from Colombia
Beatriz Peña Dix and Anne-Marie de Mejía 140

13 Academic Perspectives from Colombia
Anne-Marie de Mejía 149

USA
The authors 158

14 Policy Perspectives from the USA
Jacqueline Bott van Houten 159

15 Academic Perspectives from the USA
Heidi Byrnes 169

Asia-Pacific

China
The author 182

16 Perspectives from China
Zou Weicheng 183

Japan
The authors 197

17 Perspectives from Japan
Masako Sugitani and Yuichi Tomita 198

Taiwan
The authors 212

18 Policy Perspectives from Taiwan
Jessica Wu 213

19 Academic Perspectives from Taiwan
Hintat Cheung 224

New Zealand
The authors 231

20 Policy Perspectives from New Zealand
Glenda Koefoed 233

21 Academic Perspectives from New Zealand
Adèle Scott and Martin East 248

Commentary on Cases beyond Europe
Lynne Parmenter and Michael Byram 258

Conclusion
Lynne Parmenter and Michael Byram 262

A note on the publication of the CEFR

A draft of the *CEFR* was widely circulated by the Council of Europe from 1996 (*Common European Framework for Language Teaching and Learning*) with requests for comments. Some authors of chapters in this book refer to this action and to the fact that the ideas of the *CEFR* were already known before publication. Publication in the two official languages of the Council of Europe, French and English, took place in 2001 in cooperation with the publishing houses Didier and Cambridge University Press.

Reference to the *CEFR*.
All contributors refer to one of the versions of the *CEFR* as below:

Council of Europe (2001) *Common European Framework of Reference for Languages: Learning, teaching, assessment.* Cambridge: Cambridge University Press.

Conseil de l'Europe (2001) *Cadre européen commun de référence pour les langues: apprendre, enseigner, évaluer.* Paris: Didier.

Europarat (2001) *Gemeinsamer europäischer Referenzrahmen für Sprachen: lernen, lehren, beurteilen*. Published by: Goethe Institut Inter Nationes, ständige Konferenz der Kultusminister der Länder der Bundesrepublik Deutschland (KMK), Schweizerische Konferenz der Kantonalen Erziehungsdirektoren (EDK) and österreichisches Bundesministerium für Bildung, Wissenschaft und Kultur (BMBWK). Berlin *et al.*: Langenscheidt.

Series Editor's Preface

2001 marked the publication of *Common European Framework of Reference for Languages: Learning, teaching, assessment* (CEFR). It also marked the publication of the first of the publications in this Multilingual Matters book series Languages, Intercultural Communication and Education. The book, fittingly, was edited by Michael Byram, Adam Nichols and David Stevens and entitled *Developing Intercultural Competence in Practice*. A decade on from the publication of the CEFR many publications in this series have engaged with the Framework and many authors have reflected on its place in their practice as well as its role in creating national policy norms. It is therefore fitting that this book brings together some of those authors and others from around the world to reflect critically and comparatively on the impact of the CEFR at a global level.

The book contains twin concerns; firstly to be relevant to practitioners both in the classroom and at policy level and secondly to enable a comparative understanding of the influence of the CEFR worldwide. The book begins by assessing the different and varying ways in which the CEFR has been used within Europe and also in the new accession states. Europe itself has undergone an expansion during the last decade so the assessments in the first section of this volume allow for comparison between member states in 2001 (Germany; France) and those who joined the European Union after the publication of the Framework (Poland: 2004; Bulgaria: 2007). The second half of the volume turns its attention to case studies and national policies in the Americas and in Asia-Pacific. Critics may suggest that these reflections the CEFR beyond Europe are not comprehensive and do not include, for example, African or Middle Eastern states. However, this is a direct result of the research which produced the structure of the volume, where those contacted could not identify a policy impact of the CEFR in Africa or the Middle East. Consequently, the editors have given considerable thought to the design of this comparative study and opted to draw on contexts where there is strong evidence of impact and policy work which is directly relevant. A sister volume to this one which focuses on the ways in which language polices develop in contexts of international development would be welcome at a later date. How and where policy resonates and the kinds of policy infrastructures which enable a global policy to reach into certain areas is clearly an important question, which the editors address in their opening chapter.

The richness of the contributions in this volume, together with their reach, demonstrate the extent of the development of a globally orientated policy on language education and the normative place the CEFR has attained in its first ten years of existence. Interrogating the conditions, worldwide and locally, which have enabled this to occur and the kinds of dispositions teachers and policy makers have developed to accommodate the recommendations of the CEFR is a serious task. The scholarship in the book demonstrates the pitfalls and problems which policy and its interpretation encounters in a global context and the extent to which the Framework is re-made, culturally, and in policy terms, in each different teaching and learning context.

Consequently this book is an exhilarating read, documenting the process of globalisation and policy reach in a technological, performative educational age. It does not shirk the difficult questions or the perplexing issues which are thrown up through policy implementation, and the comparative dimension and structure of the book allow the reader to dip into and make the comparisons which are of immediate interest or relevance to themselves. Linked to earlier publications by the authors collected here, and to their contributions to this series this volume marks a watershed in scholarship on the CEFR and a definite contribution to the ongoing work to develop comparative education in policy and on language education.

Alison Phipps
Series Editor

Introduction

Michael Byram and Lynne Parmenter

The purpose of this book is twofold: to focus upon the *Common European Framework of Reference for Languages: Learning, teaching, assessment* (*CEFR*) because of its significance for language teaching and learning, and to see the *CEFR* as an example of what is now frequently referred to as the globalisation of education policy. We therefore believe that the book will be of interest to at least two broad groups of readers: those from the world of language education, and those who are interested in comparative education and the processes of what is usually referred to as 'borrowing and lending' (e.g. Steiner-Khamsi, 2004) among states and their education systems.

The *CEFR* is widely known among language teaching professionals, as will quickly become apparent from a glance at the list of contents of this book, which is only a selection of the countries from which we could have invited contributions both in Europe and beyond. There have in fact been some surveys of influence and use of the *CEFR* by the Council of Europe. The most recent survey with returns from 30 out of 47 member states was carried out in 2006 on 'The use of the *CEFR* at national level in Member States of the Council of Europe', and summarised by Martyniuk and Noijons for the intergovernmental Policy Forum of February 2007. Their summary included the following conclusions:

> In general, the *CEFR* seems to have a major impact on language education. It is used – often as the exclusive neutral reference – in all educational sectors. Its value as a reference tool to coordinate the objectives of education at all levels is widely appreciated. ... In some countries the *CEFR* has helped to develop both strategic language policy documents and practical teaching materials. In others, it is becoming the most reliable reference for curriculum planning. ... On the other hand, some respondents view the *CEFR*'s impact as quite modest so far. They point out that it does not yet play an important role for the teaching profession at the school level, although it has undeniably contributed to more transparency and coherence in general. (2007: 7)

This kind of questionnaire survey is a useful and necessary starting point, but it is one which we think needs to be enhanced by case studies that reveal the process as much as the effect. Some cases can be found in accounts from a number of countries in the proceedings of a conference in France (Le Cadre européen, une référence mondiale?, 2007) and in an article about Japan (Nishiyama, 2009). The present book will complement and enhance these because of its more systematic approach and wider range.

From the language teaching perspective, surveys and case studies help us to know what the impact of the *CEFR* is and how this varies, and what perhaps can be learnt from looking at other people's use of the *CEFR*. In this process, the heuristics of comparison is based on the intention of gaining more insight for ourselves by seeing what others do. It is also useful for the Council of Europe to know how its documents are being used.

The second, wider comparative perspective is also important. Comparative studies in all disciplines are well established and education is no exception, tracing its ancestry, in its modern form, to the 19th century. Within Comparative Education, the question of 'borrowing/lending' is a crucial one, and the *CEFR* offers a specific case of 'borrowing' that can be traced in considerable detail. It is also a case that has evolved within the period of globalisation of education policy in the last three decades. For as Ball *et al.* (2007: x) argue, education policy during the recent past can be understood as a political response to globalisation in its many forms, and thus the *CEFR* borrowing phenomenon has the potential to show how globalisation and education policy are related in a specific, detailed case. Indeed, as we shall see, the notion of bilateral 'borrowing' in its more traditional sense from one country to another has to be reconsidered.

On the other hand, the *CEFR* is not self-evidently a policy document. It presents itself from the very beginning as a 'common basis for the elaboration of language syllabuses, curriculum guidelines, examinations, textbooks, etc. across Europe' and a description of 'what language learners have to learn in order to use a language for communication and what knowledge and skills they have to develop so as to be able to act effectively'. If, from our comparative education perspective, we are to analyse the 'borrowing' of the *CEFR*, it is first necessary to clarify what is borrowed, and whether this is a case of 'policy-borrowing' or something else.

The *CEFR* and Policy

As Rizvi and Lingard (2010: 5) point out, definitions of 'policy' vary. They range from the inclusive description of policy as decision and action, as emphasised in Ball's inclusive statement that 'Policy is both text and action, words and deeds, it is what is enacted as well as what is intended', to definitions of policy, such as Easton's, which highlight the role of decision making: 'A policy ... consists of a web of decisions that allocates values' (Rizvi & Lingard, 2010: 7).

At first sight, the way the *CEFR* is written does not impose particular approaches and methods. In that sense the *CEFR* is not well described by definitions that emphasise policy as the stimulant to specific action. For throughout the text there are invitations to readers to consider the options and to make their own decisions: the formula is 'Users of the Framework may wish to consider and where appropriate state...' followed by a number of questions arising from the preceding text. This chimes with what Martyniuk and Noijons report in their 2007 survey cited above, namely that the *CEFR* 'is used – often as the exclusive neutral reference – in all educational sectors' (2007: 7). The emphasis is on 'reference' and this emphasis is reflected in the shift from '*CEF*' as the acronym to '*CEFR*', which took over in the first five to six years after its publication. Jones and Saville argue that such emphasis is entirely in agreement with the stated purposes, in contrast to which 'application' would be a more direct realisation of policy as action:

> people speak of *applying* the *CEFR* to some context, as a hammer gets applied to a nail. We should speak rather of *referring* a context *to* the *CEFR*. The transitivity is the other way round. The argument for an alignment is to be constructed, the basis of comparison to be established. (2009: 54)

For Jones and Saville, the *CEFR* is an 'instrument' of policy, which echoes the statement near the beginning of the *CEFR* itself (Section 1.2 on 'The aims and objectives of Council of Europe language policy') that it '*serves* the overall aim of the Council of Europe' (our emphasis).

However, and in contrast to first impressions, the phrase used by Martyniuk and Noijons also includes the word 'neutral' – 'the exclusive neutral reference' – which suggests that the people whose views they are summarising have not noted the 'allocation of values' quoted above by Rizvi and Lingard as a feature of a policy document. The *CEFR* embodies values, and this is what characterises policy as intention, text and action. Yet the value base of the *CEFR* is evident from the following statement on the opening page:

> In an intercultural approach, it is a central objective of language education to promote the favourable development of the learner's whole personality and sense of identity in response to the enriching experience of otherness in language and culture.

This might have come directly from a Humboldtian analysis of *Bildung* as the development of the individual, and in particular from Humboldt's views on language:

> By the same act whereby (man) spins language out of himself, he spins himself into it, and every language draws about the people that possess it a circle whence it is possible to exit only over at once into the circle of another one. To learn a foreign language should therefore be to acquire a new standpoint in the world-view hitherto possessed, and in fact to a certain extent is so, since every language contains the whole conceptual fabric and mode of presentation of a portion of mankind. (1836/1988: 60)

The *CEFR* continues with an emphasis on – and the 'allocation of value' to – the themes of the autonomy of learners, the significance of 'learning to learn' and the 'rich heritage of (linguistic) diversity' in Europe. These values are, furthermore, formulated explicitly in the Council of Europe's formal statement of policy in 2005, four years after the publication of the *CEFR*. They are on the first page of the website www.coe.int/lang and include the following:

> Plurilingualism: all are entitled to develop a degree of communicative ability in a number of languages over their lifetime in accordance with their needs
> Linguistic diversity: Europe is multilingual and *all its languages are equally valuable* modes of communication and expressions of identity; *the right to use and to learn* one's language(s) is protected in Council of Europe Conventions ...
> Social cohesion: equality of opportunity for *personal development*, education, employment, mobility, access to information and *cultural enrichment* depends on access to language learning throughout life. (Council of Europe, 2005: 4 – emphasis added)

The *CEFR* is clearly a policy document bearing values and intentions.

Yet, like any text, the intentions of its authors may not be read by its users, and the text may not be taken in entirety but only used in part for the purposes of the users. The text has indeed been reported as difficult to read, for example in the survey by Martyniuk and Noijons (2007: 7) and in a report of working with different groups of trainee teachers by Komorowska (2004). The difficulty is illustrated in a French collection of articles, intended mainly for teachers, by the presence of an introductory article that provides an explanation of the *CEFR* since there is said to be much confusion 'in the field'. The article is introduced as follows:

> Le Cadre européen commun de référence pour les langues, c'est un document de 375 pages dont Luc Collès, de l'université de Louvain en Belgique nous propose une lecture suivie. Cette synthèse nous a paru indispensable avant toute réflexion ou toute discussion des effets sur les pratiques des enseignants.
> (The *Common European Framework of Reference for Languages* is a document of 375 pages of which Luc Collès of the University of Louvain in Belgium provides us with a systematic reading. This synthesis seemed to us necessary before any reflection on or discussion of the effects on teachers' practices.)
> (Abdelgaber & Médioni, 2010: Chapter 1)

The editors also entitle one section of their collection as 'Perplexity in the field', which further reinforces the impression that teachers have difficulty with the text.

It became evident to authors and others at the Council of Europe that this was often the case. When people referred to 'the *CEFR*' they were often thinking only of the scales of proficiency, and this was not helped by academic debate about the validity and reliability of the scales, which turned attention from the rest of the *CEFR* (Fulcher, 2008). There was a fear that the technical use of the *CEFR* in processes of developing assessment systems was dominating its dissemination, and the purpose of a conference for representatives of member states of the Council of Europe in 2007 was to rectify imbalances in interpretation and use. The conference report argued that a more comprehensive analysis, enhanced by reports of practice – which may not otherwise be published and visible in the way that academic debate is – in fact showed a balanced usage:

> the discussions during the Forum, and even on its sidelines, a number of the statements made during the plenary sessions and the wide range of implementation examples described during the group work made it possible, in a very mutually-enhancing manner, to *clarify the status and the purpose of the CEFR - as a descriptive rather than a standard-setting document it allows all users to analyse their own situation and to make the choices which they deem most appropriate to their circumstances, while adhering to certain key values.*
> (Council of Europe, 2007: 7 – emphasis in original text)

Again it is worth noting here the phrase 'whilst adhering to certain key values' as an indicator of the *CEFR* as a value-bearing text – as a statement of policy – and it is as such a text that we propose to treat it in the following pages, and in our comments on its borrowing and reception in a number of countries within Europe and beyond.

Comparative Education Perspectives

The analysis of the effect of globalisation processes on education policy in general terms has been pursued increasingly in recent years (e.g. Ball *et al.*, 2007; Edwards & Usher, 2000; Steiner-Khamsi, 2004). The ways in which globalisation facilitates the movement of policy are variously described as 'borrowing', 'migration' or 'transfer' and Dale (2007) offers a typology of 'mechanisms of external effects on national policies'. Dale's discussion focuses on the question of whether globalisation has created a new phenomenon, different from what has usually been called 'borrowing' where the level of action is national and bilateral, with one country borrowing, imitating or copying from another. The novelty of the globalisation of policy lies in the fact that the locus is not bilateral and national but 'extra-national', that the power involved is indirect, that the initiative for change comes from outside the state, and that the scope includes not just policy goals but also processes (Dale, 2007: 76). There are characteristics of the *CEFR* and how it has been used which correspond, at least at first sight, to what Dale describes. Although the Council of Europe is an association of member states, the initiative for the *CEFR* came largely from within the Council and then led to recommendations to member states, and thus is an indirect power, as is emphasised in the *CEFR* itself in its explanation in the opening pages of the meaning of formal 'recommendations'. Here it refers to the concern to 'encourage, support and co-ordinate the efforts of member governments and nongovernmental institutions to improve language learning'. Furthermore, the *CEFR* and related documents deal not only with policy goals, but above all with processes of teaching, learning and assessment, as the sub-title makes clear. We shall be able to see through this book whether this first concern is upheld in practice, and particularly what kind of power or influence is present outside Europe where the recommendations have no particular status.

Whether we use the term 'borrowing' or some other term which reflects the characteristics just mentioned, it is insufficient simply to refer to globalisation and its processes if we are to understand the impact of a document such as the *CEFR* and what it stands for. It is common to talk of the immediacy of communication through the internet or of the mass of information on the web, but it is more important to ask who uses the opportunities that this technology provides. To describe the process,

Edwards and Usher (2000) use the metaphor of disease and a virus that may be spread through many channels. It is interesting that they first refer to reports and books and then to online postings. If written a decade later, they might have listed internet-based sources of information first, including list-serves and the currently powerful forces of Facebook and the like. The crucial feature here is the networks of which people have become more conscious; the term itself becoming far more frequent in the vernacular. There is therefore at least prima facie support for the use of network theory to aid our understanding of the impact of the *CEFR*.

Steiner-Khamsi also refers to this use of medical metaphors in connection with networks, but she argues that 'research on educational transfer lags behind network analysis ... we have not provided concrete empirical evidence' (2004: 214).[1] She suggests a number of factors which help an 'epidemic' to spread through networks: 'deterritorialisation' (i.e. when a policy is no longer associated with a particular country), 'critical mass' (when the numbers of conferences, lists, journals etc. reach a tipping point) and 'exposure' (i.e. the significance of highly visible and respected institutions or individuals who promote a policy, notably through 'elite networking'). The Council of Europe is certainly highly visible and promotes elite networking within Europe through its conferences for national representatives of governments, as opposed to conferences open to all researchers. Beyond Europe the situation may be different, and we shall be able in the course of this book to see if any of these features are present in the impact reported by our contributors within and beyond the continent.

The Book – Process and Product

The origins of this book lie in conversations among the series editors and the publishers, but also in discussions from time to time at the Council of Europe about the frequent but varied indications of the impact of the *CEFR*: invitations for speakers on the *CEFR* at conferences, surveys initiated at the Council of Europe among member states, references in academic and professional journals and so on. A more systematic analysis seemed appropriate some ten years after the first informal circulation of the *CEFR* drafts among representatives of member states of the Council of Europe, and by the time the project is brought to fruition it will be a decade after the publication of the *CEFR*.

Such a book could clearly not appear without a contribution from John Trim, and we as editors were delighted that he agreed to provide the introductory chapter, which is more than a description of the origins and process of the production of the *CEFR*. His explanation of the intellectual history of the *CEFR* is, we think, presented here in a comprehensive way for the first time.

From the conversations mentioned above, it was evident that a systematic analysis of the influence of the *CEFR* in all the countries where we knew it was influential was out of the question. The book would have been too long. The necessary selection of countries was a combination of a search for geopolitical range, for countries where we knew the impact was strong, others where we knew there was resistance and others where the *CEFR* was well known to academic researchers but its influence on policy uncertain. Selection was also a matter of opportunity, of whom we knew or whom we could find able to carry out the brief we planned, but we also made active attempts to discover potential influence – for example in African countries – which we knew nothing about. Add to this the usual pressures of work which mean that some contributors were not available or had to drop out or had to delay their writing, and the outcome is the present volume which we believe is representative and comprehensive without attempting to be exhaustive.

Our first concern was to chart the *processes* of influence in more detail than had been hitherto possible through the questionnaire survey mentioned earlier, and for this we thought it necessary to have descriptions of events. We therefore sought authors closely involved in the development of language education policy, some of whom work in ministries of education, others of whom work in universities and function as academics and policy-makers simultaneously. The brief given was as follows:

'For each country, the first contribution will be a description by the 'policy-maker' contributor. The 'policy-maker' will describe the processes involved in taking the *CEFR* into consideration in curriculum development (in a broad sense: aims, methods, materials, assessment, evaluation/inspection). Please consider the following issues and questions:

- How is curriculum usually developed in your country? (e.g. is it a rolling programme, a periodical review, a consequence of international comparisons, or something other?)
- How did the *CEFR* come to the notice of curriculum developers and why was it considered important?
- To what extent have policy-makers and curriculum developers been influenced by the adoption of the *CEFR* in other nations?
- What are the main areas of debate and negotiation in discussions of the *CEFR* in your national context? (e.g. influence on teaching methods or on assessment or numbers of languages to be learnt and age at which to begin.)

- What was the actual process of taking account of the *CEFR*, for example: who might have analysed it and how it was made known in detail to curriculum developers; the stages involved in curriculum development including consultation with teachers and others; in what degree of detail was the *CEFR* used? In other words, please could you provide a close description of the processes and the stakeholders in the processes.
- How was the *CEFR* made known to teachers – and to what degree of detail – as part of curriculum innovation?

This kind of description and explanation of the influences and processes will probably be unusually detailed, but therefore all the more important for this kind of book.'

Secondly, since this book is not only an account of the *CEFR* but also intended to be a contribution to the study of educational borrowing and the globalisation of educational policy, we also wanted contributors to analyse the intellectual traditions and practices which might favour or hinder the impact of the *CEFR* on a global scale. For this we sought authors from academe who would know the details of policy-making but who would also provide a historical, explanatory perspective. Here our suggestions were as follows:

'Please consider the following questions in the planning of your contribution – we recognise that not all are relevant for every country:

- Which aspects of the theoretical basis of the *CEFR* have been accepted/criticised/adapted/emphasised? What might be the explanation with respect for example to intellectual traditions in your country?
- Which aspects of the *CEFR* have been ignored or downplayed in education policy in your national context? Why?
- What are the motivations for incorporating aspects of the *CEFR* in education policy and practice in your national context?
- What are the restraints that limit the influence and adoption of the *CEFR* in education policy and practice in your national context?

The purpose here, in addition to contextualising the influence of the *CEFR*, is to provide a basis for the comparative analysis across countries which will be undertaken in the book by ourselves as editors.'

In practice, as the book eventually evolved, there are two exceptions to this general design of having a policy perspective and an academic perspective. These are the cases of Japan and China. In the first case we knew that there is a strong academic influence but as yet no traceable effect on policy, and in the case of China we were informed that it would be difficult to obtain a policy perspective.[2] As the chapter from China shows, this proved to be the case, but we are grateful to Zou Weicheng for carrying out an empirical investigation to investigate the situation for us in detail. In the case of Colombia, it proved impossible to have a contribution directly from policy-makers and we are very grateful to Beatriz Peña Dix and Anne-Marie de Mejía for carrying out interviews and for writing the policy perspective.

We decided from the beginning that the eventual collection of chapters would be presented in two groups – European countries and countries beyond Europe – because of the historic origins and the clear intentions that the *CEFR* should be a document for Europe. Its influence was in a sense ensured when it was taken up in recommendations to member states, and in the various channels of dissemination used by the Council of Europe. It is evident that its influence beyond Europe was a consequence of its quality; not all Council of Europe documents have had comparable impact.

Alternative groupings were also possible, for example into those countries where borrowing has been positive and strong and those where there has been resistance, and this would have reflected more the dimension of the book devoted to analysis of borrowing and globalisation of policy. However, we hope that these themes are given sufficient prominence in our comments after each section.

The final stage was to write the introduction, comments and conclusion. We decided to involve our contributors in this and sent them all a copy of a first draft of the introduction and the conclusion, asking them to what extent they agreed with our approach and whether they 'recognised themselves' in the account we gave. We have taken their comments into account as much as we can, but of course the final text is our responsibility only.

It remains for us to acknowledge with many thanks the patience of our contributors and their willingness to meet our requests and guidance.

Notes

(1) More recently a collection edited by Daly (2010) uses social network theory to analyse education, but it does not include policy in its scope.
(2) We are grateful to Anwei Feng, University of Bangor, for his help with this chapter, and to Glenda Koefoed for providing contacts.

References

Abdelgaber, S and Médioni, M-A. (eds) (2010) *Enseigner les langues vivantes avec le Cadre européen*. Cahiers pédagogiques. Collection des hors-série numériques 18.
Ball, S., Goodson, I. F., and Maguire, M. (eds) (2007) *Education, globalisation and new times.* London: Routledge.

Council of Europe (2005) *Plurilingual Education in Europe. 50 Years of International Cooperation.* Strasbourg: Council of Europe.
Council of Europe (2007) Report. Intergovernmental Language Policy Forum. 'The *Common European Framework of Reference for Languages* (*CEFR*) and the development of language policies: challenges and responsibilities' Strasbourg, 6–8 February 2007. Strasbourg: Council of Europe. Online at www.coe.int/lang.
Dale, R. (2007) Specifying globalization effects on national policy: A focus on the mechanisms. In S.J. Ball, I.F. Goodson and M. Maguire (eds) *Education, Globalization and New Times.* London: Routledge.
Daly, A.J. (2010) *Social Network Theory and Educational Change.* Cambridge, MA: Harvard Education Press.
Edwards, R. and Usher, R. (2000) *Globalisation and Pedagogy.* London: Routledge.
Fulcher, G. (2008) Testing times ahead? *Liaison Magazine* (1). Southampton: University of Southampton, Subject Centre for Languages, Linguistics and Area Studies.
Humboldt, von W. (1836/1988) *On Language.* Cambridge: Cambridge University Press.
Jones, N. and Saville, N. (2009) European language policy: assessment, learning and the *CEFR*. *Annual Review of Applied Linguistics* 29, 51–63.
Komorowska, H. (2004) The CEF in Pre- and In-Service Teacher Education. In K. Morrow (ed.) *Insights into the Common European Framework* (pp. 55–64). Oxford: Oxford University Press.
Le Cadre européen, une référence mondiale? (2007) *Dialogues et Cultures* 54.
Martyniuk, W. and Noijons, J. (2007) *The use of the CEFR at national level in the Council of Europe Member States.* Online at http://www.coe.int/t/dg4/linguistic/Forum07_webdocs_EN.asp#TopOfPage.
Nishiyama, N. (2009) L'impact du *Cadre européen de référence pour les langues* dans l'Asie du Nord-Est: pour une meilleure contextualisation du *CECR*. *Revue japonaise de didactique du français* 4 (1), 54–70.
Phillips, D. and Ochs, K. (2003) Processes of Policy Borrowing in Education: some explanatory and analytical devices. *Comparative Education*, 39 (4), 451–461.
Rizvi, F. and Lingard, B. (2010) *Globalizing Education Policy.* London: Routledge.
Steiner-Khamsi, G. (ed.) (2004) *The Global Politics of Educational Borrowing and Lending.* New York: Teachers College.

The Common European Framework of Reference: Learning, Teaching, Assessment

The author

John Trim graduated in German at University College London in 1949 and held a Lectureship in Phonetics there until 1958, when he was appointed to one in the University of Cambridge, where he became a Fellow of Selwyn College in 1962 and first Director of the Department of Linguistics in 1965. From 1963 to 1978 he directed the university's vacation courses in Linguistics and the English Language and from 1970 to 1978 chaired the Executive Committee for its international Examinations in English as a Foreign Language. From 1978 until his retirement in 1987 he was Director of the Centre for Information on Language Teaching and Research (CILT) in London. In 1969 he organised the Second International Congress on Applied Linguistics and became involved in the Modern Languages Projects of the Council of Europe, which he directed from 1971 to 1997, with responsibility for the development of the Threshold Level series in 25 languages, 72 international workshops for teacher trainers and the composition, piloting and publication of the *Common European Framework for Languages* (*CEFR*), of which he was part-author.

1 The Common European Framework of Reference for Languages and its Background: A Case Study of Cultural Politics and Educational Influences

John L.M. Trim

The Common European Framework for Languages: learning, teaching and assessment (*CEFR*) was published, simultaneously in English and French – the two official languages of the Council of Europe – in February 2001 as a contribution to the European Year of Languages. Many of the values and attitudes which it embodies can be traced back at least to the Protestant reformers of the 16th century, with their concern for mass literacy and direct access to the Bible as the basis for independent thought and action, and particularly to the ideas of the great Czech educational thinker, Jan Amos Komensky (Comenius) (1592–1670). Comenius saw his contemporaries in a war-torn Europe as trapped by ignorance in a labyrinth of appearances. Escape would only come through education, to make people aware of the unity and harmony of God's creation, into which human life should fit with spontaneous creativity, free from violence. Education should be a lifelong process, open to all, both men and women, on equal terms. Comenius saw language education as fundamental, starting with mother tongue literacy and oracy, then going on to the language of a neighbouring people and then to a language of universal communication, which in his time was still Latin. Language learning should not be a matter of formal exercises, but should be built upon sensory experience – where possible the experience and handling of real objects. Where not, as is most often the case in the world of the classroom, pictorial images must suffice. His *Orbis Sensualium Pictus* (*the World of the Senses in Pictures*, 1639) was not only a richly illustrated presentation of the vocabulary (words, phrases and sentences) of whatever language it was translated into, but also a guide to the exploration of the harmonious, divinely ordered world, from God, through the mineral, vegetable and animal kingdoms, to man, first as a biological, then a social and then a moral and spiritual being, and thus back to God. *Orbis Pictus,* which remained popular in successive printings and adaptations for over a century (it was the only illustrated children's book available to Goethe as a boy), was essentially an illustrated version of *Janua Linguarum Reserata* (*The Gate of Languages Unlocked*, 1631). In a striking image, Comenius compared the progress of a language learner in stages, from infancy to full maturity, to the exploration of a palace, dealing successively with the skeletal structure of a language (*vestibulum*), the substantial body of the language and associated areas of knowledge and experience (*janua*), stylistic refinements bringing life and colour (*atrium*), then the works of more suitable and accessible authors (*palatio*) and finally the unlimited wealth of writings in the arts and sciences, to which language learning gave access (*thesaurus*). This was perhaps the first attempt to provide a comprehensive framework for language learning. In *Didactica Magna* (1633–38), and later *Novissima linguarum methodus* (1644–46), Comenius elaborated his educational theories in a systematic way, expanding simple but powerful concepts (language learning should be speedy, solid and enjoyable) into 187 axioms, many of which foreshadow contemporary thinking. The role of the learner is central. That of the teacher is to organise, motivate and direct learning in a disciplined, cooperative atmosphere. This demands the highest standards of morality, knowledge and understanding, and should be accorded a correspondingly high social status. Comenius' breadth of vision, humanity and common sense were an inspiration four centuries after his birth.

A more direct influence on the development of the *CEFR* was the great reform movement at the end of the 19th century, which was based on the Neogrammarian revolution in linguistics in the 1870s. The explosive development of comparative philology in the earlier part of the century had as its aim the reconstruction of the prehistory of the Indo-European languages. Around 1870, emanating from the University of Leipzig, the focus of scholarship shifted to the investigation of the historical processes leading to the present-day condition of languages. It became clear that the forces for change lay in the everyday use of spoken language. Written language was shown to be conservative, concealing the processes of change at least until it was established. Following the publication of Edouard Sievers' *Grundzüge der Lautphysiologie* (1871), phonetics became a powerful tool for the observation, notation and analysis of language in everyday use, an essential basis for understanding the dynamics of language change. Sound change was not arbitrary, but seemed to follow 'laws' that were analogous to those being discovered in the natural sciences: *Gleiches wird unter gleichen Umständen gleich behandelt* ('under the same circumstances the same entities are treated in the same way'). Phoneticians saw themselves as pioneering a scientific approach to human behaviour. This profound change in values, attitudes and beliefs was not confined to linguistics. It was part of a more general cultural movement, evidenced in the spread of Darwinism, positivism and the naturalist movement in literature, and driven by the sociocultural forces released by the Industrial Revolution.

This paradigmatic change brought the new linguists into sharp conflict with the values, attitudes, beliefs and practices of language teaching in the educational system. Since Latin had ceased to be the lingua franca of educated people across Europe, its teaching had become isolated from practical concerns, and it was seen as an intellectual discipline leading to an appreciation of the literary heritage of classical antiquity, existing only in the form of written texts. This pattern of study was transferred to modern languages, whose place in the curriculum was justified by the development in the modern era of national literary traditions which could stand alongside those of antiquity. The International Phonetic Association (IPA), formed in 1884, had the reform of language teaching as one of its main goals. To emphasise this aspect, its journal was entitled (until the 1960s) *Le Maître Phonétique* and always included a section *Pour nos élèves*, with brief phonetically transcribed texts for use in the classroom. The IPA attracted a number of leading linguists, notably Henry Sweet, Otto Jespersen and Wilhelm Viëtor, the title of whose pamphlet *Der Sprachunterricht muss umkehren!* (*Language teaching must make a new start!*) resounded through the educational world.

The differences between the classical and modern paradigms can be summarised in the following table:

Table 1.1 The classical and modern Paradigms of language teaching and learning

Issue	**The Classical Paradigm**	**The Modern Paradigm**
Aim	to gain access to higher culture	to become a member of the language community
Objective	to provide a strict mental discipline	to develop communicative ability
Attitude to language	puristic	naturalistic

Table 1.1 continued

Type of language to learn	the best, correct form of cultivated usage	everyday usage
Preferred medium	priority to written language	priority to spoken language
Model presented	works of good authors	full range of (native) usage
Text-types	literary and philosophical writings	newspapers, broadcasts, popular writings
Criteria for expression	careful, controlled, accurate	spontaneous, fluent, appropriate
Criteria for comprehension	detailed, exact	extracting relevant information
Relation knowledge/ action	knowledge is fundamental	action is fundamental
Skill development	translation is most important	balanced development of four skills
Work style	individual study, receptive, reactive	group interaction, active, participatory
Relation among learners	competitive	cooperative
Role of teacher	authoritative and authoritarian	facilitator of learning
Approach to learning	subject-centred	learner-centred
Teaching style	magisterial	animating
Means employed	lectures, grammatical exposition, exercises, reading and translation of texts, essays	experiment, discover, games, role play, simulations, projects, discussions
Language of instruction	mother tongue	target language
Approach to grammar	a systematic body of rules to be learnt and observed	means to construct and convey meaning

Table 1.1 continued

Concept of culture	the training and refinement of mind, tastes and manners	the beliefs, attitudes and values which inform a society
Attitude to change	conservative, retrospective	innovative, prospective
Social values	aristocratic, meritocratic	democratic, populist
Where stronger	grammar schools, 'public' schools, older universities	comprehensive schools, newer universities, adult education
Claimed to be	humanistic, serious, deep, scholarly	practical, realistic, balanced, dynamic
Accused of being	remote from life, elitist, over-intellectualised, impractical	utilitarian, banal, superficial
Criteria for success	error-free performance, proof of knowledge	success in communicating message

It will be seen that the differences are profound and far-reaching. The reform movement encountered strong resistance and had mixed success. Perhaps under the influence of Otto Jespersen, or more probably owing to the differences in the respective cultures, the take-up of the modern paradigm was faster and longer-lasting in Scandinavia than in the Mediterranean countries and in the teaching of English as a foreign language than in that of other languages. In some countries, modern aims and methods were considered suitable for those destined to fill the middle ranks of society, but not for its higher echelons (perhaps an echo of Plato's distinction between *techne* and *episteme*). Foreign languages were, in any case, considered irrelevant and unsuitable for the broad mass of the working population. In Britain, over a period of time between the two world wars, modern aims and methods were introduced widely into lower secondary education, but not into higher education. Upper secondary education lay between the two, but, since school-leaving qualifications were in the hands of university examination boards, the forms of assessment that were used strongly favoured the classical approach. Under Paul Passy and Daniel Jones, the influence of the IPA was strong but limited. Many schools used a phonetic method in the first months of teaching French, and the Department of Phonetics at University College London continued to hold courses for language teachers for many years, but its influence in university teacher training departments waned in the late 1930s. UCL also offered research into language teaching methodology at postgraduate level, though the offer was rarely taken up. This probably dated from Harold Palmer's tenure of a lectureship in the department from 1914 to 1923, when he left for Japan. Though his tenure was short, his influence was long-lasting. His *Grammar of Spoken English on a Strictly Phonetic Basis* (1924) was still being used as the core text for courses held in the 1950s, as was his *Everyday Sentences in Spoken English* (1935), which was written with Blandford. The sentences were functionally categorised and provided with intonation patterns in Palmer's own notation, developed, probably under Henry Sweet's influence, for the *Grammar of Spoken English.* These works, together with his robust promotion of the modern paradigm in his published lectures and his work on vocabulary control, leading to *The Oxford Advanced Learners' Dictionary*, (1952), completed, edited and published by A.S. Hornby, and the *General Service List of English Words,* edited by Michael West in 1953, were an important background and provided input to the work of the Council of Europe.

The two world wars in the first half of the 20th century seriously disrupted international communication at all levels, as did continuing financial and administrative restrictions during the period of post-war reconstruction. In the absence of opportunities for genuine communication with native speakers, foreign language teaching in schools became introverted and reverted to the classical paradigm, to which qualifying examinations were orientated. In Britain and the United States, this tendency increased due to their physical isolation from the continent of Europe and the fact that many teachers were émigrés, out of sympathy with contemporary life in the countries concerned. In Eastern Europe, following the collapse of the wartime alliance and the lowering of the 'Iron Curtain' in 1948, international communication for ordinary citizens became impossibly difficult. In the immediate post-war situation, the main impetus for modernisation came from the United States, under the influence of Leonard Bloomfield, whose work *Language* (1933) was the primary linguistic textbook. Bloomfield was essentially a Leipzig-trained neogrammarian, and a staunch adherent of the modern paradigm, as the greater part of his work shows. Late in life he embraced behaviourist psychology and its doctrine of learning by habit formation. His pupils and successors developed this into 'post-Bloomfieldian structuralism'. Languages were analysed as an ascending series of systems, in which distinctive units were combined into permitted structures, starting with the phonemes of the language and their permitted combination into syllabic structures. Then came the morphemes, the minimal meaningful units and their combination into words and finally the combination of words into a hierarchically ordered sequence of syntactic structures to form sentences. Language learning was thought to follow the same path. First the learner should master the phonemic system, overlearning to the point at which habits of sound recognition and production were so well established that they no longer required conscious attention. Then the same methods led to the mastery of the morphemic system and of syntactic structures of increasing complexity. The aim (similar to that of military weapon training) was to make the basic mechanisms of language so instinctive that all attention could be concentrated on how best to express and understand meaning. The main problems in learning appeared to be caused by differences between the units and structures of the learner's mother tongue and the target language, which could be identified by contrastive analysis and given special attention in the learning programme. This theory provided the basis for the 'audio-lingual method' developed by linguists, notably Charles Fries, Robert Lado and Charles Ferguson, and taught by them and their followers with energy and enthusiasm to language teachers, particularly of English as a foreign language, around the world, funded by various aid programmes and notably the Fulbright scheme. Audio-lingual courses, with tapes containing dialogues to be repeated and learnt by heart, followed by appropriate structural exercises, were marketed on a large scale.

In Europe, the teaching of languages other than English was at first little affected by these developments. However, the learning and teaching of English as a language of global communication made enormous strides in the post-war period. The outcome of the war had left Anglo-American forces in control of the major lines of communication across the globe. The language was in increasing use in ports and airports everywhere and hence in international trade. Firms found it economical to use one single language in dealing with clients in a number of different countries and the growing number of multinational concerns found it useful to have that language as its operating language, internally as well as externally. The process, once under way, was of course self-reinforcing, so that growth in the use of English language was exponential. The reason for the increasing learning and use of English was utilitarian, strongly favouring the modern paradigm, despite resistance from older teachers concerned with the maintenance of educational values and standards. In adult education, in which the demand for English was very strong, there were no such inhibitions. There was, however, some tension between the tightly controlled American structuralist approach and the less formal methods, which were strongly influenced by Palmer and Hornby, promoted by the British. Since it was universally accepted that foreign learners should model themselves on native usage, the tension also extended to which native model, general American or British RP, should be followed.

The first formal proposals to modernise language teaching in European educational systems came from the Council of Europe on the initiative of the French government, taken perhaps as a reaction to the rapid erosion of the position of French as the language of diplomacy and international institutions and in international relations more generally. The Council of Europe was founded in 1949, in the uncertain conditions following the divisive and ominous events of 1948, with the main aim of protecting human rights, the rule of law and pluralist parliamentary democracy. Membership was and is open to all European countries accepting these principles and it has steadily grown over the years, particularly since 1990, to include all European states, including all members of the European Union (from which it is quite distinct) and the successor states to the USSR (except those in Central Asia). As an intergovernmental organisation it has no directive powers and works mainly by consensus, but its Committee of Ministers can make Recommendations to member states and its work can lead to European Conventions, in the light of which national legislation is harmonised and amended. As the European political situation has stabilised, the Council has increasingly worked to promote and coordinate international cooperation in tackling common problems facing European society in all fields except defence and to foster social progress in Europe. Its work in the language field is based on the European Cultural Convention, signed in Paris in 1954. Under Article 2, each member state undertakes to promote the study of its own language, history and civilisation and that of other contracting parties in its own territory and that of others, and to grant similar facilities to them. This formulation indicates that the Convention was conceived within the classical paradigm, but in fact the activities of the Council have consistently promoted modernisation. In many ways, their purpose and effect may be seen as the achievement of the aims and objectives of the reform movement.

In 1959, impressed, perhaps, by the success of American efforts to promote the learning of English, the French government set up the *Centre de Recherche et d'Étude pour la Diffusion du Français* (CRÉDIF), which developed and published *le Français fondamental,* listing the most frequent words and grammatical structures of French as a basis for the setting of priorities in the early learning and teaching of the language. In cooperation with Petar Guberina of the University of Zagreb, CRÉDIF adopted the audio-visual method, publishing *Voix et Images de la France* and *Bonjour Line* for use in this way with different age groups. The method was similar to the audio-lingual method with an added visual component, except that the ideology was holistic, with greater emphasis on the memorisation of dialogues in whole and in part. In the early 1960s, following a meeting of experts and an influential *stage* organised by the French government to present the work of CRÉDIF to a European audience, the Council of Europe launched a major, 10-year project for the modernisation of language teaching at all levels across Europe. The programme aimed to modernise all parts of the educational system and in particular to encourage: (a) the extension of language teaching to all sections of the school population and its encouragement in adult education; (b) the development of applied linguistics at university level, with closer cooperation between university researchers and practitioners in the field of language teaching; and (c) the adoption and further development of audio-visual technology and methodology. By 1969, the International Association for Applied Linguistics had been founded and was approaching its Second Congress, at which it progressed from a purely European to a global scale. Work was sufficiently advanced for the Council of Ministers to issue Recommendation R(69)2, setting out a programme of reform to be carried out at the national level.

In 1971, the Swiss government, in association with the Eurocentres organisation and with support from the *Volkshochschulverbände* (DVV) – the principal providers of adult education in the German-speaking countries – hosted an Intergovernmental Symposium at Rüschlikon on behalf of the Council of Europe to consider: 'The linguistic content, means of evaluation and their interaction in the teaching and learning of modern languages in adult education'. The symposium centred on the possibility of setting up a European unit-credit system, which would allow learners to build up language qualifications in a modular fashion over time according to the uncertain conditions of study in adult life. In accordance with the recommendations of the symposium, the Committee for Out-of-school Education and Cultural Development of the Council of Europe set up a small working party under my chairmanship to investigate the feasibility of such a system. The group felt that it should first consider carefully its aims and methods of working. This process led to a profound reorientation, the effects of which have lasted until now and within which the *CEFR* was conceived and produced. The successive Modern Languages Projects of the Council of Europe have been highly influential in the learning, teaching and assessment of languages over this period, thanks largely to the enthusiasm and dedication of the Council's administrators, Antonia de Vigili and her successor Joseph Sheils.

The group were agreed that, as a Council of Europe project, its aim was to promote language learning not as an end in itself – though for many learners, especially perhaps the more gifted ones, that might be sufficient motivation – but rather as a contribution to the over-arching political aims of the Council. It should serve to improve international understanding and cooperation, promote methods that strengthen democratic practices and develop the learner's independence of thought and action combined with social responsibility. We accepted the ideological viewpoint of the Committee for Out-of-school Education and Cultural Development that the teaching of one or more European foreign languages should be available to all on a lifelong basis and that it should be centred on learner needs, rather than being teacher- or subject-centred. We then had to consider what the acceptance of this approach would entail for our work in terms of its aims, principles, strategies and methods. The outcome may be summarised as follows:

Aims

- To facilitate the free movement of people, information and ideas in Europe with access for all and to encourage closer cooperation by providing the linguistic means of direct interpersonal communication, both face-to-face and at a distance.
- To build up mutual understanding and acceptance of cultural and linguistic diversity in a multilingual and multicultural Europe, with respect for individual, local, regional and national identities, developing a common European intercultural identity by unforced mutual influence.
- To promote the personal development of the individual, with growing self-awareness, self-confidence and independence of thought and action combined with social responsibility as an active agent in a participatory, pluralist democratic society.
- To make the process of learning itself more democratic by providing the conceptual tools for the planning, construction, conduct and evaluation of courses closely geared to the needs, motivations and characteristics of learners and enabling them so far as possible to assess, steer and control their own progress.
- To provide a framework for close and effective international cooperation in the organisation of language learning.

Principles

- A systems development approach, interrelating aims, objectives, methods, materials, assessment and evaluation should be adopted.
- Objectives should be appropriate, desirable and feasible:

- appropriate in the light of the characteristics of the learners;
- desirable in the light of the needs, (vocational, recreational, cultural and personal) and motivations of learners and the interests of society;
- feasible in the light of the human and material resources which can be brought to bear.

- Methods and materials should be selected and/or developed which are appropriate to learners, teachers and the learning situation and used so as to achieve the agreed objectives.
- Methods of assessment and evaluation should be employed and developed which are directly related to learning objectives and provide accurate and relevant information to learners, teachers and other interested parties.

Strategies

- To identify and win the cooperation of the most advanced and effective institutions and individual workers in the member countries engaged in the various aspects of the planning, organisation and conduct of language learning, teaching, assessment and research.
- To engage these institutions and individuals in collaborative projects and to make the results of their work available to their counterparts in all member countries.
- To bring institutions with similar interests and problems into structured working relationships, and thus steadily develop mutual confidence and mechanisms of cooperation.
- The approach to language learning and teaching should be learner-centred rather than subject-centred or teacher-centred.
- The function of teachers and other partners is to facilitate appropriate and effective learning.
- There should be consultation and agreement on aims, objectives and methods among all the partners for learning.
- A permanent education perspective is needed, as the developing individual learns to understand and to communicate in diverse ways for diverse purposes in a multilingual and multicultural Europe.
- All educational programmes should involve preparation for future independent learning.

Methods

- Commissioning studies under contract from individuals, dealing with areas of importance for systems development.
- Establishing subgroups and working parties to develop key areas.

- Engaging institutions, or groups of institutions, in case studies and pilot experiments.
- Issuing a series of documents as conceptual tools to assist administrators, publishers and authors of textbooks and other teaching materials, as well as course developers, media producers, teacher trainers, examiners, teachers and learners in educational planning.
- Preparing Recommendations of the Committee of Ministers to member governments.

In the light of this basic approach, which became known as 'the Council of Europe approach', we decided not, at that time, to attempt to build on the work of CRÉDIF and the American structuralists in constructing a scale of ascending levels defined in terms of frequency of vocabulary and complexity of structure. The reasons for this decision were partly based on scepticism as to the validity and reliability of lexicostatistics as a basis for vocabulary selection. For one thing, apart from the highly frequent members of closed sets with grammatical functions, lexical items did not appear to reach statistical stability from one text to another. For another, word frequency in a written corpus was very different from that in a spoken corpus (e.g. the frequency of 'Yes'). We were interested in direct face-to-face interaction and no substantial spoken corpora were available for most European languages. Moreover, information theory showed that information value was inversely proportional to frequency of occurrence. In any case, lexical ordering could only be proposed for one particular language at a time. Grammatical ordering, too, varied from one language to another and the problems this presented varied not only from one target language to another, but also from one L1 background to another. A pan-European system could not be built on that basis. In any case, we did not wish to impose a top-down system on all adult learners across Europe, but rather to empower teachers and learners to plan courses as close to the point of learning as possible, in light of the needs, motivations, characteristics and resources of the particular learners involved in their local situations. Also, while we held that the teaching methods to be employed should be contingent on these factors and agreed between teachers and learners rather than imposed from above, we were well aware of Chomsky's critique of behaviourism and, having had some experience of the deadening effect of the overlearning of dialogues and endless structure drills, wished to see attention shift from excessive formalism to the processes of communicative face-to-face interaction. In setting this as our goal we were motivated by a desire to enable the broad mass of Europeans, whose lives had up to now been spent within their national boundaries, to take full advantage of the rapidly expanding means of communication and the lowering of financial and bureaucratic barriers to international mobility for educational, vocational and leisure purposes. We wished them to be able to meet the challenges of living in a foreign language environment with confidence, not only transacting the business of everyday living, but also building personal relations and working relationships. We were also made aware of the very real problems posed by the rapidly increasing numbers of refugees and migrant workers and their dependants in most member states. Since we regarded the setting of appropriate objectives to be at the centre of the systems approach to educational planning derived from educational technology, we made the definition of such a learning objective our highest priority, terming it 'the Threshold Level'.

In preparation for this task, we commissioned a number of studies that drew upon the experience of different members of the group. René Richterich, of Eurocentres, had worked on the analysis of learner needs. Jan van Ek had specialised in the grammar of English and had worked with DVV and the associated International Certificate Commission (ICC) on an English equivalent to *le Français fundamental.* David Wilkins, as an applied linguist, had developed a strong interest in notional analysis. Under the influence of D.B. Fry, I considered the primary task of linguistics to be the detailed investigation of 'what happens when people talk to each other'. Following also the teachings of J.R. Firth and in discussions with Del Hymes, I had long been interested in the pervasive role of language in human life and in the processes of speech communication and the many competences (areas of knowledge and skill) which underlay them. In assembling the raw material for the Threshold Level, we supplemented these studies from published sources, such as J.L. Austin (1962) and Palmer and Blandford (1935). We also co-opted onto the group Anthony Peck and Svante Hjelmström, whose work, respectively, on *Sprechintensionen* for the Schools Council and Nuffield German course *Vorwärts* and the Linköping distance course in English: *In the Air* were valuable sources of functional categories and descriptors, alongside a first classification of language functions I had prepared as an appendix to the report of the Rüschlikon Symposium. The Netherlands government then gave van Ek a substantial period of study leave to complete and organise this material as an exemplification of a functional-notional objective for a given learner constituency.

The success of *The Threshold Level* was beyond our expectations. It rapidly established itself as a basis for the renewal of adult education courses, textbooks and examinations in English as a foreign language. Within the Council of Europe it rapidly eclipsed the unit-credit scheme itself, which was never implemented. Instead, following the publication of van Ek's *The*

Threshold Level for Modern Language Learning in Schools, commissioned by the Committee for General and Technical Education, and similar modifications of *Un Niveau-seuil* to schools as well as to migrant workers, the main attention shifted for a generation to the application of the threshold level concept and the 'Council of Europe approach' more generally to the modernisation of language teaching in schools across the continent. A series of 72 international workshops directed to teacher trainers, identified as the key agents for change, had a strong influence, direct and indirect, on classroom practices, particularly in Central and Southern Europe in the 1980s and in the former Eastern Bloc countries in the 1990s. The reason for this phenomenal success was that it came at the right historical moment. By the mid-1970s, the accelerating growth of global communications was already apparent to employers and parents and the demand from all sectors of society, especially for English as a means of communication in daily life, was strong and still increasing. There was an increasing impatience with traditional methods of teaching and testing. The profession was in need of change and it was largely ready for change. In the words of Goethe, *die Lampe harrt der Flamme, die entzündet* ('the lamp awaits the flame that will ignite it'). The concrete and detailed specification contained in *The Threshold Level* of what a learner needed to know and to do in order to meet the challenges of everyday life in another country offered a practical tool for the various agents engaged in the planning of language provision and they seized upon it with enthusiasm. Versions of *The Threshold Level* for other European languages were soon produced. CRÉDIF devoted a major research effort into the compilation of *Un Niveau-seuil,* a work of 663 pages, expounding the principles on which the enterprise was based, greatly enlarging the section on language functions (renamed *Actes de parole)* and adding an innovative functional grammar. The authors did not wish to set out a single objective for a defined audience, which they thought might prejudice the diversity of learner-centred provision, but to survey the overall reservoir of linguistic resources for the learning and teaching of French at a relatively modest level, from which course designers and teachers would be obliged to make a principled selection. *Un Niveau-seuil* remains an invaluable source book, if still underused, but practitioners found the demands made on them somewhat forbidding and only the Portuguese, with help from René Richterich, and to a much lesser extent the German *Kontaktschwelle,* attempted to follow that model. In the course of the 1980s, versions based fairly closely on *The Threshold Level* model were produced for almost all the national and some major regional languages represented in the Council. They were of particular value to the small groups with severely limited resources providing services to immigrants, students and business people in the smaller languages not taught in schools abroad. In the 1990s, production of a version for the language concerned was undertaken as a central aspect of the renewal of language teaching in the new member countries of Central and Eastern Europe that were opening their doors to the world, from Russian to Slovenian and the languages of the Baltic states. Overall, versions were produced for some 25 European languages.

As the threshold level concept became part of mainstream thinking, demand grew for similar specifications at other levels and descriptions were produced using the same model at Waystage below, and Vantage above Threshold. Practical considerations overrode the theoretical misgivings as to the validity of the concept of 'level'. We had used the term 'level' originally despite deep misgivings about the concept. We could see no reason to break the process of language learning into a series of steps and did not like the image of learning poured into an empty vessel, with skills and knowledge rising like sand in an hourglass. In a learner-centred approach, the diversity of needs, motivations and characteristics might lead in many different directions. Why force everyone to follow the same set of *gradus ad Parnassum*? However, we thought an exception might be made at the point where the early learning of bits and pieces of language cohered into a generally usable communicative competence, producing a 'threshold' effect. Over time, it became apparent that our reasoning took too little account of the realities of the social organisation of language learning. State education systems were organised into primary, lower secondary and upper secondary, further and higher educational sectors, and their interfaces called for assessments of proficiency that would provide objectives for one sector and starting points for the next. Similarly, the major institutions of adult education had to cater for large numbers of students at different stages of development, to sort them into financially and organisationally viable groups with realistic common objectives. *Waystage* was developed to provide a first year objective for the Anglo-German multimedia English course *Follow me!,* when Threshold proved to require a longer period of study in an adult education context. In the 1980s, the need became apparent for a further objective for students who had reached Threshold and wanted to develop their powers of self-expression further. At the same time, the development of the communicative approach indicated the need to take into account a wider range of factors contributing to communicative competence. A series of studies on different aspects led to a major study by van Ek on the scope and levels of language proficiency in the specification of learning objectives. This led to the revision of *Waystage* and *Threshold* and the formulation of a higher-level objective, *Vantage,* resulting in a three-level series using the same descriptive model.

At the same time, the Swiss federal government asked the Council of Europe to convene an intergovernmental symposium to consider more closely the question of language qualifications. The symposium, held in November 1991, once more in Rüschlikon in cooperation with the Eurocentres organisation, was entitled *Transparency and coherence in language learning in Europe: objectives, assessment and certification.* It was asked to consider: (a) the introduction of a Common European Framework of Reference (CEFR) for the description of objectives and methods for language learning and teaching, curriculum and course design, materials production and language testing and assessment, and (b) the introduction of a European Language Portfolio (ELP), in which individual learners could record not only institutional courses attended and qualifications gained, but also less formal experiences with respect to as wide a range of European languages and cultures as possible. The symposium agreed that it was desirable to develop a Common European Framework of Reference at all levels in order to:

- promote and facilitate cooperation among educational institutions in different countries;
- provide a sound basis for the mutual recognition of language qualifications;
- assist learners, teachers, course designers, examining bodies and educational administrators to situate and coordinate their efforts. It should be useful both as a common basis for the exchange of information among practitioners and as a basis for critical reflection by practitioners on their current practice and the options open to them.

In order to fulfil its functions, a framework should be comprehensive, transparent and coherent. A CEFR should attempt to specify as full a range of language knowledge, skills and use as possible. All users should be able to describe their objectives and so on by reference to it. A CEFR should differentiate the various dimensions in which language proficiency is described, bearing in mind that the development of communicative proficiency involves other dimensions than the strictly linguistic (e.g. sociocultural awareness, imaginative experience, affective relations, learning to learn, etc.). A CEFR should also provide a series of reference points (levels or steps) by which language proficiency and progress in learning can be calibrated. Information should be clearly formulated and explicit, available and readily comprehensible to users. It was also agreed that the Framework should be flexible, open, dynamic and non-dogmatic, since the aim was not to prescribe how languages should be learnt, taught and assessed, but to raise awareness, stimulate reflection and improve communication among practitioners of all kinds and persuasions as to what they actually do. As such, it was not intended to be definitive, set in tablets of stone, but was expected to evolve further as knowledge and experience expanded.

The Swiss initiative, partly motivated by its own internal concerns, was taken in response to the growing need for qualifications to be 'portable'. Within the European Union (EU), freedom of movement for educational and vocational purposes was guaranteed to all and it was clearly in the interest of university admissions authorities and employers on the one hand, and of individual students and job-seekers on the other, that qualifications awarded by one authority should be readily evaluated and recognised by others. There was a call in some quarters for some authority to certify the level of language proficiency guaranteed by the possession of a particular qualification. This was not a role the Council of Europe wished, or indeed was in any position, to play. It did not have the powers, structure or resources to do so and in any case it will be clear to the reader by now that its commitment to voluntary cooperation, diversification and grass-roots empowerment led in a different direction. As developed with extensive field consultation over a decade and published, simultaneously in French and English, in 2001, the European Year of Languages, the Scales of Proficiency were part of a threefold structure alongside a taxonomy of language use and competences and the presentation of methodological options for learning, teaching and assessment, the whole being conceived primarily as an instrument for reflection and empowerment of learners as well as teachers and other professionals.

In the event, it was the six-level scaling of language proficiency, with descriptors carefully selected from existing scalings, which had the greatest impact on the field, not only in Europe but on a global scale. Again, the instrument was produced at the right moment, as authorities awarding and having to evaluate qualifications felt the need to situate themselves in a global market. It may well have been the permissive nature of the Council of Europe's approach, offering a tool for calibration without arousing fears of bureaucratic direction, which made it easier for independent agencies to accept its descriptive system. In 1998, the Committee of Ministers issued Recommendation R(1998)6 to member governments. Among the many recommendations on different aspects of language policy were three on 'the specification of objectives and assessment'. Whilst advocating the use of CEFR, they make it clear where the responsibility for action lies:

> Section G: *Specification of objectives and assessment*
>
> 25. For all European national and regional languages, develop realistic and valid learning objectives – such as are to be found in 'Threshold

Level' type specifications – so as to ensure quality in language learning and teaching through coherence and transparency of objectives.

26. Encourage institutions to use the Council of Europe's Common European Framework of Reference to plan or review language teaching in a coherent and transparent manner in the interests of better international co-ordination and more diversified language learning.

28. Encourage institutions engaged in assessment and certification – especially those which award recognised qualifications – to make their objectives, criteria and procedures clear both to candidates and teachers, thus facilitating the comparability of qualifications and European mobility.

By 2008, the use of the six-level scale A1–C2 to indicate the level of courses, textbooks, examinations and qualifications had become so widespread as to be expected by users and almost routine. In response to doubts expressed as to the validity of some claims, the Council of Europe came under pressure to provide stronger guidance to the field than the *Guide for users* already produced. In 2008, the Committee of Ministers issued Recommendation CM/Rec(2008)7, accompanied by explanatory notes, covering the range of uses of *CEFR* for curricular guidelines, textbook and course construction, teacher training and, particularly, tests and examinations leading to recognised qualifications. Again, the formulation of the relevant paragraphs lays the responsibility for action on the governments and institutions concerned:

- 4.5. ensure that all tests, examinations and assessment procedures leading to officially recognised language qualifications take full account of the relevant aspects of language use and language competences as set out in the *CEFR*, that they are conducted in accordance with internationally recognised principles of good practice and quality management, and that the procedures to relate these tests and examinations to the common reference levels (A1–C2) of the *CEFR* are carried out in a reliable and transparent manner;
- 4.6. ensure that full information regarding the procedures applied in all tests, examinations and assessment systems leading to officially recognised language qualifications, particularly those used to relate them to the common reference levels (A1–C2) of the *CEFR*, is published and made freely available and readily accessible to all the interested parties;
- 4.7. encourage all other bodies responsible for foreign/second language assessment and certification to adopt measures that guarantee the provision of fair, transparent, valid and reliable tests and examinations

in conformity with the principles set out in paragraph 4.5 above and to publish their procedures, particularly those used to relate these tests and examinations to the *CEFR* common reference levels (A1–C2) as outlined in paragraph 4.6 above.

It also became clear that, for authorities and institutions to meet these responsibilities, the level descriptors provided in *CEFR* were inadequate. Designed to meet the criteria of positiveness, definiteness, clarity, brevity and independence, their user-friendliness made an immediate appeal to learners, teachers, parents, employers, educational authorities and other users, but, perhaps for that very reason, they could not meet the criterion of operational adequacy for those charged with the actual construction and conduct of tests and examinations leading to recognised qualifications in specific languages. The Language Policy Division of the Council of Europe therefore set up a working party to prepare a manual for relating examinations to the *CEFR*, supported by recorded performances by learners at successive levels, and encouraged the preparation of Reference Level Descriptions (RLD) for individual languages. The first of these was *Profile Deutsch,* a specification of learning objectives for German at all six levels, produced by a trinational team. A multi-faceted long-term project for English: *English Profile* is currently under way. In addition, a project is in the course of elaborating a framework for the languages of school education.

It will thus be seen that *CEFR* represents a significant step forward in a long process of educational reform, firmly rooted in a developing tradition under a wide-range of intellectual, cultural, socio-economic and political influences and pointing forward to a period of further educational advance.

References

Austin, J.L. (1962) *How To Do Things with Words.* Cambridge: Cambridge University Press.

Baldegger, M., Müller, M. and Schneider, G. in Zusammenarbeit mit A. Näf (1980) *Kontaktschwelle Deutsch als Fremdsprache.* Berlin: Langenscheidt.

Coste, D., Courtillon, J., Ferenczi, V., Martins-Baltar, M. and Papo, E. (1976) *Un Niveau-Seuil.* Paris: Hatier.

Council of Europe (1982) *Recommendation no.R(82)18 of the Committee of Ministers to member States concerning modern languages.* Appendix A to Girard and Trim (1988).

Council of Europe (1997) *European language portfolio: proposals for development.* Strasbourg: Council of Europe.

Council of Europe Committee for Out-of-School Education and Cultural Development (1971) *Modern language learning in adult education: linguistic content, means of evaluation and their interaction in the teaching and learning of modern languages in adult education. (Report of a Symposium held in Rüschlikon, Switzerland 3–7 May 1971).* Strasbourg: Council of Europe.

Council of Europe Committee of Ministers (1998) *Recommendation no.R(98)6 of the Committee of Ministers to member States concerning modern languages*. Strasbourg: Council of Europe.
Ek, J.A. van (1976) *The Threshold Level for Modern Language Learning in Schools.* London: Longman.
Ek, J.A. van (1985–86) *Objectives for Foreign Language Learning: vol. I Scope. vol. II Levels.* Strasbourg: Council of Europe.
Ek, J.A. van and Trim, J.L.M. (1998) *Threshold 1990* (revised and corrected edition). Cambridge: Cambridge University Press.
Ek, J.A. van and Trim, J.L.M. (1998) *Waystage* 1990 (revised and corrected edition). Cambridge: Cambridge University Press.
Ek, J.A. van and Trim, J.L.M. (2001) *Vantage.* Cambridge: Cambridge University Press.
Ek, J.A. van and Alexander, L.G. (1980) *Threshold level English.* Oxford: Pergamon,
Ek, J.A., van, Alexander, L.G. and Fitzpatrick, M.A. (1980) *Waystage English*. Oxford: Pergamon.
Firth, J.R. (1964) *The Tongues of Men* and *Speech*. London: Oxford University Press.
Fries, C.C. (1945) *Teaching and Learning English as a Foreign Language.* Ann Arbour: University of Michigan Press.
Fry, D.B. (1977) *Homo Loquens.* Cambridge: Cambridge University Press.
Girard, D. and Trim, J.L.M. (eds) (1988) *Project no.12 'Learning and teaching modern languages for communication': Final Report of the Project Group (activities 1982–87).* Strasbourg: Council of Europe.
Glaboniat, M., Müller, M., Rusch, P., Schmitz, H. and Wertenschlag, L. (2005) *Profile Deutsch.* Berlin: Langenscheidt.
Hymes, D.H. (1972) On communicative competence. In J.B. Pride and J. Holmes (eds) (1972) *Sociolinguistics*. Harmondsworth: Penguin.
Jespersen, O. (1904) *How toTeach a Foreign Language.* London: G. Allen & Unwin.
Kingdon, R. (1958) *The Groundwork of English Intonation.* London: Longman.
Komenský, J.A. (Comenius) (1658) *Orbis Sensualium Pictus.* Nuremberg.
Lado, R. (1961) *Language Testing: the Construction and Use of Foreign Language Tests*. London: Longman.
North, B. (ed.) (1992) *Transparency and Coherence in Language Learning in Europe: Objectives, Evaluation, Certification: Report of a Symposium held in Rüschlikon, Switzerland, 10–16 November 1991.* Strasbourg: Council of Europe.
O'Connor, J.D. and Arnold, G.F. (1961) *The Intonation of Colloquial English.* London: Longmans.
Oskarsson, M. (1980) *Approaches to Self-Assessment in Foreign Language Learning*. Oxford: Pergamon.
Pride, J.B. and Holmes, J. (eds) (1972) *Sociolinguistics*. Harmondsworth: Penguin.
Riddy, D.C. (1972) *The Work of the Council of Europe in the Field of Modern Languages.* Strasbourg: Council of Europe.
Schools Council (1968) *Vorwärts: Nuffield introductory German course.* Leeds: E.J. Arnold.
Searle, J.R. (1976) The classification of illocutionary acts. *Language in society* 51 (1), 1–24.
Sheils, J. (1988) *Communication in the Modern Language Classroom*. Strasbourg: Council of Europe (also available in German, Russian and Lithuanian).
Sweet, H. (1899) *The Practical Study of Languages.* New York: H. Holt and Co.
Trim, J.L.M. (1998) The Gate of Languages and its threshold. In J. Hendrich and M. Prochazka (eds) *J.A. Comenius' Heritage of Man for the 21st Century: Section Five: Comenius and the Significance of Languages and Literary Education* (pp. 46–63). Prague: nakladatelstvi Univerzity Karlovy.

Trim, J.L.M. (1976) 'Die Junggrammatiker nach 100 Jahren', in 'Akten des V. Internationalen Germanisten-Kongresses, Cambridge 1975'. *Jahrbuch für Internationale Germanistik,* Reihe A, Band 2,1. *75–96.*

Trim, J.L.M. (1980) *Developing a Unit/Credit Scheme of Adult Language Learning*. Oxford: Pergamon.

Trim, J.L.M. (2000) The Birth and early Development of AILA. In AILA '99 Tokyo Organizing Committee (eds) *Selected Papers from AILA '99 Tokyo.* Tokyo: Waseda University Press.

Trim, J.L.M.(ed.) (undated) *Common European Framework of Reference for Languages: Learning, Teaching, Assessment; a Guide for Users.* Strasbourg: Council of Europe Language Policy Division.

Trim, J.L.M. (undated) *Modern Languages in the Council of Europe 1954–1997.* Strasbourg: Council of Europe Language Policy Division.

Trim, J.L.M., Richterich, R., van Ek, J.A. and Wilkins, D.A. (1980) *Systems Development in Adult Language Learning.* Oxford: Pergamon.

Trim, J.L.M. (1988) *Consolidated Report on the Programme of International Workshops for Trainers of Teachers of Modern Language 1984 – 87.* Council of Europe: Strasbourg

Trim, J.L.M. (1997) Council of Europe workshops 1990–1996 (conclusion). *Language Teaching* 30 (2), 88–90.

Trim, J.L.M., Richterich, R., van Ek, J.A. and Wilkins, D.A. (1980) *Systems Development in Adult_Language Learning*. Oxford: Pergamon.

Trim, J.L.M., Holec H., Coste, D. and Porcher, L. (eds) (1984) *Towards a more Comprehensive Framework for the Definition of Language Learning Objectives. Vol. I Analytical Summaries of the Preliminary Studies. Vol. II Preliminary studies*. (contributions in English and French). Strasbourg: Council of Europe

Viëtor, W. (1902) *Die Methodik des Neusprachlichen Unterrichts.* Leipzig: Teubner.

Wilkins, D.A. (1972) *Linguistics in Language Teaching*. London: Edward Arnold.

Wilkins, D.A. (1976) *Notional Syllabuses*. Oxford: Oxford University Press.

Part 1

THE *CEFR* IN EUROPE

France

The authors:

Francis Goullier has been a General Inspector of National Education since 1997 and in this capacity he is associated with changes in language education policy in France. In particular, he was appointed specialist adviser for modern languages to the minister of education from 2000 to 2002.

As an expert with the Language Policy Division, he has been involved in various Council of Europe projects and was chair and then vice-chair of the European Committee for the validation of the *European Language Portfolio.*

Véronique Castellotti is a Professor in Language Sciences and Language Education at the University François Rabelais in Tours (France), where she has been teaching since 1998, first in the department of French as a foreign language, then in the department of Sociolinguistics and Language Education.

She chairs the Master's programme 'Languages, Education, Francophonies' and the Tours Research Team DYNADIV (Dynamics and challenges of diversity: languages, cultures, formation). Her research interests focus on the study of migrations, international mobility, multilingualism and multiculturalism in various situations of contact, language learning and teacher training, from the points of view of sociolinguistics, language education and epistemology.

2 Policy Perspectives from France

Francis Goullier

In France, the *CEFR* has become the reference document for the teaching of foreign languages as a consequence of a governmental decree of August 2005. This decree officially adopts the *CEFR* for three purposes: first for defining the level of competence it is expected pupils will achieve at different stages in their schooling; second for introducing modes of assessment linked to these levels of competence (certification linked to the countries concerned for each foreign language); and third for recommending a new kind of organisation of language learning groups which takes into account the actual competences of pupils rather than the number of years they have learnt a particular language ('competence groups').

This high-level of political decision-making is very rarely concerned with questions dealing with a discipline; more often it is focused on the general organisation of the educational system. It has been reinforced since then by important new regulations or even new laws. These decisions of a political nature have had a rapid effect: the evolution which began in 2002 in the curricula has accelerated, and since then all the texts defining the contents of teaching for foreign languages for all stages of the education system have introduced references to the *CEFR*. No text dealing with the teaching of languages or the assessment of what has been learned in this discipline is without reference to this Council of Europe document.

This coherence between regulatory and pedagogical texts (curricular documents) is not surprising insofar as the decision to renew curricula is the responsibility of ministerial authorities, and texts and documents written within this framework are necessarily validated by the same authorities; with respect to the contents of teaching, the French education system is highly centralised. The rapidity with which texts that organise language teaching pedagogically have been made to conform with legal texts clearly shows the importance that the ministry attaches to this reference to the *CEFR*.

Entry into the *CEFR* Took Place Through the Scales of Levels of Competence

The introduction of the *CEFR* into language teaching began, almost exclusively, as the contents of the governmental decree mentioned above show, by reference to the levels of competence. This can be explained quite easily. Language teaching in France does not achieve the results that society expects of it. The relatively recent realisation in this country of the importance of a mastery of languages was accompanied by concern about the actual level of competences of pupils leaving the education system. This concern has to be understood in the light of the ambition of the education system in France to ensure that all pupils of a particular age group acquire competences in at least one foreign language, and that the majority do so in two foreign languages. The vague feeling of inadequate performance in the education system led the ministry to undertake international comparisons which only confirmed the 'suspicion' that France was lagging behind in the overall results in languages in comparison with pupils of other European countries. This preoccupation with comparison to legitimise the effort required in the mastery of languages is probably also the origin of French support for the implementation of the indicator of linguistic competence of young Europeans, which was decided at the European Union's Barcelona summit.

The publication of the *CEFR* and of its scale of language competences in 2001 happened at the very moment when the French Ministry of Education was looking for a means to give new impetus to the teaching of languages. It quickly saw in this scale of levels a response to its expectations of a tool, which at the same time provided comparability and a check on the results achieved.

Thus like most European countries, France fixed the linguistic objectives of its teaching with the help of the levels of the scale of competences of the *CEFR*. However, it is important to note the perspective from which this was undertaken. It is not a question here, in contrast to what has happened in other countries, of fixing these levels in relation to the actual competences achieved by pupils in the classes in question, but rather of clarifying the nature of the ambition which each teacher and each school should have for the pupils in their care. These levels, fixed for each stage of schooling, are not levels required for passing into the next class above or for success in an examination, but rather the levels that are aimed at. Let us take one example: whilst the level *aimed* for at the end of obligatory schooling is level B1 in the first foreign language, the *requirement* for obtaining the diploma which certifies this stage of schooling is level A2. The levels aimed at are an expression of the collective need for a noticeable improvement of the general level in foreign languages in France and a 'horizon' towards which all language teachers and their pupils should progress.

The rapid and enthusiastic adoption of the *CEFR* in the French education system is thus due essentially to a chronological coincidence of the political and collective realisation of a need, and the provision for member states of the Council of Europe of this scale of levels of competence. In large part it was motivated by reasons different from those that underpinned the development of the *CEFR*. One might even risk saying that this adoption was decided upon without a detailed analysis of the contents of this document and of its pedagogical and didactic implications.

For a long period of time and for most of those involved, the *CEFR* was thus limited to its scale of levels of competence. But the scale of levels proposed by the *CEFR* offered the additional, valuable advantage of emphasising the notion of competences and of making the development of these competences measurable. Foreign languages were from that point onwards destined to play a pioneer role in the implementation of European recommendations concerning basic competences to be taught during obligatory schooling, which were translated in France into a 'common core of knowledge and competences'. This interpretation of this particular role attributed to the adoption of the *CEFR* is supported by the fact that, from 2008, partial mastery of this 'common core' has been assessed for all pupils only in the subject foreign languages; the assessment of other components of the common core is planned for later.

The Convergence of Political Purposes and Considerations of a Pedagogical and Didactic Nature

If this succinct analysis explains the political decision and the rapid commissioning of new curricula, it does not in itself allow us to understand the reasons for the success of this decision in the collective representations of all those involved in the teaching of foreign languages in France.

This success is due in a very obvious way to the very strong convergence of the preoccupations of political decision-makers on the one hand, with the analyses, the discourse and the documents produced by recognised authorities on the teaching of foreign languages in France on the other. The interconnecting of the country through a dense network of language inspectors made it possible to make all teachers aware of the convergence of views between these two levels of responsibility, and thus to give these political decisions the credibility and effectiveness that might have been lacking in the contrary case, and which might have reduced their impact on the teaching and assessment of languages.

The people who are the 'bearers of pedagogical discourse' saw in the *CEFR* and in its scales of levels of competence elements of a response to the difficulties of language teaching in France that had been recognised for some time. These can be summarised as follows: weak motivation for language learning among a substantial number of pupils, due in large part to a lack of confidence in their own ability to learn a foreign language effectively; lack of ability in the discipline to formulate clearly what it proposed to teach all pupils, which led to a naive collective evaluation of the results of teaching based on a comparison with an expected level of almost 'perfect' mastery of the languages studied; difficulty in elaborating and assessing progression in the operational mastery of a language; reluctance to take account of the different degrees of progression of pupils with respect to different linguistic activities of comprehension and expression, and as a result, missed opportunities to valorise progression and to make pupils aware of it; and attempts, sometimes vain, to go beyond the artificial character of the use of a foreign language in formal education and to make its use in class meaningful.

It is easy to identify the specific contribution of the *CEFR* for each of these problems: the definition of levels which legitimate an intermediary degree of competences which no longer needs to be valued in relation to its distance from that of the native speaker; strongly positive assessment of competences emphasising success, even partial; use of the scale of levels for each linguistic activity independently and recognition of the naturally uneven character of the individual's linguistic profile; and an action approach.

Over the course of time it is moreover noticeable that the focus on the levels of competence – which was probably excessive – is giving way in the teaching and in the discourse on the *CEFR* to the dimensions of the action approach. Debates in the community of language teachers in France now focus essentially on the understanding of this pedagogical approach and the means of its implementation in the school situation.

Different and complementary discourses have thus been grafted onto the promotion of the *CEFR* and have had the effect of making this document and its scale of levels of competence a *sine qua non*. The doubts and resistance that were evident in the early stages have rapidly given way to acceptance of the necessity of these tools for all concerned.

The most obvious sign of this rapid evolution and of its overall acceptance by teachers is the process of ensuring that all pedagogical materials published by educational publishing companies conform. Thus textbooks and accompanying documents for teaching and learning claim to be based upon the action approach which underpins the definition of competences in languages in the *CEFR*. They usually make reference to one of these levels of competence to define the level of expectation at which they aim, and they quote descriptions of these levels to formulate the objectives pursued in a unit of learning or in proposing activities for self-assessment. The adoption by private publishing companies of this reference can only be motivated, in addition to the didactic convictions of the authors, by acceptance of this reference by the body of language teachers who, in France, are the ones who have the exclusive right to choose textbooks in an educational establishment without interference by the institution.

Taking into Account the Specificity of Modern Language Teaching in France

In order to facilitate such a profound and rapid evolution in representations concerning levels of competence, assessment and pedagogical approaches to the teaching of languages, it was of course necessary to take into account the concerns that appeared. The first, and undoubtedly the most important, concerned the exclusively operational character of the definition of levels of competence in the *CEFR*. It is clear that even if it is an important element of the purpose of language teaching in schooling and university education, the mastery of linguistic pragmatic and strategic skills in the languages learnt does not cover all the objectives of this teaching. It does not take into account the contribution of this discipline to the general education of pupils or the indispensable nature of cultural contents and intercultural competencies that must be acquired by pupils in the course of this teaching. This explains the importance of a strong initiative taken at the national level, from the moment of introduction of reference to the *CEFR* in texts determining the teaching of languages, to substantially reinforce the emphasis on these cultural contents in the curricula of the primary school, of the lower secondary school (*collège*) and of the upper secondary school (*lycée*). The link between language and culture has always been emphasised in the teaching of languages in France, but since 2002 these contents have been reinforced and made explicit for each stage of schooling. It would be wrong to see in this merely a means of counteracting possible reticence from teachers with respect to the *CEFR*. On the contrary, it is based on the conviction that only these cultural contents, linked to the action approach, can give teaching the meaning necessary to win the interest and commitment of pupils.

Let us note, however, that the weight given to cultural content in the teaching of languages does not explicitly include the intercultural dimension recommended in the *CEFR* and in the publications of the Council of Europe. It is a matter essentially in the language curricula in France of giving all pupils cultural knowledge that allows them to identify and understand explicit or implicit cultural references in a text, or in the individual or collective behaviour of speakers of the language being learnt. The next step, which consists of seeking, on this basis, in a focused and structured way to develop a tolerant and responsible attitude towards the expression of diversity, and to contribute in this way to the educational purposes of the school is undertaken by many teachers, but is not explicitly included in the objectives given to the teaching of cultural contents.

In an area close to that which we have just commented upon, one also notes another choice being made from the different contents of the *CEFR*. The very innovative definition of plurilingualism as a single competence of the individual, a repertoire of knowledge and skill in different languages and cultures at diverse levels of competence, has not yet been included in what has been borrowed from the *CEFR* in France. Even though almost all pupils in schools are obliged to learn at least two foreign languages for a part of their schooling, and even though the vast majority of those who are in general and technical secondary education continue learning both languages until the final examination, there is no trace in the current curricula of strong encouragement to exploit the convergences between the languages learnt, to develop competencies in the linguistic activity of mediation or to help pupils manage in an effective way their individual plurilingual repertoire. The choice was made, perhaps in order to take account of the capacity of the education system to implement the formulated recommendations, to limit the focus to the separate teaching of each language.

Reactions to some Misunderstandings in the Introduction of the *CEFR* into the Practice of Teaching and Assessment

The introduction of the *CEFR* into the practice of teaching and assessment, forcefully supported by political and pedagogical authorities on language teaching, created an enormous demand for explanations from teachers. The latter were split between an understandable concern about the required evolution in their practices by reference to an instrument known by very few on the one hand, and enthusiasm for a text to which many tended to attribute, almost with a sense of 'magical thinking', all the qualities of innovation on the other.

Efforts made to 'train' language teachers for the *CEFR* – which in fact consists of presenting them with the main arguments of the text and, in many cases, above all the levels of competence – were immense. They facilitated the creation of a common discourse for all teachers of all languages and the de-dramatisation of its introduction.

These efforts also removed certain misunderstandings as to the nature of the document to which some people wrongly – in order to criticise its introduction – attributed an obligatory dimension for all member states of the Council of Europe, which is often confused with the European Commission. This training also contributed to the demystification of this text, which some people had difficulty in understanding as a basis for mutual and formalised reflection in Europe at a given point in time.

Another confusion was more difficult to eradicate, namely that between the *CEFR* and the European Language Portfolio (ELP). Although these two instruments are complementary, one cannot be identified with the other. In fact, the ELP often served as an introduction to the logic of the *CEFR*. It is more easily accessible and its contents speak immediately to teachers in so far as it is anchored in learning. For many teachers or teacher educators, the ELP was synonymous with the *CEFR* and, as a consequence, the assessment of levels of competence expected by the education system was confused with self-assessment as proposed in the ELP. It was necessary for the education system to respond to this confusion. The response took the form of a strict distinction in the discourse of pedagogical authorities between the obligatory nature of the *CEFR* for all teaching and assessment situations, and the affirmation of the status of the ELP as being a pedagogical instrument which, like all pedagogical material in France, is chosen by pedagogical teams and cannot be officially promoted by the educational institution.

Conclusion

In concluding, we will consider just three points. As a consequence of the ways in which it was introduced into the French educational system, the *CEFR* was seen to be more an instrument of language policy than a technical document: above all, it was a matter of giving a new impetus to teaching. The second point concerns the conclusions that can be drawn. It is certainly too early to draw a global conclusion from the introduction of the *CEFR* beyond the increasing number of teachers who are successfully implementing the action approach of the *CEFR*. However, we can be satisfied with a first major effect rich in pedagogical potential: work across languages has rapidly become self-evident in pre- and in-service language teacher training and in shared thinking in educational establishments.

Furthermore, all curricula are now common to all languages. Finally, certain criticisms are beginning to be formulated concerning certain aspects of the *CEFR* by those involved in pedagogy or by teachers of languages. This phenomenon is very encouraging because it shows that the adoption of the *CEFR*, which is not in general questioned, is no longer simply submitted to or naively accepted as the remedy for all the ills of modern language teaching. It is being assimilated progressively in a critical fashion, which is the basis for its effectiveness.

3 Academic Perspectives from France

Véronique Castellotti

In order to analyse the reception of the *CEFR* in France, we need first to paint a rapid picture of the educational and linguistic traditions which prevail and which strongly influence attempts to practise and to theorise about, to renew and to reform the teaching and learning of languages. These traditions are strongly characterised by centralising and normative conceptions, which have settled like sediment over the course of centuries in the construction of a national language, tolerating neither competition nor deviation. In addition, there are the characteristics of a form of teaching that has progressively developed from a model originally elaborated for the transmission of Latin, and then of a grammar grounded in scholarly, written French, the purpose of which is to allow all French children to spell the national language correctly. We will need to consider in particular the interactions between the weight of these inheritances and the initiatives of the *CEFR* that are susceptible of encouraging possible evolutions.

Conceptions of Languages and Language Teaching

The teaching of foreign languages in France is influenced by their relationship to French, the history of which is a matter of political construction that overlaps with the history of the spatial and ideological unification of a state in which the linguistic dimension is sacred. It is the linguistic dimension which constitutes the yeast of national unity par excellence, and this is not without consequence 'in as much as prescriptivism . . . and purism . . . in France have acquired an extension and importance of a particular nature with, more firmly anchored than anywhere else, the conviction that uniformity represents the ideal state of a language and that heterogeneity can only be an obstacle to communication' (Lodge, 1997: 12).

Until recently, these ideas have led to the eradication of all other language varieties present on French territory, forbidding in public the use of regional languages and varieties as well as the languages of migration. This eviction has taken place more particularly thanks to schooling: France has a long tradition of literacy and the teaching primarily of the national language, and then of foreign languages, developed from the pattern of the teaching of classical languages. This philosophy, which still exists, favours a scholarly orientation more grounded in 'science' and 'reason' than in usage. This is also a form of teaching which is founded on the absolute supremacy of the written word, reinforcing purist ideas, with the oral dimension only appearing as a second best, a bastardised form of the ideal norm. This development was complemented by a refusal of otherness. First applied to French with respect to other 'dialects' present in France, it was also applied to foreign languages, the learning of which became widespread only towards the end of the 20th century, having been the subject of profound resistance and demonstrations of rejection for more than fifty years (Clavères, 1985).

The spread of language teaching in schools developed throughout the 20th century, being extended to primary schooling in the course of the 1990s. The labels are also significant: it is in fact a question of *modern* languages (*langues vivantes*) but above all of *foreign* languages, and it is important to note the emphasis on the 'foreign' character, whereas in other countries more importance is given to the characteristic of being 'second' in acquisition (e.g. *English as a Second Language*).

Finally, French also became, outside its frontiers, a dominant colonial language, reinforcing existing ideas of a form of 'intrinsic superiority' of French and of the importance of a normative grammar, which is explicit in the modes of its dissemination.

This combination of concepts, linked to the principles of the organisation of the education system, influences the context of reception of an instrument such as the *CEFR*, part of which has been adopted in France as a stimulus to bring a new dynamic into the teaching of languages, as pointed out in the previous chapter.

Consequences for the Reception and Integration of the *CEFR*

As has been shown, France is strongly centralised in linguistic terms; it is also centralised, in contrast to many of its neighbours, in administrative and educational terms. As Goullier notes in the previous chapter, this has positive consequences in that it permits the rapid transmission of new ideas that are to be implemented in a unified way.

However, these two complementary characteristics also constrain the context of the reception of educational changes. The organisation of the highly hierarchic education system, where the disciplines are carefully separated and demand strong and distinct 'identities', contributes to the difficulty of developing thinking which calls into question what exists in order to introduce change.

As Goullier also reminds us, the French authorities took from the *CEFR* what coincided with their primary preoccupations with respect to language teaching (i.e. above all the reference to the 'levels of competence' and the discourse on the 'action approach'), with the hope of renewing language teaching practices and improving their effectiveness.

This approach is not limited to the French context. As Coste comments in more general terms, 'referring to the *Framework*, in fact means only making reference to the scales of competences and their descriptors. This is a kind of inverse metonymy: instead of defining the whole by a part – as we used to say "the sail" to mean "the ship" – people refer to a part by the whole – "the ship" to refer to "the sail" – "the *Framework*" to speak about the scales of competence' (Coste, 2007: 6).

What we propose to do here, therefore, is to provide an interpretation of the modes of acceptance (or not) by France of the main orientations of the *CEFR*.

The action perspective and the competences

The action approach is explicitly mentioned as a main characteristic of the *CEFR* and is presented as a means of making language teaching more communicative, this being a fundamental objective given the unsatisfactory results achieved by French pupils in international surveys. In France it is undoubtedly a useful lever to question practices that are sometimes too heavily centred on the metalinguistic dimension and even on the transmission of contents, neglecting the involvement of the pupil in active learning. However, it is also often perceived by some people in the field as a utilitarian conception of language, to the detriment of the educational and cultural dimensions (especially literary) which are highly prized in France.

In the same vein, the development of a competence approach defined in terms of capacities, skills and attitudes is sometimes suspected of leading to an abandonment of fundamental disciplinary knowledge for the sake of an impoverished communicative practice. These criticisms stem from a tradition that strongly values the intellectual dimensions of learning in school to the detriment of abilities focused more on pragmatic aspects. Schooling in France has always favoured a strong metalinguistic culture, a 'knowledge about' languages considered to stem from the purposes of schooling, more than the transmission of language usage itself.

From this perspective, the *CEFR* is often presented as a break: a break which is welcomed by some because it favours the value attributed to practical communication, and seen as damaging by others because it could lead to a kind of abandoning of broader and more fundamental educational objectives.

The action perspective, both supported and simultaneously rejected, also valorises forms of transversality and continuity in learning together with support for principles of autonomy that are seldom put into operation in reality.

Learner autonomy and life-long learning

In the thinking throughout the evolution of Council of Europe's 'modern languages' projects since the 1970s, the underlying principles of the *CEFR* have largely been developed on the basis of a perspective of lifelong learning, based on the needs and the involvement of motivated learner groups such as people in adult education or university students.

School environments, however, are in general different, with quite different situations: on the one hand, learners only rarely have functional motivations, and, on the other, the modes of learning do not favour continuity of learning or access to autonomy. The contents are determined by the length of each stage of schooling and by limiting curricula, and the breaks between the stages are reinforced by 'teaching cultures' that are different from each other, especially those of primary and secondary education, and even those of different language teaching traditions.

Furthermore, assessment practices are essentially underpinned by the presence of examinations at the end of a stage of schooling, in particular by the *Baccalauréat* at the end of secondary schooling, where the tests do not encourage, in the backwash effect, the development of diversified approaches that would support autonomous learning.

These issues are not limited to France, but they are probably reinforced here by the belief in the superiority of a hierarchical education system, egalitarian and centrally organised, where principles such as those of continuous assessment, of taking into consideration the diversity of pupils, or reliance on experience in the determination of competences, have great difficulty in finding recognition.

The practices that can be observed in the use of European Language Portfolios (ELP) are revealing in this respect. Their purpose is often undermined, reducing them merely to their assessment aspect, of a summative assessment nature, and making them a kind of verification booklet for the teacher. In fact, they could be used more as a formative process focusing on pupils' awareness and recognition of their progress (cf. Huver & Springer, 2011).

Forms of interdisciplinarity between language learning and other disciplines are also made difficult after primary education, especially because of a form of teacher training which is narrowly focused on disciplinary contents. Within the 'languages' area there are the beginnings of new thinking, as Goullier notes. There is nonetheless a need to reinforce transversalities in order to envisage the formation and use of transferable strategies that have not been much researched so far.

Asserting a plurilingual and pluri/intercultural purpose

The basic philosophy of the *CEFR*, rooted in its plurilingual and pluri/intercultural purpose, is the political underpinning of its development. In contrast to the national structures of the 19th century, Europe has chosen not to impose a common language but, in its principles, to valorise linguistic diversity. In this context, which is explained in detail in the *Guide for the Development of Language Education Policies in Europe* (Beacco & Byram, 2007), the importance of the plurilingual and pluri/intercultural dimension of learning is very evident.

Despite the repeated support for these possibilities in official discourses, this philosophy was not taken up when the *CEFR* was adopted in France, as Goullier says. There may be several interpretations – party interrelated – for this decision:

- the first interpretation suggests that this is a matter of taking a realistic decision, taking into account the current, little developed competences of French people in the use of languages; this would then be a matter of operationalising a gradual policy, with the intention of filling the gap by taking one language at a time;
- the second interpretation is based on the ideological dimension which has already been explained. This leads to the conclusion that in fact it is better to master one language perfectly than several in an approximate way, that one can only learn a language 'completely' without hesitation, without making errors and that the aim of all learning is of this nature;
- the third interpretation comes from the suspicion that this choice is a consequence of a lack of understanding of the concept of plurilingualism found in the *CEFR*, which interprets it as an aim for a high-level competence in a significant number of languages. In fact, the notion of plurilingual competence was developed precisely as the contrary of this idea, as

a single competence, plural, partial and unbalanced, which operates by using the multiple resources of a complex repertoire (Coste *et al.*, 1997). It is therefore not a matter of the juxtaposition of several languages that have been mastered to perfection, but above all of the management of plurality (Castellotti, 2010).

In France and Elsewhere

The action perspective that underpins the *CEFR* is a concept which is ambitious and demanding in the role of language and languages in social relations. And the notion of 'task' to be found in curricular documents and textbooks represents it in only a weak way (Chiss, 2005). In France as elsewhere, and especially in school environments, it is difficult to envisage a general implementation of this kind of approach, the implications of which are scarcely compatible with institutional obligations and the time available for learning.

The way in which the *CEFR* was conceived also contributes to emphasising the importance of the assessment dimension which, given the objectives of European harmonisation, has rapidly changed into an obligation to certificate. We can see this in many places, in forms of 'blind' application of the scales, and of excessive standardisation where there is no reflection on the modes of assessment and the necessarily relative and situated nature of the competences in question.

The other purposes of the *CEFR*, especially those of a political nature, have rapidly become a lower priority in the minds of most potential users who tend to only consider it as a technical tool.

This also explains why the intercultural dimension is 'forgotten'. It is usually marginalised, leaving emphasis on the 'knowledge about' cultural aspects, which is more compatible with forms of learning in schools, and easier to assess. The development of new tools such as the *Autobiography of Intercultural Encounters* (Conseil de l'Europe, 2009) could lead to change in this conceptualisation.

Conclusion

In France the *CEFR* has undoubtedly contributed to the analysis of some 'certainties' in language teaching in schools, especially with respect to the methodological approaches used. In particular, the focus on action, even if it is based on a very weakened version compared to the research that emphasises the complexity of the links between language and action (Filliettaz, 2002), is contributing to giving more meaning to language learning in school contexts. From this point of view, we can only be glad of the stimulus role that the *CEFR* is playing.

The production of reference level descriptions for French, making concrete the levels of the *CEFR* in order to operationalise them, is also an important process carried out by Beacco and his collaborators. In particular, the interest in individuals who have a low-level of education, recognising and valorising what they already know (Beacco *et al.*, 2005) is an original initiative that is in full coherence with the philosophy of the *CEFR* and could transform its use with respect to the question of plurality.

The difficulty French people have – which is frequently criticised – in using other languages is not in fact due to the methods so much as the inability, sometimes carefully cultivated, to accept difference, to venture into uncertainty, into heterogeneity and the impure.

However, largely as a consequence of a French initiative, there is a development under the aegis of the European Centre for Modern Languages in Graz, of *A Framework of Reference for Pluralistic Approaches / Cadre de référence pour les approches plurielles*, which is intended to favour the recognition of the construction of plurilingual and pluricultural competence (Candelier *et al.*, 2007). It is in France too that approaches are being developed for the study of the more concrete conditions for a general education for plurilingualism in the primary school (Castellotti *et al.*, 2008).

If, at the moment, France has not adopted the plurilingual philosophy of the *CEFR*, it may find in it a stimulating opportunity to develop ideas and shake the inertia, to promote methods of teaching and learning languages which are truly changed, within a context of a linguistic policy capable of favouring approaches which are both active, inclusive and 'diverse'.

References

Beacco, J-C. and Byram, M. (2007) *Guide pour l'élaboration des politiques linguistiques éducatives en Europe*. Strasbourg: Conseil de l'Europe.

Beacco, J-C., De Ferrari, M., Lhote, G. and Tagliante, C. (2005) *Niveau A1.1 pour le français. Référentiel et certification (DILF) pour les premiers acquis en français*. Paris: Didier.

Candelier, M., Camilleri-Grima, A., Castellotti, V., de Pietro, J.-F., Lörincz, I., Meissner, F-J., Schröder-Sura, A. and Noguerol, A. (2007) *A travers les Langues et les Cultures. Cadre de Référence pour les Approches Plurielles des Langues et des Cultures*. Graz: Centre européen pour les langues vivantes.

Castellotti, V. (2010) Attention! Un plurilinguisme peut en cacher un autre. Enjeux théoriques et didactiques de la notion de pluralité. *Les cahiers de L'ACEDLE* 7 (1), *181–207*. Online at http://acedle.org/spip.php?article2864.

Castellotti, V., Coste, D. and Duverger, J. (coord.) (2008) *Propositions pour une éducation au plurilinguisme en contexte scolaire*. ADEB et Université François Rabelais. Online at www.adeb.asso.fr/publications_adeb/brochure_Tours2007.pdf.

Chiss, J-L. (2005) Réflexions à partir de la notion de tâche: langage, action et didactique des langues. In M.A. Mochet, M-J. Barbot, V. Castellotti and J-L. Chiss (eds) *Plurilinguisme et Apprentissages. Mélanges Daniel Coste* (pp. 39–48). Lyon: ENS Editions.

Clavères, M-H. (1985) 1884 ou la lassitude du corps. In D. Thomières (ed.) *Le Citoyen de Demain et les Langues*. Paris: Colloque de Cerisy /APLV.

Conseil de l'Europe (2009) *Autobiographie de rencontres interculturelles*. Online at http://www.coe.int/t/dg4/autobiography/default_FR.asp

Coste, D. (2007) Contextualiser les utilisations du CECR. *Rapport du forum intergouvernemental sur les politiques linguistiques*, Strasbourg, 6–8 February 2007. Online at www.coe.int/t/dg4/linguistic/Source/SourceForum07/D-Coste_Contextualise_FR.doc

Coste, D., Moore, D. and Zarate, G. (1997) *Compétence Plurilingue et Pluriculturelle.* Strasbourg: Conseil de l'Europe.

Filliettaz, L. (2002) *La Parole en Action. Eléments de Pragmatique Psycho-Sociale*. Québec: Nota Bene.

Goullier, F. (2007) Faut-il 'appliquer' le Cadre Européen Commun de Référence pour les Langues (CECRL)¿ Conférence au CRDP de Bourgogne, 26 September 2007. Online at http://crdp.ac-dijon.fr/Faut-il-appliquer-le-Cadre.html#outil_sommaire_4.

Huver, E. and Springer, C. (2011) *L'Évaluation en Langues.* Paris: Didier.

Lodge, R.A. (1997) *Le Français. Histoire d'un Dialecte devenu Langue.* Paris: Fayard. (For the English version, see: *French, from Dialect to Standard*. London: Routledge).

Germany

The authors:

Henny Rönneper works in the fields of foreign language education, bilingual education, international graduation and supervision of schools. A certified interpreter for French and Russian, she worked as a French and Russian teacher at a grammar school *(Gymnasium)* for more than 20 years. She acted as coordinator with the UNESCO school project and has professional experience in primary school education and in institutions of further education. She has been head of the Foreign Language Division at the Ministry of Education and Further Education of North Rhine-Westphalia since 2001.

Adelheid Hu was Professor for Foreign Language Pedagogy at the University of Hamburg and is now at the University of Luxembourg. Her work includes the topics of intercultural learning and intercultural competence in the context of language learning, plurilingualism, foreign language teaching in migrant societies and foreign language curriculum planning and policies. From October 2005 to October 2009 she was head of the German Association for Foreign Language Learning Research (DGFF). She began her career at the Ruhr-University Bochum, where she studied German and French linguistics and literature, as well as applied linguistics (Sprachlehrforschung) and Chinese. She spent six years in Taiwan teaching German and French at university level. She also spent one and a half years in France, teaching German at a French school and later applied linguistics at the University of Franche-Comté (Besançon). She has published many books and articles and supervises doctoral students, mainly in the field of intercultural studies, plurilingualism and foreign language teaching and learning in school contexts.

4 Policy Perspectives from Germany

Henny Rönneper

The political, cultural and economic development of Europe in the context of international cooperation and global competition is leading to changes in societal conditions. The starting point and purpose of the *CEFR* is to enable people in a multilingual and pluricultural Europe to take action, to develop mobility and their ability to communicate in decisive ways, and to offer them opportunities for lifelong learning. The diversification and intensification of language learning support the attention paid to and the maintenance of linguistic and cultural diversity in Europe, more intensive communication and interaction, better access to information and deeper mutual understanding.

In order to meet these demands, foreign language guidelines and curricula in Germany as in many other countries of Europe place communicative, intercultural and strategic competences at the heart of modern foreign language teaching, and are orientated to the *CEFR* and its descriptions of competence.

Above all, the description of the linguistic capacities and skills in terms of the six levels of reference of the *CEFR* based on a communicative-action orientated concept of language learning provide an orientation for foreign language learning in all kinds of education, in schools and beyond, and comparability and recognition of certification and examination levels throughout Europe. They thus form an important basis for the development of curricula, textbooks and language examinations in Europe and allow for international cooperation of educational institutions.

The Influence of the *CEFR* on the Development in North Rhine-Westphalia of Education Standards and Competence-Orientated Curricula

The *CEFR* is a decisive signpost for foreign language learning and teaching in which foreign language competences are described operationally, partial competences are defined and levels of competence determined.

The 'Einheitliche Prüfungsanforderungen in der Abiturprüfung' (EPA) ('Uniform examination requirements for the final examination at upper secondary school level (Abitur)') adopted by the Konferenz der Kultusminister (KMK) – the organisation of all ministers of education of the 16 states of the Federal Republic of Germany – and valid for all states of the Federal Republic of Germany, were already an early recognition of the internationalisation of foreign language standards. The *CEFR* has been fundamental to the EPA since 2002. This is the basis for the strengthening of the focus upon application and real-world use of languages, as well as the emphasis on oral communication skills, particularly presentation, discourse and interaction skills.

The EPA defines qualifications and competences that are both subject-specific and transversal across subjects as the framework conditions for university entry qualifications at the end of upper secondary school, and these are orientated to the levels of reference and the formulations of the *CEFR* (see Table 4.1). The *CEFR* also provides the basis for the education standards adopted in 2004 by the KMK for the first foreign language (English and French) in lower secondary schooling. The standards are valid for all lower secondary leaving qualifications, and in this way obligatory levels of attainment (so-called 'regulated standards') were fixed for the end of this level of schooling as A2 for those leaving school after nine years and B1 for those leaving school after 10 years, including grammar schools (*Gymnasien*) (see Table 4.1).

Even before the modification of the EPA and the development of education standards, the *CEFR* had decisively influenced the development of teaching in North-Rhine Westphalia (NRW) since it was the basis for competence-orientated curricula from 1999 onwards, and it thus had a significant influence on the development of curricula. The reason for this decisive influence was that the development of the *CEFR* coincided with the development of the curriculum for the upper secondary grammar school in NRW. It was the aim at that time to take into consideration the most recent results from the Council of Europe. Since this point, a comprehensive appendix with the *CEFR* reference levels for functional communicative competences, the availability of linguistic means and accuracy and the capability of expression and the communicative range in foreign language curricula has been developed for all school types in NRW. This means that NRW was the first federal state to devise curricula and syllabi in a systematic way from the *CEFR*. Since the level descriptions of the *CEFR* are not specifically related to school or institutional foreign language learning, the production of curricula was not a matter of simply adopting the levels of reference. It was rather a matter of introducing into the curricula specifications of competence descriptions appropriate as outcomes of school-based foreign language learning, which were orientated to the competence descriptions of the *CEFR*.

Only the consistent application of foreign language skills leads to the attainment of foreign language competences and to the level of independent language use. This level is set in the competence orientated core curricula for lower secondary education as the final certification level – equivalent to *CEFR* level B1, as indicated in Table 4.1 – and is operationalised through curricula developed within schools, examples of which can now be downloaded for English and French from the Internet.

In NRW the central authorities determine core curricula that are then enriched with further details by individual schools. These core curricula are competence based where the expected outcomes of learning are presented as obligatory education standards, and these learning outcomes are described in the form of subject-specific competences. The competence fields described in foreign language curricula comprise capacities in substantial knowledge and skills in the areas of 'communicative competences', 'intercultural competences', 'competences in the application of language skills and language awareness', 'competences in handling texts and media' and 'strategic competences in independent and cooperative learning'. The competence areas are thus directed towards language use in situations of everyday life and employment as well as intercultural capacity for action, attitudes and commitments. These areas of competence are at the same time the framework for complex situations of learning in the foreign language classroom and help teachers to plan concrete teaching processes.

Competence-orientated curricula are now available for all foreign language subjects and for teaching heritage languages. Pupils have a wide choice of languages in addition to English as an obligatory first foreign language: from French, Spanish, Italian, Portuguese, Dutch, Russian, modern Greek and Turkish, to Japanese and Chinese.

The implementation of the *CEFR* is also supported by the fact that extracts from it are included in the appendices to the core curricula, the education standards and the EPA, as indicated above. The fields of competence described in the core curricula are furthermore the basis of the criteria for the formal recognition of textbooks in NRW. Thus the *CEFR* is also indirectly the framework for the construction of foreign language teaching materials, the planning of which has to be orientated to the core curricula.

The links of the core curricula of NRW to the *CEFR*, to the national education standards and to the EPA of the KMK ensure that solid foreign language competences are attained at internationally defined and comparable levels.

Table 4.1 The *CEFR* stages and the corresponding school leaving certificates in NRW

	CEFR	**Curricula in North-Rhine Westphalia**	**Einheitliche Prüfungsanforderungen im Abitur (EPA)**	
Elementary language use	A1 Breakthrough	Primary school curriculum English After Form 4		European Language Portfolio / EUROPASS
	A2 Waystage	Education Standards KMK Hauptschule/lower secondary leaving certificate after Form 9 Core Curriculum English		
Independent language use	B1 Threshold	Education Standards KMK Middle school leaving certificate after Form 10 Core Curricula for Foreign Languages	EPA Foreign Languages GK (n) LK (n) Curricula for Foreign Languages GOSt	
	B2 Vantage	EPA Foreign Languages GK (f) LK (f) Curricula for Foreign Languages GOSt GK (f) LK (f)		
Competent language use	C1 Effective Operational Proficiency			
	C2 Mastery			

Explanations:
GK – Basic Course; LK – Major Course; GOSt – Grammar school upper secondary; (f) – Foreign language carried forward in Grammar School upper secondary section from lower secondary; (n) – new language beginning in Grammar school upper secondary.

European-based standards and competence expectations are also the basis of the surveys of learning outcomes and central examinations (lower secondary and upper secondary). Furthermore, education standards for the *Abitur* examination and learning and test tasks for the education standards

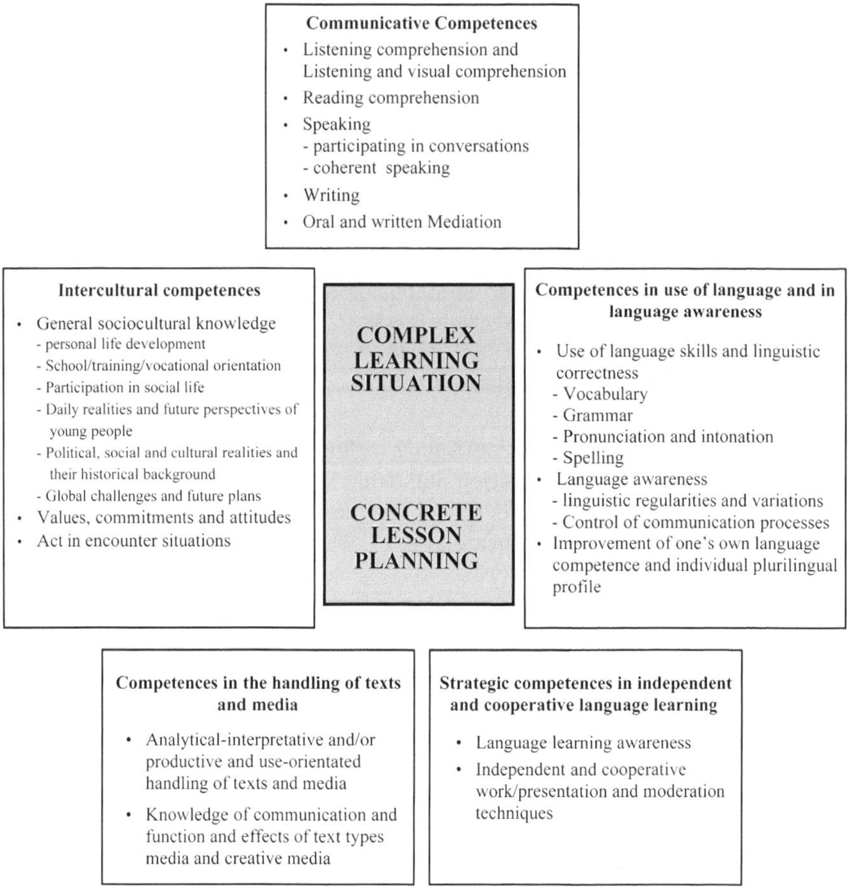

Figure 4.1 The competence areas in foreign language teaching and learning from the overview of the foreign language core curricula

of lower secondary in English and French were developed through cooperation of the federal states with the Institute for Quality Development in Education (IQB) in Berlin with participation by experts from NRW.

Furthermore, a network for the development of teaching methods was formed for the development of competence-oriented teaching and learning with participation of schools, of teacher educators in universities, in-service institutions and in the school inspectorate for English and French. The network deals with the development of learning tasks and offers support and further impulses for the development of teaching and learning in all foreign languages. The over-arching aim of the network is to make teachers more competent in creating learning and assessment tasks which correspond to the descriptions of competence in the core curricula and the *CEFR*, and to strengthen their capacity for diagnosing and developing individual pupils.

Competence-orientated exercises and examples of good practice have been developed which support teachers in their work and which can be downloaded from the internet pages of the Ministry for Schools and Further Education of North Rhine Westphalia (http://www.standardsicherung.schulministerium.nrw.de/cms/angebote/unterrichtsentwicklung-englisch/angebot-home/uebersicht.html). The detailed descriptors of the *CEFR* stimulate teachers to check whether adequate conditions have been created in their classrooms and whether the chosen methods and the texts they use are appropriate for the attainment of the expected competences. Pupils have the opportunity to evaluate their language level themselves to reflect on their course of learning and to plan and check their progress.

Further Development of Foreign Language Teaching and Learning

The further development of foreign language teaching and learning has taken place on several levels. In addition to a very broad offer of foreign languages which contributes to the diversification of foreign languages (at the moment 11 modern languages, three classical languages and 19 heritage languages are being learnt), measures have been taken for the intensification of foreign language learning which are decisive for the development of the plurilingual and intercultural competence in our schools.

Since 2009, English, as the first foreign language, has been learnt by all pupils from Grade 1 in the primary school through to the end of lower secondary school. This ensures that all pupils acquire communicative competence relevant to everyday use in English and can make themselves understood orally and in written language in international contexts.

From Grade 6 in the three kinds of secondary school (*Gymnasium*/grammar school, *Realschule*/middle school and *Gesamtschule*/comprehensive school), and in certain grammar schools in Grade 5, a second foreign language is added. Preparations are being made to offer a second foreign language, for example Turkish and Russian, in the fourth kind of lower secondary school (basic school/*Hauptschule*). In grammar schools a third foreign language can be taken from form eight, and in comprehensive and middle schools a second or third foreign language can be learnt. A further foreign language may be introduced at the beginning of the upper secondary stage.

It is thus the aim of foreign language learning to promote the plurilingualism of pupils and to ensure that all young people learn at least two foreign languages in addition to their mother tongue. The aim of intensification is to use the whole of the time of schooling so that as high competences as possible will be reached, forming a secure basis for further learning after schooling is complete. It is here that the B-levels of the *CEFR* have a key role since all pupils should learn at least one language to level B1 by the end of lower secondary schooling and B2 by the time of the *Abitur* at the end of upper secondary. There are many initiatives to provide impulses to broaden the spectrum of languages learnt in schools as well as to improve the competence levels reached. These include the promotion of lessons where a foreign language is used as the medium of instruction and the offer of internationally recognised language and plurilingualism certificates.

Intensification of Foreign Language Learning by Foreign-Language Certificates

In order to strengthen education in general and vocational schools, and to ensure the expected competences are obtained, several thousand pupils per year have been taking part in international certification examinations in many languages since the 1990s. In 2010/11, approximately 30,000 pupils were successful in these examinations in English, French, Italian, Spanish, Dutch, Russian, Japanese, modern Greek and Chinese. Pupils can also take a language certificate for Turkish from 2010. The evaluation report of the University of Cambridge shows that there have been above average results for NRW pupils in international comparison, and a 97% pass rate of pupils taking the French *DELF* examinations.

It is particularly motivating for pupils to be able to demonstrate attainments at *CEFR* levels through internationally recognised language certificates, which are taken to complement school-based examinations. Participation in such examinations means testing their own achievements in an international comparison. Pupils learn to estimate their achievements and to improve their ability in oral expression through this experience of another kind of examination and with native speaker examiners. In this way they simultaneously acquire personal competences and an important additional qualification for vocational training and study at home and abroad. Pupils and their parents are very much interested in earning international language certificates, and consider it a significant merit if their schools include preparation for and organisation of these certificates as a regular part of their curriculum. Schools also obtain a price reduction for their pupils.

From the school's point of view, these external foreign language examinations provide a substantial contribution to the development of quality and quality assurance in foreign-language teaching, since preparation for the examinations corresponds to the aims set for foreign language teaching and provides clear goals within the competences that are to be achieved. The format of the examinations requires the ability to deal with authentic contemporary texts as well as the production of appropriate texts for use in real life. This also means that there are opportunities for teachers for further training, which leads to an improved understanding of the *CEFR* among those who participate. For example, the week-long DELF/DALF teacher training course at the *Centre international d'études pédagogiques* in Sèvres strengthens the professionalisation of teachers. The conceptualisation and evaluation of test tasks analogous to the levels of the *CEFR* is a central focus of such training carried out by DELF/DALF specialists, and similar courses are offered by Cambridge ESOL, DELE, the Nederlandse Taalunie und the Turkish TÖMER Institute.

Because of the motivational power of these certification examinations and their positive effects on foreign language learning, they are being integrated into the NRW school system. Furthermore the process of decision-making at institutional level concerning the awarding of language certificates encourages a more intensive international cooperation at administrative level.

Strengthening of orality in foreign language teaching and learning

Communicative tasks are characteristic of everyday activity in private and public life and the world of work. Skills in oral expression, competence in presentation and discourse skills thus have an important place in the preparation of pupils for employment and study. The emphasis on the role of communicative tasks in the *CEFR* has directed attention to the breadth of areas of communication and the high value of orality, and this in turn has led to a significant strengthening of orality in foreign language teaching in NRW. Pupils shall have the opportunity to build up and try out their oral competences in systematic ways. The legal framework for education and examination regulations was altered so that, in lower and upper secondary education, written tests and examinations can be fully or partially replaced by oral examinations. The demonstration of oral competences in the areas 'participate in conversations' and 'coherent speaking' can take place in single, pair or group examinations. Teachers have developed guidelines for oral examinations that contain examples of competence-orientated tests for upper secondary education school in English and French on the basis of evaluations of the practical operationalisation of such examinations (see http://www.standardsicherung.schulministerium.nrw.de/cms/front_content.php?idart=1907andidcat=923).

Changes to the regulations for examinations and existing offers of support have also had a positive effect on foreign language teaching, which is increasingly structured in communicative ways and thus creates more space for complex expression by pupils and opportunities for authentic speaking.

Creating Greater Fluidity in Transfer between Schools

The *CEFR* is strongly anchored in the school system as a consequence of issues thrown up in practice by the introduction of early foreign language learning from Grade 1, and the transfer from primary to lower secondary school through its contribution to continuity in the language acquisition process. As a consequence of the introduction of foreign language teaching in the primary school at national level, there have been wide-ranging issues for foreign language teaching in secondary schools. It is vital to carry further the fruits of early foreign language learning and to build on them in continuation of teaching in lower secondary schools. This means there is a need to document the competences from one level of schooling to the next and to develop further the competences acquired at the end of primary school. There is an even greater need for a formal documentation in this context because oral language work tends to be foregrounded in the primary school. This can only be successful if evaluations by learners and teachers are linked to descriptions of learning in the *CEFR*.

The German European Language Portfolio (basic and continuation) is an instrument with which foreign language skills and competences can be documented and differentiated accurately so that they can also be understood and accepted in other countries. The Portfolio was developed at national level and provides a means of describing pupils' individual competences at the transition phase by reference to the *CEFR*. On the pages for self-evaluation of one's language knowledge, the basic Portfolio defines, in terms appropriate to the age range, competences in the areas of listening comprehension, speaking, reading comprehension and writing. The level of ability is formulated at the end of each page with a summarising descriptor. The continuation Portfolio uses these descriptions and enables pupils to bridge the transfer from one school level to the next. Furthermore, the areas of intercultural learning and strategic learning build on each other in both Portfolios. In this way, the basic and continuation Portfolios complement each other and can be used as accompaniments to transfer between forms of schooling. The process of foreign language learning becomes transparent for both pupils and teachers in the logic of the organically linked competence acquisition in increasingly complex stages.

New Forms of Documentation of Foreign Language Competences

A further contribution to the demonstration of acquired language competences at a European level is provided by the Language Passport, one of the five elements of the Euro-Passport (www.europass-info.de/EN/). This is orientated to the *CEFR* and provides for competence profiles to describe foreign language skills and competences, so that it is possible to document in a differentiated and precise way what a language learner can achieve in the areas of 'listening', 'reading', 'participating in conversations', 'coherent speaking' and 'writing'. The European dimension of the Language Passport depends on the fact that this is linked to the European Language Portfolio where the parts 'language biography' and 'dossier' support the work with the Language Passport and make it concrete, for example by the provision of further indicators which provide a reliable basis for self-evaluation and evaluation by others of language competences.

The German versions of the European Language Portfolio and the Language Passport act as resources and initiatives for the development of quality in education by the Council of Europe and the European Union at a European level. Both instruments are important opportunities to speed up the development of standards and quality in teaching and learning of languages in all areas of education. At the same time, they offer a starting point for international cooperation between educational institutions in Europe.

Influence of the *CEFR* on School Development: CertiLingua

An example of increased international cooperation is provided by the CertiLingua label of excellence for plurilingual, European and international competences developed by North Rhine-Westphalia together with other European partner countries, and currently awarded by 17 European ministries of education.

The aim of the initiators was to link and combine more intensively the different levels of development of multilingualism with the teaching of interpersonal and intercultural competences in a European perspective, and to stimulate pupils to use the education opportunities offered by their schools to develop high foreign language and international competences.

Those who hold the CertiLingua certificate, awarded as a complement to the examinations at the end of schooling giving access to higher education, which are the responsibility of national authorities, can demonstrate high competences in two, and in some cases more, modern foreign languages, bilingual competences and European and international competences.

The preconditions are:

- the demonstration of foreign language competence at level B2 of the *CEFR* in at least two modern foreign languages;
- the demonstration of bilingual competence in approximately 90 lessons at the final, qualification phase of upper secondary level or 180 lessons in the last four years before the *Abitur;*
- the demonstration of European and international competences at level IV of the draft reference framework for Europe competences in the partial competences of knowledge, critical reflection and task competence (European ELOS Network; www.europelearning.info).

CertiLingua could hardly have been conceived without the *CEFR* since it defines the access level to higher education as B2 independently of the multiplicity of European assessment systems. The *CEFR* makes a particular contribution in the development of plurilingualism in the CertiLingua framework, since competences in several languages can be compared and clear competence profiles described.

Agreements with many partners at different levels are necessary in the organisation, evaluation and further development of the CertiLingua label of excellence. An international CertiLingua network has been created to coordinate these multifarious tasks (www.certilingua.net). The members of this network are the ministries of education of the partnership countries that have signed a common Memorandum of Understanding defining the cooperation of countries in the CertiLingua network. By signing this document, ministries of education state that they are ready to underwrite the CertiLingua quality criteria in the award of the label of excellence in schools by appropriate instruments of quality assurance. The quality standards for the award are determined in the international network of the CertiLingua schools and guarantee a Europe-wide comparability of competences acquired in the CertiLingua framework. The CertiLingua network is led at European level by an international steering group which, in addition to the organisation of the annual CertiLingua meeting, is responsible for the coordination of the evaluation and development and decision-making about further processes with the purpose of ensuring quality and the further development of the label of excellence.

CertiLingua thus offers specially gifted and high-achieving pupils the opportunity to achieve and demonstrate above average capacities in the area of foreign language and intercultural competences. The certificate motivates pupils to use existing education opportunities in their schools that facilitate access to international courses of study, to universities abroad and to the European world of work.

Conclusion

All in all, it is clear that the *CEFR* has influenced the NRW educational landscape in many ways. The *CEFR* has contributed decisively to the development of curricula and of teaching approaches, which is evident from the professionalisation of teachers, a further extension of competence-oriented foreign language teaching and learning tasks, and from forms of centralised examinations. The further development of the strengthening of oral competences and an 'applied' approach to language teaching is particularly clear. New forms of documentation and certification of foreign language achievements offer pupils impulses to develop their individual competences in systematic ways and motivate schools to continue to offer foreign language and international courses.

5 Academic Perspectives from Germany

Adelheid Hu

Introduction

From the very beginning, the *CEFR* both challenged and changed the teaching and learning of languages in Germany in school contexts and beyond. Its influence became even stronger with the passage of the regulations on education standards for the first foreign language (English/French) by the Kultusministerkonferenz (The organisation of all ministers of education of the 16 federal states of the Federal Republic of Germany – KMK) in 2003 (Kultusministerkonferenz, 2003) since this document adopted the skills of the *CEFR* to a large extent. What was not originally intended by the authors of the *CEFR* took place: the reference levels were used for the description of standards and therefore gained even more normative weight. If one looks today at foreign language textbooks, at recently introduced comparisons of test results, at surveys of standards of learning, at language certificates or tests, the levels A1-C2 are present everywhere and determine the ideas of many teachers concerning language learning processes.

This development is all the more surprising in that, in the scientific community of those concerned with foreign language teaching and research, the *CEFR* is controversial and has been received critically and with some ambivalence. The same was the case with respect to the introduction of the education standards by the KMK, an event which also stimulated serious debates about its meaning and purpose and the consequences of such a development in educational policy. Two things become clear from this development: the tension between local concepts in language education, stemming from a specific cultural history, and the dynamics of neo-liberal, international, political-economic developments, not least in the education sector. At the same time, the implementation process reveals the power relationships and the various interests that influence educational institutions: economics, politics and science. At the moment, science has a critical but also to a large extent legitimising and supporting role.

In the first part of this chapter I will consider the relatively critical early reception of the *CEFR* in the scientific methodology of foreign language teaching. In the second part I will show how and why, despite the contentions of the scientific community, the *CEFR* was so quickly and fundamentally introduced into the practice of foreign language teaching. In the third part I will address some themes which underlie the discussion of a competence-orientated foreign language teaching: the problems involved in taking over the reference levels as standards, the question of intercultural competences and the question of the languages of migration. I will conclude with some considerations concerning the hegemony of a specific neo-liberal educational discourse, and plead for a multiplicity of discourses and alternative visions.

The Early Reception of the *CEFR* in German Foreign Language Teaching

In March 2002, shortly after the appearance of the German translation of the *CEFR*, the '22nd Spring Conference on Research into Foreign Language Teaching and Learning' was devoted exclusively to a discussion of the *CEFR*. The main emphases were its underlying concept of language, its approach to language acquisition and/or foreign language theory, the descriptors and their role in the future of assessment and/or curriculum development work, and the consequences for research in foreign language teaching (Bausch *et al.*, 2003: 7). Twenty-two well-known foreign language experts in German universities presented their views on the *CEFR* in the conference. The proceedings of this conference can thus be seen as a significant account of the early reception of the *CEFR* in Germany.

First, the positive aspects. There was a general welcome for the fact that the *CEFR* had led to a fundamental discussion of the teaching and learning of languages. It was clearly accepted as a stimulus to rethinking traditions and to considering in innovative ways the principles of language learning and teaching (cf. Barkowski, 2003: 22; Bausch, 2003: 29). Many also saw the potential for international transparency and comparison in a positive light, especially with respect to processes of assessment (e.g. Vollmer, 2003). The concept of pluricultural plurilingualism, which is developed in particular in Chapter 1 of the *CEFR* (Council of Europe, 2001: 17), was readily accepted, as was the constructively positive development of the 'can-do descriptors' (instead of the usual deficit-orientated judgements made hitherto). The especially constructive potential of the language portfolio was also noted, since this was linked to the hope of making possible complex, individually tailored descriptions of language levels (Gogolin, 2003: 89).

On the other hand there were many aspects that were criticised, the most frequent and important of which were:

- The underlying concept of language was considered to be one-sidedly instrumental-functional; the aesthetic, affective, creative, moral and cultural dimensions of language and language learning seemed underdeveloped to many people (e.g. Barkowski, 2003: 23; Krumm, 2003: 125; for criticism of a trivial concept of reading competence see Bredella, 2003).
- The concept of pluricultural plurilingualism, first developed in the *CEFR* and which was judged very positively, was thought not to be carried through consistently; in the scales, on the other hand, there were isolated partial competences in a traditional native speaker combination of first and foreign languages (cf. Barkowski, 2003; Bausch, 2003; Christ, 2003; Krumm, 2003); scales for intercultural and plurilingual competences were missing; and the languages of migration as first languages seemed to be neglected (Legutke, 2003: 132).
- The concept of communicative action was criticised on the one hand for being instrumental (without consideration of mutuality and understanding) (Bredella, 2003: 45), and as idealistic on the other since it took no account of politico-linguistic power and relationships of inequality (Barkowski, 2003: 23f.).
- *Processes* of language learning seemed to be underemphasised; by contrast it seemed that the question of assessment was foregrounded, despite the subtitle 'learning, teaching, assessment' (Tönshoff, 2003: 183).
- The needs, interests and aims of learners seemed to be neglected (Königs, 2003: 115).
- The danger of the Macdonaldisation of foreign language research was raised: language learning and teaching was being taken only from the viewpoint of efficiency, predictability, calculability and control measures (Schwerdtfeger, 2003: 178).
- The descriptors seemed to many people to be unsystematic and insufficiently precise (e.g. Quetz, 2003).

Many authors also expressed prognoses about the future influence of the *CEFR*, and for most of them the main worry was that there would be undesirable effects. There was a fear of a strong norm-setting influence, even though this was explicitly not the intention of the authors of the *CEFR*. It was thought that there was a danger in the schematic representation of language development of submission to a compulsory system (Christ,

2003: 62). There would be 'no escape' because of the close-meshed can-do definitions (Krumm, 2003: 124), and individuality and variety would be abandoned in favour of transregional processes of standardisation (Krumm, 2003: 125). There was also fear about the increase in a trend to certification and quality control, which considers learning processes from the point of view of assessment (Königs, 2003: 115).

In summary, the enormous significance of the *CEFR* for the development of foreign language teaching was duly recognised and predicted. There were certainly hopes, but worries and fears were also expressed. The main concern was about the reductionist, one-sided instrumental-functional concept of language learning, which ignores educational dimensions (intercultural, aesthetic, critical and creative). The high-value of pluricultural plurilingual language development and its requirements appeared only as 'decoration' (Quetz, 2003: 145), since the scales did not include the characteristic competences of plurilingual people (transfer, reference to internationalisms, code-switching, maintenance of communication with the help of other languages). There seemed to be a danger that individual learners with their own interests and purposes would not be taken seriously.

Given this thoroughly critical reception, the rate at and 'vehemence' (Quetz, 2003: 150) with which the *CEFR* was implemented in the German school system is all the more surprising, as is the fact that it now determines thinking about language learning in decisive ways in many places.

The History of the Implementation of the *CEFR* in Germany

The fact that the *CEFR* could develop such a strong dynamic in the practice of language teaching and learning and change foreign language teaching so fundamentally was due to the coincidence of two simultaneous developments in educational policy. First there was the European initiative for a common educational space, which included – alongside other initiatives such as the so-called Bologna process – the *CEFR*. A second decisive factor, which is at least indirectly connected to the first, was in the OECD studies, in particular the PISA study (Deutsches PISA-Konsortium, 2001). The discrepancy revealed by these comparative studies of proficiency between the claims of the German education system and the actual results obtained led not only to a general shock (the 'PISA shock'), but also to a reform agenda in educational policy which was expected to lead to an improvement in the proficiency of German pupils in international comparisons (cf. Klieme & Leutner, 2006: 876). The education standards which were produced by the KMK in 2003 for the subjects of mathematics, German and the first foreign language form the heart of the envisaged general strategy for education policy. The Institute for Educational Progress (IQB), founded by the KMK in 2001, had the task of further developing education standards and of implementing and verifying them (cf. for the first foreign language, Tesch *et al.*, 2008). The plan in the medium and the long term was to establish for the whole education system, schools and universities, aims for every subject in the form of competence-orientated and assessable catalogues of expectations.

The overall strategy of the KMK (cf. Sekretariat der Ständigen Konferenz der Kultusminister, 2006: 6) included: the establishment of education standards; regular participation in international investigations of school achievement; central testing of the attainment of education standards in a comparison across the German federal states; comparative studies linked with the education standards in testing nationally or across federal states; the efficiency of all schools; and a common form of educational reporting at a national and federal state level. The aim of this major education policy project is 'evidence-based policy and practice' (Klieme & Leutner, 2006: 877) (i.e. learning results are to be surveyed on a wide scale by evaluation agencies on a regular basis, compared and, according to need, reported back to schools, federal states or countries). The heart of this kind of system of monitoring is a so-called 'output orientation' instead of the 'input' hitherto common in Germany (i.e. the content-orientated curricula are to be replaced by an orientation to 'output', namely the assessable competences of pupils at various stages).

When the KMK decided on the basis of the PISA results to implement education standards, foreign languages were a special case insofar as a system of levels already existed from the *CEFR*. Since there were no other empirically based models of competence development in foreign languages, it was not surprising that, under strong political pressure for action, this existing work was taken up without hesitation, and the B1 level used as the basis for the expected level at the end of lower secondary school. Though not intended by its authors as a norm-setting document, the *CEFR* now acquired, having been transformed into education standards, a high normative significance. The framework curricula provided for the first time in the federal German system for the whole country could be developed in ways specific to each federal state, but the link to the defined areas of competence and above all the levels was nonetheless obligatory. Thus through the coincidence with the results of the PISA study, the *CEFR* became a central part of a radical reorientation of education policy in Germany.

Some Fundamental Issues

It is clear that, after the appearance of the education standards for the first foreign language, the critics did not remain quiet, with the view that the problems already identified in the *CEFR* were now being definitively implemented in teaching practice. At the same time, after the PISA results it was also increasingly recognised that there was a need for a redirection, with the result that the new political strategy now appeared to be promising for many people (cf. Bausch *et al.*, 2005). In addition, there was an immense wave of research funding in the area of empirical educational research, for work on the development of empirically founded models of competence structures and competence development. Similarly, research on tests and test development was strongly emphasised. Competence orientation became the central concept or buzzword, not least for the teaching and learning of languages.

The major project of competence orientation is driven forward on many levels (research, test theories, teacher education, in-service teacher education, development of textbooks and tasks). As before, there remains much controversy and the earlier expressed critical points are still relevant (cf. Hu, 2008). Positions range from euphoric recommendation of the new paradigm (some people do in fact speak of a paradigm shift in this context, see for example Helbig-Reuter, 2006) to, on the other hand, fundamental doubters about the new direction, not only with respect to teaching but also education itself. Many authors express their increasing discomfort at current ways of thinking and speaking about education as a consequence of the Bologna process and in the context of school policy. This discourse about education, as for example Simons and Masschelein (2006: 19) argue, is producing a 'culture of performativity', which does not take into consideration many aspects of learning and education. The learning subject who is created by this discourse is an enterprising individual, with an objectifying attitude towards him/herself (Simons & Masschelein, 2006: 82f). At the heart of the criticism there is the observed tendency to industrialisation, capitalisation and economisation of knowledge. Teaching and learning processes and the relationships between teachers and learners, understood as human capital, are thereby becoming calculating and calculable, functionalised and capitalised.

According to these authors, what is significant in these processes of economisation is the rhetoric with which learning and teaching processes are addressed. According to Liessmann (2006: 174), the current dominant metaphors of *quality, competence, modularisation, autonomy, evaluation, standardisation, efficiency, knowledge management* and so on are developing a normative power which is leading to a 'desire for affirmation' that scarcely anyone can resist without being considered a denier, a refuser, a troublemaker, an antediluvian or a ditherer. On the other hand, there is the 'admiration for rankings', which is corrupting serious thinking (a very similar argument can be found in Rizvi & Lingard, 2010 and in Block & Cameron, 2004).

Alongside this fundamental criticism of contemporary currents in education policy, there are also individual areas in foreign language research that are under critical consideration; these do, however, more often target the education standards for the first foreign language rather than the *CEFR* itself. For example, Vogt and Quetz criticise the inconsistency of the descriptors and above all the sudden and uncritical adoption of them for the standards. In their eyes, the reference levels develop into 'travelling concepts', which, bereft of their theoretical basis, are being used in the competition for market share (2009: 66; see also Harsch, 2007).

Intercultural competences, included in the *CEFR* and in the education standards, are another unresolved problem. The debate whether intercultural competences are scalable or assessable or whether they should better be dealt with and reflected upon in autobiographical portfolios still continues (Hu & Byram, 2008). With a strong emphasis on testing and a rather functional-pragmatic concept of language and communication in the *CEFR* and the education standards, there remains the danger that precisely these educationally relevant aspects of language learning are underdeveloped in teaching.

A further important theme is the question of languages of migration in relationship to languages taught at school and/or the question of plurilingual competences. This is an issue that is being vigorously addressed in many parts of the world as a consequence of globalisation and mobility (cf. Hu 2003, 2010). There is a need for further development with respect to research on and recognition of specific plurilingual competencies on the one hand, and with respect to research into processes of transfer in plurilingual constellations on the other, particularly in the context of typologically distant languages (cf. the Hamburg research project Linguistic Diversity Management in Urban Areas (LiMA) where inter alia these questions are being addressed).

Conclusion

If one considers the German development in the wider context of the globalisation of education systems and education policies, and the linear processes and phases of policy implementation as described for example by

Rizvi and Lingard (2010: 9), the German case seems to be prototypical. On the one hand, the critical discussion reflects the conflict between long-established, culturally-anchored beliefs about the purpose and aims of language education and the spreading of neo-liberal 'social imaginaries', which are being established economically and politically. On the other hand, the extent to which the global project of the economisation of education has gained a footing in Germany and is being established on many levels is equally clear. It is desirable that in spite of the obvious power of a specific globally functioning education discourse, alternative discourses can be pursued which, besides economic viewpoints, also emphasise and include cultural, ethical, identity-related and ecological aspects of language education and human communication (cf. Block & Cameron, 2004; Heller, 2004). The further development of the *Common European Framework of Reference* should take these aspects into consideration and deal with them seriously.

References

Barkowski, H. (2003) *Skalierte Vagheit* – der europäische Referenzrahmen für Sprachen und sein Versuch, die sprachliche Kommunikationskompetenz des Menschen für Anliegen des Fremdsprachenunterrichts niveaugerecht zu portionieren. In K.-R. Bausch, H. Christ, F.G. Königs and H.-J. Krumm (eds) *Der Gemeinsame Europäische Referenzrahmen für Sprachen in der Diskussion. Arbeitspapiere der 22. Frühjahrskonferenz zur Erforschung des Fremdsprachenunterrichts* (pp. 22–28). Tübingen: Narr.

Bausch, K-R. (2003) Der gemeinsame europäische Referenzrahmen für Sprachen: Zustimmung, aber...! In K-R. Bausch, H. Christ, F.G. Königs and H-J. Krumm (eds) *Der Gemeinsame Europäische Referenzrahmen für Sprachen in der Diskussion. Arbeitspapiere der 22. Frühjahrskonferenz zur Erforschung des Fremdsprachenunterrichts* (pp. 29–34). Tübingen: Narr.

Bausch, K-R., Christ, H., Königs, F.G. and Krumm, H-J. (eds) (2003) *Der Gemeinsame Europäische Referenzrahmen für Sprachen in der Diskussion. Arbeitspapiere der 22. Frühjahrskonferenz zur Erforschung des Fremdsprachenunterrichts*. Tübingen: Narr.

Block, D. and Cameron, D. (eds) (2004) *Globalization and Language Teaching*. London and New York: Routledge.

Bredella, L. (2003) Lesen und Interpretieren im ‚Gemeinsamen europäischen Referenzrahmen für Sprachen: Die Mißachtung allgemeiner Erziehungsziele. In K-R. Bausch, H. Christ, F.G. Königs and H-J. Krumm (eds) *Der Gemeinsame Europäische Referenzrahmen für Sprachen in der Diskussion. Arbeitspapiere der 22. Frühjahrskonferenz zur Erforschung des Fremdsprachenunterrichts* (pp. 45–46). Tübingen: Narr.

Council of Europe (2007) *From Linguistic Diversity to Plurilingual Education in Europe. Guide for the Development of Language Education Policies in Europe.* Strasbourg: Council of Europe.

Christ, H. (2003) Was leistet der *Gemeinsame Europäische Referenzrahmen für Sprachen: lernen, lehren, beurteilen*? In K-R. Bausch, H. Christ, F.G. Königs and H-J. Krumm (eds) *Der Gemeinsame Europäische Referenzrahmen für Sprachen in der Diskussion. Arbeitspapiere der 22. Frühjahrskonferenz zur Erforschung des Fremdsprachenunterrichts* (pp. 57–66). Tübingen: Narr.

Deutsches PISA-Konsortium (2001) *PISA 2000, Basiskompetenzen von Schülerinnen und Schülern im internationalen Vergleich*. Opladen: Leske+Budrich.

Gogolin, I. (2003) Der Gemeinsame Europäische Referenzrahmen. In K.-R. Bausch, H. Christ, F.G. Königs and H-J. Krumm (eds) *Der Gemeinsame Europäische Referenzrahmen für Sprachen in der Diskussion. Arbeitspapiere der 22. Frühjahrskonferenz zur Erforschung des Fremdsprachenunterrichts* (pp. 85–94). Tübingen: Narr.

Harsch, C. (2007) *Der Gemeinsame Europäische Referenzrahmen: Leistung und Grenzen*. Saarbrücken: VDM Verlag Dr. Müller.

Heller, M. (2004) Globalization and the commodification of bilingualism in Canada. In D. Block and D. Cameron (eds) (2004) *Globalization and Language Teaching* (pp. 47–64). London and New York: Routledge.

Helbig-Reuter, B. (2006) Standardorientierung: ein Paradigmenwechsel des fremdsprachlichen Lehrens und Lernens. In J.P. Timm (ed.) *Fremdsprachenlernen und Fremdsprachenforschung: Kompetenzen, Standards, Lernformen, Evaluation. Festschrift für Helmut Johannes Vollmer* (pp. 35–68). Tübingen: Narr.

Hu, A. (2010) Migrationsbedingte Mehrsprachigkeit und schulischer Fremdsprachenunterricht: Forschung, Sprachenpolitik, Lehrerbildung. In H. Faulstich-Wieland (ed.) *Umgang mit Heterogenität und Differenz* (pp. 115–133). Hohengehren: Scheider.

Hu, A. and Byram, M. (eds) (2009) *Interkulturelle Kompetenz und fremdsprachliches Lernen. Modelle, Empirie, Evaluation / Intercultural Competence and Foreign Language Learning. Models, Empiricism, Assessment*. Tübingen: Narr.

Hu, A. (ed.) (2008) Kompetenzorientierung, Bildungsstandards und fremdsprachliches Lernen. Positionspapier der DGFF. Online at http://www.dgff.de/fileadmin/user_upload/dokumente.

Hu, A. (2003) *Schulischer Fremdsprachenunterricht und Migrationsbedingte Mehrsprachigkeit*. Tübingen: Narr.

Klieme, E. and Leutner, D. (2006) Kompetenzmodelle zur Erfassung individueller Lernergebnisse und zur Bilanzierung von Bildungsprozessen. *Zeitschrift für Pädagogik* 52 (6), 876–903.

Königs, F.G. (2003) (K)Eine Referenz für den Referenzrahmen? Überlegungen zum 'Gemeinsamen europäischen Referenzrahmen für Sprachen. In K-R. Bausch, H. Christ, F.G. Königs and H-J. Krumm (eds) *Der Gemeinsame Europäische Referenzrahmen für Sprachen in der Diskussion. Arbeitspapiere der 22. Frühjahrskonferenz zur Erforschung des Fremdsprachenunterrichts* (pp. 113–119). Tübingen: Narr.

Krumm, H-J. (2003) Der Gemeinsame europäische Referenzrahmen – ein Kuckucksei für den Fremdsprachenunterricht? In K-R. Bausch, H. Christ, F.G. Königs and H-J. Krumm (eds) *Der Gemeinsame Europäische Referenzrahmen für Sprachen in der Diskussion. Arbeitspapiere der 22. Frühjahrskonferenz zur Erforschung des Fremdsprachenunterrichts* (pp. 120–126). Tübingen: Narr.

Kultusministerkonferenz (2003) *Bildungsstandards für die erste Fremdsprache (Englisch/Französisch) für den mittleren Schulabschluss (Jahrgangsstufe 10)*. München: Wolters-Kluwer.

Legutke, M.K. (2003) 'Das begonnene Sprachenlernen weiterfuhren...' Was leistet der *Gemeinsame europäische Referenzrahmen für Sprachen* im Schnittfeld von Grundschule und weiterführenden Schulen? In K-R. Bausch, H. Christ, F.G. Königs and H-J. Krumm (eds) *Der Gemeinsame Europäische Referenzrahmen für Sprachen in der Diskussion. Arbeitspapiere der 22. Frühjahrskonferenz zur Erforschung des Fremdsprachenunterrichts* (pp. 127–134). Tübingen: Narr.

Liessmann, K.P. (2006) *Theorie der Unbildung. Die Irrtümer der Wissensgesellschaft*. Wien: Paul Zsolnay Verlag.
LiMA (*Linguistic Diversity Management in Urban Areas)*. Online at http://www.lima.uni-hamburg.de/index.php/en
Masschelein, J. and Simons, M. (2005) *Globale Immunität oder Eine kleine Katastrophe des Europäischen Bildungsraums*. Zürich/Berlin: Diaphanes.
Quetz, J. and Vogt, K. (2009) Bildungsstandards für die erste Fremdsprache: Sprachenpolitik auf unsicherer Basis. *Zeitschrift für Fremdsprachenforschung* 20 (1), *63–89*.
Quetz, J. (2003) Der *Gemeinsame europäische Referenzrahmen*: Ein Schatzkästlein mit Perlen, aber auch mit Kreuzen und Ketten. In K-R. Bausch, H. Christ, F.G. Königs and H-J. Krumm (eds) *Der Gemeinsame Europäische Referenzrahmen für Sprachen in der Diskussion. Arbeitspapiere der 22. Frühjahrskonferenz zur Erforschung des Fremdsprachenunterrichts* (pp. 145–155). Tübingen: Narr.
Rizvi, F. and Lingard, B. (2010) *Globalizing Education Policy*. London: Routledge.
Schwerdtfeger, I.C. (2003) Der europäische Referenzrahmen – oder: Das Ende der Erforschung des Sprachenlernens? In K-R. Bausch, H. Christ, F.G. Königs and H-J. Krumm (eds) *Der Gemeinsame Europäische Referenzrahmen für Sprachen in der Diskussion. Arbeitspapiere der 22. Frühjahrskonferenz zur Erforschung des Fremdsprachenunterrichts* (pp. 173–179). Tübingen: Narr.
Sekretariat der Ständigen Kultusministerkonferenz der Kultusminister (2006) *Gesamtstrategie der Kultusministerkonferenzzum Bildungsmonitoring*. München: Wolters Kluwer.
Tesch, B., Leupold, E. and Köller, O. (eds) (2008) *Bildungsstandards Französisch konkret. Sekundarstufe I: Aufgabenbeispiele, Unterrichtsideen und Fortbildungsmöglichkeiten*. Berlin: Cornelsen.
Tönshoff, W. (2003) Referenzrahmen: Zwischen Ansprüchen und Erwartungen. In K-R. Bausch, H. Christ, F.G. Königs and H-J. Krumm (eds) *Der Gemeinsame Europäische Referenzrahmen für Sprachen in der Diskussion. Arbeitspapiere der 22. Frühjahrskonferenz zur Erforschung des Fremdsprachenunterrichts* (pp. 180–191). Tübingen: Narr.
Vollmer, H.J. (2003) Ein gemeinsamer europäischer Referenzrahmen für Sprachen: Nicht mehr, nicht weniger. In K-R. Bausch, H. Christ, F.G. Königs and H-J. Krumm (eds) *Der Gemeinsame Europäische Referenzrahmen für Sprachen in der Diskussion. Arbeitspapiere der 22. Frühjahrskonferenz zur Erforschung des Fremdsprachenunterrichts* (pp. 192–206). Tübingen: Narr.

Bulgaria

The authors:

Maria Stoicheva is Associate Professor at the Department of European Studies, Sofia University 'St. Kliment Ohridski'. Her principal research interests are language policy, the European dimension of education, language education policy and the comparative study of education and language policies in the context of European integration and cooperation. She is currently a member of the Bureau of the Council of Europe's European Language Portfolio Validation Committee and a member of several European Union independent expert groups.

Pavlina Stefanova is Associate Professor, Doctor Habil. in pedagogy at the Department of Foreign Languages and Literature at the New Bulgarian University, Sofia. Her research interests are in the field of methodology of modern languages teaching and her main academic courses are in foreign languages methodology, early language acquisition, education theories, didactics, foreign language learning strategies, analysis and development of language teaching materials, teacher training methods, adult language learning and teaching materials assessment. She is the editor-in-chief of *Foreign Language Teaching*, a professional journal published by the Ministry of Education and Science since 1996.

6 Policy Perspectives from Bulgaria

Maria Stoicheva

Introduction

The period preceding and following the publication of the *Common European Framework of Reference* can be characterized as a period of transition for Bulgaria to democracy, a market economy and the establishment of democratic institutions and civil society organizations. Bulgaria became a member of the Council of Europe in 1992. In 1995, the process of negotiations for membership of the European Union began, leading to Bulgaria's full membership in 2007. The dominant discourse since 1989 has centred on 'Europeanization' reflecting the broader influence of factors of internationalization and globalization on the policy discourse in education. It is closely related to the liberalization of the educational services market, including foreign language training provision, and to higher expectations in society concerning the outcomes of education and training. In this respect, the dynamics of the languages offered in the education system are not bound to particular political and economic circumstances, although Bulgaria's accession to NATO in 2006 and to the EU increased the importance of English. By and large, language education is not therefore a direct effect of economic and political influences, but rather a reflection of the general market dynamics of language choice – both individual and institutional.

Another important factor has more overtly shaped the configuration of the languages offered and choice: mobility for educational and employment purposes. Employment purposes usually make English the first choice, while educational mobility has an impact on the choice of language for access to higher continuing education in other European countries.

The *CEFR* is central to this discourse in advocating the communicative approach to language teaching and emphasizing the relation between language teaching, learning and assessment and the performance of tasks in the context of educational and employment mobility. From its circulation in draft versions in 1996, and especially after its commercial publication in English and French in 2001, the *CEFR* became the most innovative aspect of new developments in foreign language learning in the Bulgarian case, mostly with its clear response and proposed paths for 'converting language teaching from structure-dominated scholastic sterility into a vital medium for the freer movement of people and ideas' ('Preface' to the 1980 edition of *Threshold Level English* (van Ek, 1980)).

CEFR as a Legitimization and Validation Tool

'Europeanization' today is most often associated in Bulgaria with domestic adaptation to the pressures emanating directly or indirectly from European sources or policy centres, in particular those of the European Union. There are many uses of the term 'Europeanization' in a range of sectors and policy applications. It is typically viewed as a process reorienting the direction and shape of politics, with the result that European political (or economic) dynamics have become a part of the organizational logic of national politics and policy-making. Traditionally, issues relating to domestic education were immune to being radically affected by globalization or Europeanization processes. According to Rizvi and Lingard (2010), education policy studies have tended to focus on almost all aspects of educational processes except those relating to curriculum, pedagogy and assessment. The reception of the *CEFR*, though, refers to a policy area of education 'intimately linked to the ways curriculum, pedagogy and evaluation are being reframed' (Rizvi & Lingard, 2010: 94). We can therefore relate the process of the Europeanization of education policy to the processes in other areas of redefinition of interests and behaviour to meet the imperatives, norms and logic of membership of international organizations, notably the European Union, but also other governmental and non-governmental bodies and associations.

The scope of the *CEFR*, as recorded in its title and covering 'learning, teaching, assessment', indicates the extent of adaptational pressure and raises the issue of 'goodness of fit' between European processes, policies and institutions and those found at domestic level. The type of political discourse in which the *CEFR* is embedded reveals a mechanism of Europeanization that demarcates the scope of potential domestic change. The propensity to apply the *CEFR* levels and approach shows an attitude of 'positive integration' in which the *CEFR* is viewed as prescribing a framework model to which domestic arrangements have to be adjusted with limited national discretion. There is evidently a lack of research on whether the *CEFR* approach entails absorption and transformation of the setting in foreign language learning. The overriding attitude of the education authorities and language teaching community seems to be in line with an accommodation to the domestic traditions and reality, an ambition to prove that there is conformity with it as standard setting and a process of exploring and finding every possible link with it. In this respect, the *CEFR* is largely considered to be a legitimization and validation tool for practices. However, unless there is a process of practical reflective and research work on the *CEFR*, some of its creative and transformational influence could be diminished, ignored and downplayed in education policy.

Introduction of the *CEFR* through the European Language Portfolio Concept

There are some peculiarities concerning the introduction and circulation of the *CEFR* in the Bulgarian context. These peculiarities explain some of the academic and theoretical issues that are the main focus of research. First, we should present the sequence in which the *CEFR* and its companion piece, the European Language Portfolio, was introduced.

The *CEFR* became a research topic in 2001 through a large academic project on the development of the first Bulgarian European Language Portfolio.[1] The project included substantial survey, research and development components that fed the design and applicability concept of both the 'ELP thinking' and aspects of the *CEFR*. The interconnectedness between the two tools was one of the main foundations of the adoption of the *CEFR*. This interconnectedness can be considered as still being dominant in the Bulgarian context.[2] The translation of the *CEFR* text into Bulgarian in 2006 (edited by Maria Stoicheva and Pavlina Stefanova) was a logical consequence of the ELP development work. This path also determined a rather heavy emphasis on the descriptors and the *CEFR* levels, and the translation of the self-assessment grid was made under the ELP Project. A series of eight workshops, seminars and conferences were organized, some of which had a wide participation of researchers, teachers, educators and central and local authorities (Stoicheva, 2002; Stoicheva, 2004). Special emphasis was laid on the following aspects: partial language skills; variegated description of language proficiency; individual language profiles; and response to identified language needs in various education and training contexts; and the setting of objectives for language learning.

There was a basic assumption behind this approach to the introduction of the *CEFR* in the Bulgarian context. The approach reflected the need for innovative pedagogical tools for a reform in the language teaching practices in the country in response to a radically changed language environment and language learning context and objectives, as is explained in more detail in the next chapter.

Nonetheless, the initial discussions of the ELP development team on the *CEFR* content and before that on the content of the Threshold levels clearly identified the issue that the direct application of the *CEFR* to the learning context as a pedagogical tool was not possible. The main concern of some of the initial discussions referred to the question of whether the *CEFR* can be considered as standard setting or a framework of reference, whether it should be applied as a compulsory document if adopted or as a descriptive illustration of a new approach. As a result of these discussions, a view was clearly adopted that other tools were needed and attention was in particular focused on the European Language Portfolio as a tool closely linked – and conceived as linked – to the *CEFR*, in which some important aspects of the *CEFR* could find appropriate elaboration and clarification. The ELP development set the objectives of elaborating a Bulgarian ELP model in its complexity of functions and application (i.e. as a complex toolkit, this term being taken from Little, 2010: 20).

There are thus two tendencies in the acceptance and introduction of the *CEFR* in the Bulgarian context. First, there is the attitude of utilizing it as a tool that can emphasize and in certain aspects validate existing good practices and foreign languages teaching traditions. For example, this includes more than 50 years' experience in the so-called 8th form intensive foreign language year in specialist and vocational upper secondary schools,[3] bilingual training practised in specialist language schools,[4] introduction of early foreign language learning[5] and the compulsory teaching of two foreign languages in mainstream schools as a solid tendency towards plurilingual education.

Against this background, the reality of 'Europeanization' could be questioned in surveys and research as merely labelling and validating the contemporary aspects and appropriateness of foreign language learning and teaching traditions. Yet by using this term we emphasize a complex reality of application of rather asymmetrical patterns of absorption and accommodation of the *CEFR* as a conceptual framework. And this represents a second tendency in the process of reflection and adoption of the *CEFR* approach. It is evident that even in their limitations the above-mentioned developments necessitate at least two prime types of innovation: first, the revision of existing conceptual frameworks in a much broader context than initially anticipated by the term 'language policy', and second, broadening of the scope of traditional analytical dimensions that reflect the dynamism of change in contemporary language policies. It clearly signals the emergence of new, cross-national policy networks and communities of practice and shifts of cognition and discourse that cannot be sufficiently explained merely as policy mimicry. Most notably, it highlights:

- adaptation and the need and pressure for adaptation in the broadest sense (of rules, norms, standards, practices as elaborated in learning, teaching and assessment);
- a cross-national community of practice for which the *CEFR* has become the language of exchange;
- commitment and deeper understanding by key domestic actors that can serve as a source of leverage for further and deeper embedding of the conceptual scheme that the *CEFR* exemplified.

Later in the chapter I will discuss the three main areas that constitute the key research agenda. However, there are gaps and shortages of in-depth surveys and analyses and those conducted and used are often marked by partial outcomes.

Assessment and Self-Assessment

From the first research projects in Bulgaria, the topic of assessment and self-assessment became a key area of further analysis and investigation. This work produced examples of good practices in adapting the generic descriptors of the *CEFR* for various occupational domains and for learners with special needs. There is research and practical work on specific vocational descriptors for the hotel and catering sector, banking, finance and local administration that are closely linked to curriculum design for tertiary and upper secondary education. Other applications include those for students of medicine, economics and business administration. This approach was consistently applied in the elaboration of the legislative requirements for acquiring professional qualifications or state education requirements in the section of Key Competences gained during general compulsory vocational training – standardized for all occupational areas, for example, in the practices of the National Agency for Vocational Education and Training between 2002 and 2003 in the elaboration of state vocational requirements that serve as the basis for developing training programmes and the main learning and training goals of vocational curricula.

Assessment and self-assessment is a principal topic in academic courses in initial teacher training both in Bachelor and Master programmes; it is used as a standard action research assignment for trainee teachers. Considered as a feasible and effective way of mastering and further understanding the specificity and demarcation of the competence levels, this has resulted in gathering valuable empirical data from various educational and school contexts. The work of researchers with students on a regular basis has produced interesting empirical material in students' reflective thinking about the process of setting objectives following self-assessment.

The tendency to label all assessment procedures and events with the *CEFR* levels (both in formal and private language provision) has produced a wide recognition and awareness of the procedure of self-assessment and assessment against checklists and discrete description of language communicative skills. In a survey conducted with first-year university students in 2009 at three Bulgarian universities, around 70% of the interviewees confidently quoted their level of language proficiency using the *CEFR* levels.[6] Broad public awareness is further enhanced by the precise labelling of all activities, language courses and the additional development work carried out by language centres of European countries' cultural institutes in Bulgaria, including their role in relationship to language testing agencies, which have widely adopted the *CEFR* levels. This effectively reinforces the aspect of Europeanization in the application of the *CEFR* in Bulgarian public life.

There is also work, although not formally presented and published as research papers, on the correlation of the Bulgarian National Curriculum for foreign languages with the *CEFR*. The first major attempt to do this was undertaken as a collective event between researchers and the three major cultural institutions of European states (British Council, Institut Français and Goethe-Institut) with the participation of the Ministry of Education and Science and regional foreign languages inspectorates in 2004 as a collaborative one-week workshop.

Although there is already a good record of events, collaborative research and practical work, it should be noted that there is not a consistent approach in applying the basic principles of the *CEFR* approach to assessment and self-assessment by tertiary education institutions and universities, in private language courses provision and in surveys of language proficiency. In this context there is a tendency to utilize and apply the *CEFR* in various external evaluation and assessment procedures of foreign language teaching.

The *CEFR* as a Reference Tool for Assessment

There is an application and anticipated need for the use of the *CEFR* in two clearly identified areas. The first is the official curriculum, although it is not entirely consistent in the formulation of goals as 'can-do' statements. The goals of the official curriculum for some stages and languages are linked to the *CEFR*, but are formulated in more general terms. The second area is the internal and external assessment of language competences applied in the course of formal education throughout mainstream schooling.

Expert assessment is sought for the official external assessment examinations carried out at the end of key stages of formal education (e.g. after the 8th grade intensive language teaching year, and after the 5th and 6th grades of lower secondary school). The external assessment format has been examined in relation to the *CEFR* levels and to the learning outcomes of the national curriculum for the relevant grade. The main conclusions refer to an inappropriate scoring emphasis on lexical knowledge and communicative competences, an imbalanced relative emphasis among the language skills in final scoring and selection of tasks and texts for the corresponding level and considerable divergences in skill levels.

However, there are considerable gaps in research related to the *CEFR*. They are not exclusively theoretical issues, although this can be identified as a major deficiency of current research. For example, there is no in-depth analysis of the reasons for and the barriers involved in the application of the *CEFR* (and the Portfolio) concepts in the context of the process of Europeanization and modernization in Bulgaria. Major aspects of the integration of the *CEFR* approach have been assumed to be relevant and consistent with the language teaching and learning traditions in the country, whether or not this is actually true. By and large the *CEFR* has not been viewed as creating change in the domestic rules of the game. Thus the effect of potential 'negative integration' – demanding that domestic regulations comply with international or European, supranational regulations or standards and envisaging a considerable change – have been widely ignored both in theory and practice.

The *CEFR* in Teacher Education

Broader embedding of the *CEFR* in teacher education has been considered a major area of intervention that can further enhance research, and effectively lead to a more realistic scenario for the Europeanization and modernization of foreign language learning and teaching. The issues of levels and the estimated number of hours needed to reach them has not been researched and theoretically explored, although it seems that it has been incorporated in textbook development in an ad hoc way. Levels become particularly relevant to teacher training when they are distinguished in terms of the number of 'learning hours' needed to achieve them. Yet there is no clear division of stages in the clearly identified number of learning hours for first foreign language (842 hours) and for the second foreign language (144 hours) in formal education. There is a general agreement that higher levels take progressively more effort than lower ones. This implies that a given amount of learning makes a bigger observable difference at lower levels than at higher ones. How observable, and hence measurable, proportional gain can be in language proficiency has not been explored in a systematic way. In this respect the branching approach advocated by the *CEFR* has not been widely adopted or illustrated in concrete practices of teaching and assessment. It is a difficult and complex area which requires an averaging of quicker learners, slower learners, and learners who are going nowhere and the pace of slowing down of observable differences as learning progresses. This is an example of one of the topics related to *CEFR* levels that draws attention to other issues relevant for teacher education: teaching skills like task management, classroom management, communicative language methodology and giving corrective feedback, in other words how to manage a task-based, content-oriented foreign language classroom. This also signals extended opportunities for a sustainable presence of the *CEFR* as a topic in in-service teacher training.

Conclusion

In the discussion of the Bulgarian cultural and political context and the patterns of adoption of the approach and aspects of the *CEFR*, we have seen positive and negative integration tendencies. In conclusion I can add a third, ideational or 'framing', type of integration. This is related to setting frameworks in areas where traditions and complex economic and political contexts would only allow the adoption of new policies that are not radical or have a more or less symbolic character. In this situation, the interface between existing practices and the adoption of the *CEFR* approaches do not necessarily refer to curriculum change, pedagogy development and elaboration of assessment criteria. This is an area where Europeanization, though less powerful, could proceed equally well through the framing of domestic beliefs and learners' expectations. Europeanization then becomes manifest in the transformed beliefs of domestic actors (experts, researchers, educationalists, learners, teachers) or in reconfigured domestic discourses. This is the third dimension of the *CEFR* impact at national level. The *CEFR* itself does not have a prescriptive ambition and does not endeavour to promote one particular language teaching methodology. However, this by itself allows for a much broader impact beyond its allegedly normative scope in various learning, teaching and assessment contexts.

Notes

(1) Project BG/00/B/F/LA-132078 under Leonardo da Vinci Programme: The European Language Portfolio: promoting a lifetime of vocationally oriented language learning, 2001–2003.

(2) It should be noted that a similar tendency of linking the *CEFR* and the ELP has been identified in other contexts in the course of the impact study conducted by the European Language Portfolio validation committee in 2009. 'The linking between these two basic Council of Europe tools seems unavoidable and it is the reality experienced

by those who implement them. The two instruments were initially conceived as closely interrelated in particular in relation to their possible impact' (Stoicheva *et al.*, 2009: 20).

(3) This includes a curriculum of 648 foreign language teaching hours (18 per week) and 468 teaching hours (13 per week) respectively for specialist and vocational schools.

(4) It is presented as Content and Language Integrated Learning (CLIL) mainly practised at the upper secondary stage of specialist schools and in the 13th form of vocational schools although here it is confined to teaching relevant technical vocabulary.

(5) It was adopted as part of the national curriculum in 1993/1994 from the first year at school and from 2nd school form in 2002.

(6) A student survey and review of attitudes was carried out under the project 'Students' Language Profile' in Sofia University 'St. Kliment Ohridski' in 2009. Small-scale pilot surveys were also conducted in two other public universities. More than 600 first year students participated in the survey of their competence and attitudes to languages. The survey allowed for presentation and analysis of the individual language repertoires, the dominant language combinations, level of language competence in the transition between high and higher education in Bulgaria. The survey is to be used in a pan-European context (Stoicheva, 2011).

References

Council of Europe (2006) Obshta evropeiska ezikova ramka: uchene, prepodavane, ozeniavane. Varna: Izdatelstvo Relaxa. (Bulgarian translation of the CEFR.)

Languages at Work. Description of Modules: Banking and Finance, Local administration, Tourism (English, German, French, Italian) (2003), Sofia University Press.

Rizvi, F. and Lingard, B. (2009) *Globalizing Education Policy*. London: Routledge.

Stefanova, P. (2007) *Foreign Language Learning Complex in the Theory and Practice of Foreign Language Teaching*. Sofia: Anubis Publishing House.

Steiner-Khamsi, G. (ed.) (2004) *The Global Politics of Educational Borrowing and Lending*. New York: Teachers' College Press.

Stoicheva, M. (2006) *European Language Policy*. Sofia: Sofia University Press.

Stoicheva, M. (2004) *European Language Portfolio for vocational purposes 48.2003* (The Bulgaria model), The Languages as Means for Education, Research and Professional Realization (keynote speaker paper), III International Conference Proceedings. Varna: Steno Publishing House.

Stoicheva, M. (2002) *Needs analysis in language teaching for specific purposes with a view to fostering learner autonomy*. In M. Stoicheva (ed.) *Identification of Needs and Language Competences in the Occupational Domain*. Sofia: FIUT Publishing House.

Stoicheva, M. (2004) *The Application of the Common European Framework of Reference in Bulgarian schools*. CD with training materials for teacher training, published by the Ministry of Education, Goethe Institute and the British Council (July).

Stoicheva, M., Hughes, G. and Speitz, H. (2009) *The European Language Portfolio: an Impact Study* (DGIV/EDU/LANG 1). Strasbourg: Council of Europe.

Stoicheva, M., Tschavdarova, A. and Vesselinov, D. (eds) (2011) *Language Policies: Bulgaria – Europe*. Sofia: Sofia University Press.

Tschavdarova, A. (2002) Der Fremdsprachenunterricht in Bulgarien in 20. Jahrhundert – Zwischen Kenntnisvermittlung und Ideologie. In E. Lechner (ed.) *Formen und Funktionen des Fremdsprachenunterrichts im Europa des 20.Jahrhunderts* (pp. 393–418). Frankfurt am Mein: Lang.

van Ek, J.A. (1980) *Threshold Level English in a European Unit/Credit System for Modern Language Learning by Adults*. Oxford: Pergamon Press.

7 Academic Perspectives from Bulgaria

Maria Stoicheva and Pavlina Stefanova

Setting the Historical Scene

The response to the *CEFR* in the Bulgarian context cannot be properly understood without presenting the specific traditions of foreign language teaching in the country. These traditions reflect the dominant language attitudes formed in Bulgarian society in the 20th century, and their dynamics and relationships with other relevant economic, cultural and political factors affecting education policy. Foreign language teaching can thus be viewed as influenced by the political and economic orientation of the country in a given specific historical period, and three periods can be identified in modern times concerning the specific orientation and offer of languages:

- from 1878 until 1944, the period when Bulgaria was established as an independent state after a long period of Ottoman rule;
- from 1944 until 1989, the socialist period permeating all sectors of public life;
- from 1989 onwards, the transition period of the country towards democracy, establishing the country as a democratic state, with a functioning market economy and EU membership.

The role of the economic and cultural elites of the country formed through education, training and other contacts with other European countries and traditions was markedly influential in the three periods, and can be identified as a major factor for language education policy. Intellectual and governing elites processed a vision of the economic and political future of the country and radically influenced the economic and political models to be adopted and implemented.

Three main influences marked the process of establishing Bulgaria as an independent state after a long period of Ottoman rule in the first of the three periods identified above: Russian, German and French. These in turn set the framework and explain the dynamics of the dominant foreign language policy and methodology in the educational system and in the private market for educational services. They are also defined as three sources and three constituent parts of the Bulgarian vision of the modern state that can clearly be identified as European in their source and inspiration.

The Russian element is closely associated with the process of Bulgarian nation-building, with the significant political influence of Russia and with the various aspects of the proximity of the culture of the two peoples (language, traditions, Eastern Orthodox religion, aspects of the people's psychology, long-standing mutual influences and relations, etc.). The German line of influence was salient throughout the 20th century, when a western orientation of the country was established in all areas of public life after 1886. Although it was not influential in economic and political life, the French element remained an intellectual marker. It retained its essential role in the cultural and educational areas from the Bulgarian Renaissance period of 1762–1878. French was the first foreign language introduced in the civil educational system of Bulgaria in the period before 1878 in parallel with the practical acquisition of Greek and Turkish. These two languages were of importance for trade, and Greek was the language of the church until Bulgarian church independence from the Greek Orthodox, but their acquisition did not produce notable results for language methodology and teaching traditions. French was followed by German and Russian as the other foreign languages that were taught. However, French retained a prominent position as the first 'western European' foreign language throughout the 20th century. The first books on foreign language methodology were published in close relation with and as a consequence of the teaching of French.

The new Bulgarian state was looking for reference points and for established development models to be adapted to existing cultural and educational traditions and the reality of the new Bulgarian state. This pursuit had an essential effect on culture, education and science, and through this process language teaching models and methodology were transferred and adopted. French, Russian and German were the main foreign languages taught in Bulgarian schools. Even in this early period two foreign languages were taught in the so-called 'real' and classical Bulgarian *gymnasiums* (i.e. secondary schools). This tradition constitutes an important feature of foreign language teaching in Bulgaria, sustained throughout all periods up to the present day.

In the next period of shift in the political orientation of the country (1944–1989) there was a radical change in the core languages offered. Russian was introduced as a compulsory first foreign language with a special status in relation to any other foreign language in the educational system. After 1945, the policy of two foreign languages in the school curriculum was retained, with Russian as the compulsory language together with the so-called second western European language (English, French, German or Italian). The foreign language provision included a centralised curriculum and a compulsory single textbook for all schools in the country. From 1979 until 1985, there was a period of reduction of the learning and teaching objectives in the second 'western' language, which was followed by the introduction of a more communicative school curriculum and, after 1985, an increase in the relative proportion of the second foreign language compared to compulsory Russian.

Foreign language policy, in terms of languages taught in schools and choice of languages, was thus closely related to the concrete political orientation of the country and the education of its political, economic and cultural elite. However, the role of foreign languages as a subject enjoyed a significant weight in the school curriculum throughout these different periods and was closely related to the achievement of general learning objectives and goals. It constituted a core part of the model of the educated citizen and was given special attention in all stages of the educational system. There was also a positive attitude in society towards the learning of languages, which led to a much wider provision of foreign language teaching in alternative sectors outside the official school – the private sector, religious schools, foreign schools, lyceums and so on. It also led to a sustainable tradition of early foreign language learning enhanced and fostered by parents' active support and investment in their children's language learning outside of school and through individual private lessons. By and large, Bulgarian language policy exhibited the typical features of the foreign language planning of a small state within broader geopolitical and cultural influences.

Theory and Practice Enabling and Influencing the Reception of the *CEFR*

From a historical perspective, the period after 1990 can be characterised as containing all the relevant conditions for a radical change and a shift away from the dominant model in foreign language teaching. A new model was sought as a driving force for carrying out the change. This was particularly acute in academic circles and was related to the belief in a wider and more responsible provision of FLT in formal education. The creation of a coherent and transparent structure of provision for effective language learning that was relevant to the needs of learners and to the expectations of society was considered to be of primary importance. As described in the previous chapter, there were traditions that could be enhanced and capitalised upon, such as the experience developed within the language specialist schools, the support for an early start in language learning demonstrated in the alternative educational sector and the tendency to add a second foreign language in the standard individual repertoire as a learning outcome.

Although there were many aspects in common with the other periods, some objective changes in the European context related to languages and their spread, and, in particular, the multilingual character of the European community, encouraged a different type of solution. While in other periods nationally proven and developed models were transferred and adapted to the Bulgarian context independently in the teaching of a particular target foreign language, in the beginning of the 1990s the need to fill the gap of an effective and coherent foreign language teaching system with internationally proven and tried models was acutely felt.

A salient milestone of this process was the extensive academic work for the development of the entry-exit levels for all types of schools and the new documentation consisting of state educational requirements for foreign language teaching and the detailed curriculum, including early foreign language learning piloted from 1993/1994.

The intended application of a common model for all foreign languages was conditioned by a growing internationalisation of education within the context of Europe and the radical shift of the Bulgarian political and economic orientation. Bulgaria became a member of the Council of Europe in 1992 and submitted its application for EU membership as early as 1995. The teaching of Russian was radically influenced and its status as the first and compulsory second language was abolished, but French – as the language that had occupied the top position among 'western European' languages taught in the country for a long time – was also affected. Similar to the trends in other European countries, English firmly occupied the top position in the choice of languages, a phenomenon which is not related to economic and political bilateral relations, but rather to the process of the 'Europeanisation' of English and its stable inclusion as a ubiquitous component of the modern language repertoire of European citizens.

'The Entry-Exit Levels' for the school subject 'Foreign language' were a realisation of the conception of top-down planning (i.e. from the learning language outcome for a given educational stage down to its first year of study). The incentive was to correlate the learning outcome with 'European standards'. Three educational stages define three educational boundaries within which there are different qualitative and quantitative indicators for language communicative competence. The Threshold Levels from the mid-1970s were a model in other countries for specifying objectives in operational terms of what a learner should be able to do when using the language independently. This model, which was initially elaborated for English, together with the specification developed for French, provided the basic models adapted for almost thirty other languages. By the 1990s, when the need for an international rather than a national or language-specific model in Bulgaria was acutely felt, the Threshold Level model had already proven its validity. Similar to its application in other countries, it was used in the Bulgarian educational context as a basis for new national curricula, better textbooks, popular multimedia courses and more realistic and relevant forms of assessment. However, there was a delay in the process of 10–15 years.

There was collaborative work in this process for a period of almost three years among language experts and researchers with various language backgrounds on the application of instruments for innovative language descriptions based on the concept of Threshold Level. The objective was to create a model that could be adapted to suit the peculiar features of each language whilst applying the same reference instruments, and thus provide for the comparison and transparency of the foreign language outcomes at national and European level.

'The Entry-Exit levels' were first published in the professional journal *Foreign Language Teaching* in two volumes, and they became the most debated topic among foreign language methodology experts, foreign language teachers, educational experts, policy stakeholders and educational administrators. They included a number of innovative components in the levels definitions that are also relevant as a basis for the reception of the *CEFR* after 2003. The action approach was present through the concept of the performance of speech acts, variations of topics, domains of application of communicative competence and ability to carry out tasks with the use of the target language. Additionally, a common descriptive toolkit was applied to all target languages, with the only variation being in the language material component. The Entry-Exit levels became and remain a core topic in initial and continuous teacher training. This, in fact, both facilitated and hindered the formal introduction of the *CEFR*. On the one hand, it radically changed the language and the way of thinking about foreign language teaching in the educational system conceptually, uniting all foreign languages within the same model of competence description. On the other hand, it produced the impression that what was to be done with the *CEFR* implementation, or rather correlation, had already been carried out and incorporated both in theory and practice. The fact that the application of the Threshold Level model as an instrument for language description was 10–15 years late laid the ground for the belief that no more was actually needed for the reception of the *CEFR* concept.

Although applied to descriptions of levels beyond Threshold, the Threshold concept did not entirely reflect the complexity of the philosophy of the *CEFR*. It should be noted that no specific correlation or further adaptation of the level descriptions was carried out later as a consequence of the commercial publication of the *CEFR*. The national curriculum is centred on the threshold level descriptions model, which has been used to prove the link to the *CEFR* levels.

The publication of the Entry-Exit Levels was an academic project with immediate practical implications for language teaching and learning conducted exclusively by an academic change of paradigm in foreign language learning and methodology discourse. It eventually provided for a smooth transition to the specific language, conceptual framework and understanding of the *CEFR*. The publications and the collective work of researchers and representatives of academia played a decisive role by promoting methodological innovations and new approaches to designing common language teaching programmes. The immediate outcome was a radical change in the discourse, based on the concept of communicative competence perceived to consist of six components: linguistic, discursive, sociolinguistic, sociocultural, social and strategic. There was an immediate and significant effect on foreign language education from the elaboration of the entry and exit levels as concrete learning objectives for the state educational system. The *CEFR* levels were more readily adopted and applied in the private language training organisations almost 10 years later with the incentive of easy recognition and the better location of their foreign language courses within a wider European foreign language provision market.

Reception of the *CEFR*

There was a specific sequence involved in the introduction of the *CEFR* in Bulgaria. The *CEFR* was translated into Bulgarian in 2005/2006, but at that time it was already known in its basics among university and other researchers through its versions in English, French and German. The first publications on the *CEFR* date from as early as 2002/3. *Identification of Needs and Language Competences in the Occupational Domain* (2002) introduced the topic of learner autonomy and contains courses designed in correlation with the *CEFR* levels and principles. The translation, and in particular the editing of the text, was assigned to a team of university lecturers among whom were the authors of this chapter. The editors used the three existing versions – English, French and German – although the actual translation was from French as a source language.

There are two important aspects of this work. On the one hand, the team faced difficulties in terminology adaptation, which clearly showed that the shift performed earlier with the work on the Entry-Exit school stage levels in the language and framework of thinking was not yet completed. This constituted a significant difficulty in the further application of the *CEFR* in its depth and multilayered structure. On the other hand, some of the main concepts related to the *CEFR* – such as the *CEFR* levels, the 'can-do' statements, the specific mode of language competence description, the issues of communicative language competences and methodology-related issues such as the task-oriented approach, learner autonomy and the relation between self-assessment and assessment – had already been introduced widely among academics and teachers through a very intense and many-sided process of development of the first Bulgarian European Language Portfolio model and the work in the area of developing specific vocational description, as discussed in the previous chapter.

The reception of the *CEFR* was mediated by a process of intense and growing internationalisation of education. A prominent topic of discussion became the so-called 'European dimension' of education both in academic and political circles. Another important aspect was the unprecedented growth in educational mobility. Unofficial data provided by educational NGOs and foundations suggest that 12,000–17,000 students were leaving the country every year to continue their education in other European and non-European countries.

The various educational interventions performed by international organisations and institutions in the educational sector constitute another significant component of the process of education modernisation. They had a significant impact on the development of 'indirect' educational strategies, such as the construction of categories of thought, of organising language, and in establishing procedures relevant to education and proposing solutions. The educational policy of the country was increasingly thought about and formulated within the context of pressures and requirements of globalisation, Europeanisation or internationalisation. In this context, international organisations acted as agents fuelling educational models.

The role of the language and cultural institutions of other European countries providing language courses correlated to the *CEFR* levels also contributed significantly to a growing awareness and better application of some of the basic ideas and components of the *CEFR*. In the period after 1990 there was a rapid liberalisation of educational products with a variety of teaching materials and textbooks entering the school system. It was especially in the period of the piloting of the new curriculum that new 'global' language teaching textbooks were applied with permission of the national educational authorities. Their use later became part of official tender procedures, in which three sets of textbooks are provided from which to choose for every grade of school education. Up to 7th grade most of the textbooks are developed by Bulgarian teams including academics, while most of the textbooks for upper secondary school grades are published by international and European publishers. They can be considered as another powerful source of introduction of specific aspects of the *CEFR*, related to the levels and through them to other components of the *CEFR* action approach. This process has also been gradually establishing standards of quality, task formulation, communicative competence and assessment, including self-assessment, which can be considered as a set of practically acquired criteria for assessment of domestically developed teaching materials and textbooks.

The period after 2000 has been marked by stages of reconfiguration of the educational system conceived in response to economic and developmental needs, but also as a response to the parental pressure exercised through the choices that families were making for their children. The system of streaming based on examination – particularly at 7th grade when selection for language and specialist vocational secondary schools takes place – expanded to include even entrance examinations for primary education. The *CEFR* has a particular role in this whole process. It defined the orientation and construction of a language to talk and think about language education in Europe and to harmonise categories, language and systems of reasoning, and this was significant in Bulgaria in the introduction of themes that are associated with the reform movement – quality of foreign language teaching, diversity of language offer, parental choice for children, school autonomy to preserve traditions and expand language offer and learning, responsibility to meet the needs of students. Foreign language teaching policy and academic discussions were reconstructed around ideas of 'competences' and, to a certain extent, of 'choice' – as a way to legitimise the growing pressure to make the perceived needs of the stakeholders in education into the primary goals of the school.

All these developments can be considered as incentives and motivating factors for the positive reception of the *CEFR*. In a period of the growing importance of Europeanisation, there is a clear tendency to seek to replicate patterns and solutions adopted internationally by international teams of experts. Best models in their field are promoted for adoption and the *CEFR* is classified as one of them. This is related to issues of legitimisation in a reform context, especially in adopting models regarded as innovative, modern and internationally approved. On the other hand, they are not only positively accepted as innovative, but there is a tendency to draw validity from internationally approved models rather than from local experience. In this respect the *CEFR* can often be used as a validation tool.

However, the context of the introduction of the *CEFR* concepts in the country reveals factors that set limitations and constraints for the reception of the *CEFR* philosophy. Those aspects that appear to be more easily adaptable as abstract models seem to be readily introduced and interpreted (*CEFR* levels, summaries of skills descriptions) while others remain insufficiently discussed, elaborated on and effectively introduced. Matriculation examinations and external school evaluation of language skills seem correlated to the *CEFR* levels, but they do not sufficiently address all language skills and types of language communicative competences. Basic *CEFR* concepts such as learner autonomy and plurilingual education have not become an inherent part of the necessary reflection on learning and teaching practices. The *CEFR* has not yet become a *vademecum* or a book of reference for the language teaching community. It has not yet produced and has not triggered the reflection response on our own foreign language practices, which is one of the main aims of the book with all the questions asked at the end of each chapter encouraging readers to reflect on their current practice and methodological assumptions. It is still viewed as an effective transnationally circulated model and its contextualisation has not yet started at full speed.

The concept of plurilingual education and the interaction of languages in language repertoires seem to be neglected and poorly addressed in the general reception of the *CEFR* in the domestic context. An emerging academic interest in this topic has been demonstrated in recent years, taking into account the fact that language teaching remains monolingual contrary to a reality of language use and practice that requires a plurilingual approach.

There are traditions of close interaction of education policy-making and academia. However, there is a clear tendency in policy-making to involve teachers more extensively and with priority in evaluation, tender and development procedures. However, the *CEFR* is a rather complex document that requires mediation for interpretation and can hardly be considered as directly applicable in all educational contexts. This is particularly valid for the expected process of transforming some of its ideas into practice in the process of language teaching and learning, and for triggering change, in view of the new challenges in a more diverse and interrelated multilingual world.

References

Council of Europe (2006) Obshta evropeiska ezikova ramka: uchene, prepodavane, ozeniavane. Varna: Izdatelstvo Relaxa. (Bulgarian translation of the *CEFR*.)

Gocheva, E. (2000) Chuzhdoezikovo Obuchenie. Teoria i Praktika na Uchebnika. Sofia: Lodos. (Foreign Language Teaching. Theory and Practice of Textbook Use.)

Patev, P. (ed.) (1993) *Vhodno-izhodno ravnishte na uchebnia predmet 'Chuzhd ezik' v balgarskoto nachalno uchilishte*, v spisanie 'Chuzhdoezikovo obuchenie 4/1993. (The *Entry-Exit levels of the School Subject 'Foreign Language" of the Primary School in Bulgaria*, in *Foreign Language Teaching*, 4/1993.)

Patev, P. (ed.) (1995) *Vhodno-izhodno ravnishte na uchebnia predmet 'Chuzhd ezik' za gimnazialnata stepen*, Sofia, MONT. (*The Entry-Exit levels of the School Subject 'Foreign Language" of the High School in Bulgaria*, Sofia, Ministry of Education, Science and Technology.)

Patev, P. (ed.) (1995) *Vhodno-izhodno ravnishte na uchebnia predmet 'Chuzhd ezik' za ezikovite gimnazii*, Sofia, MONT. (*The Entry-Exit levels of the School Subject 'Foreign Language" of the Specialist Language Schools in Bulgaria*, Sofia, Ministry of Education, Science and Technology.)

Shopov, T. (2002) *Chuzhdoezikovata Metodika*. Sofia: Sofia Universitetsko Izdatelstvo 'Sv. Kliment Ohridski'. (*Foreign language teaching methodology*, Sofia University Publishing House 'St. Kliment Ohridski'.)

Simeonova, Y. (2000) *Prepodavatelyat po Chuzhd Ezik*. Sofia: Firma Aktiv Comers. (*The Foreign Language Teacher*. Sofia: Active Commerce Publisher)

Stefanova, P. (2007) *Uchebniat Complex po Chuzhd Ezik v Teoriata I Praktikata na Chuzhdoezikovoto Obuchenie*. Sofia: Izdatelska kashta Anubis. (*The Teaching Complex in the Theory and Practice of Foreign Language Learning*. Sofia: Anubis Publisher)

Stoicheva, M. (2006) *Evropeiska Ezikova Politika*. Sofia: Universitetsko Izdatelstvo 'Sv. Kliment Ohridski'. (*European Language Policy*. Sofia: Sofia University Publishing House 'St. Kliment Ohridski'.)

Stoicheva, M. (2003) *The Common European Framework of Reference and the European Language Portfolio*. International conference, dedicated to the 40th anniversary of the Institute for foreign students, CD of the proceedings of the conference.

Stoicheva, M. (2002) Needs analysis in language teaching for specific purposes with a view to fostering learner autonomy. In M. Stoicheva (ed.) *Identification of needs and language competences in the occupational domain*, Sofia: FIUT Publisher.

Veselinov, D. (2003) *Istoria na Obuchenieto po Frenski Ezik prez Vazrazhdaneto*. Sofia: Universitetsko Izdatelstvo 'Sv. Kliment Ohridski'. (History of French Language Teaching in Bulgaria during the Renaissance Period. Sofia: Sofia University Publishing House 'St. Kliment Ohridski'.)

Poland

The authors:

Paweł Poszytek has been with the Foundation for the Development of the Education System since 1998, first as a coordinator of the SOCRATES-LINGUA programme and European Language Label competition, then as member of the managing board and the director of the Lifelong Learning programme. In 2010 he co-founded the Institute for Quality in Education, which serves as the National Institute for Languages in Poland. He has also been a member of several advisory boards for languages giving support to the European Commission, and was the Polish national coordinator of the Council of Europe's 'Language Policy Profile' for Poland. He is a former member of the national committee for the European Language Portfolio, and was also a member of the executive committee of the European Association of Language Testing and Assessment. He is an author of a book on language testing and a number of articles on language and education-related issues.

Hanna Komorowska is a full professor of applied linguistics at the Institute of English, Warsaw School of Social Sciences and Humanities and Warsaw University, and works in the field of pre- and in-service teacher education. As head of the curriculum development centre she built a team that designed the first set of communicative syllabus documents for second and foreign languages taught in the Polish school system. After the fall of communism she headed the Expert Committee for foreign language teaching and teacher education reform in Poland. Former vice-President of Warsaw University, the Polish delegate for the Modern Languages Project Group of the Council of Europe, and member of the European Union High Level Group on Multilingualism in Brussels, she is now a consultant to the European Centre for Modern Languages in Graz and co-author of the European Portfolio for Student Teachers of Languages. She publishes widely in the field of Foreign Language Teaching methodology and teacher education.

8 Policy Perspectives from Poland

Paweł Poszytek

Introduction

The educational reform in 1999 and its continuation in 2009 in Poland introduced new national curriculum frameworks that were based on and constructed in line with the widely-established notions of learning outcomes and language proficiency competences. Before these reforms took place, the national curriculum for languages had been content and structure based. For the purpose of this discussion, both the curriculum of 1998, implemented officially in the educational system in 1999, and the curriculum of 2009 will be taken into consideration. This approach is influenced by two factors: (i) although the *CEFR* was officially published by the Council of Europe in 2001, its main ideas and methodological assumptions were already known a few years before this; and (ii) the dissemination of approaches adopted by the *CEFR* and its growing impact on education systems coincided with reform movements in Polish education, and the beginnings of this process go back to before 2001.

Curriculum Development in Poland

In both of the above-mentioned cases, the national curricula for language education were developed as a result of broader educational reforms that had been provoked by wider political agendas. Consequently, it is difficult to perceive these two initiatives from the perspective of a rolling programme, a periodical review or as a consequence of international comparisons. Poland has very seldom used international comparisons in a really thorough and profound way as an incentive for any new national language agendas. However, to a certain degree, the 2009 national curriculum might be seen as a sort of periodical review, since it introduced only superficial changes without destroying the main construct of the previous curriculum. Yet the main impetus for this change did not come from the need to upgrade the system, but rather from a highly political orientation. Although there were some voices in the middle of the first decade of the 21st century expressing the view that the national curriculum and the attainment of standards for the national matriculation examination were not fully compatible, this discussion did not result in the introduction of changes. The educational reform in 2009 aimed at changing the national curriculum for all subjects and was politically driven.

Awareness of the *CEFR* in Curriculum Development

Polish delegates of different levels and different backgrounds had been involved in the activities initiated by the Council of Europe for many years and have brought knowledge of the *CEFR* and its ideas to Poland. Initially, this was limited to individuals, but with the initiative of the European Language Portfolio (ELP) numerous training activities took place, the main aim of which was to disseminate the ideas of the *CEFR* on a broader scale. At one stage, it even became a sort of fashion to include training sessions on the *CEFR* during all kinds of workshops, conferences and seminars for language teachers organised on different levels: local, regional and national by different kinds of institutions, such as teacher training centres, publishers, private training institutions, universities and central institutions affiliated to the ministry. However, the *CEFR* and the issues connected with it have not yet become an important or priority field for scientific research in Poland. Accordingly, general knowledge of the *CEFR* among most of the teachers and key players in the field of language teaching is common, but rather low and superficial. Moreover, although warmly welcomed at the beginning, the above-mentioned initiative of promoting the ELP has not resulted in substantial success. The ELP, in fact, is not used in practice on any considerable scale.

It has become natural for curriculum developers to take into account elements of innovation, such as the *CEFR* in this case, which have already been well rooted in the 'blood circuit' of foreign language teaching in Poland. Additionally, in the era of being a pre-accession country and later on as a new member state in the European Union, Polish decision-makers and policy-makers were eager to give a greater European dimension to different documents and legislation, and it was generally felt that one could not ignore the *CEFR* in the debates about new reforms. Paradoxically, this is more true in the case of the 1999 reform than the 2009 reform. In 1999, individuals engaged in the reform had already been aware of the current of changes and had taken the opportunity to make the curriculum as modern as possible. The curriculum of the 1999 reform was deeply rooted in the

CEFR since it was based on competences and also took into account such concepts as interaction and mediation, which are thoroughly described and developed in the *CEFR*. Yet this curriculum did not make a direct reference or link to the *CEFR* itself.

Direct reference was made in the 2009 curriculum, although only in regard to the proficiency levels described in the *CEFR*. Otherwise, *CEFR* ideas are very poorly and superficially treated and sometimes even misinterpreted. For example, language education and its development in the first three years of schooling, namely in Grades 1 to 3, is not defined with reference to any language proficiency levels. The most basic proficiency level, A1, in the *CEFR* scale, first appears in Grade 4. Consequently, it is unclear what proficiency level is supposed to be achieved by pupils at earlier stages during this period. The authors of the curriculum do not explain what level or sub-level of language proficiency they have in mind. Additionally, the development of intercultural competence, which is a fundamental element of the development of language proficiency, is treated very modestly by the 2009 curriculum. One can speculate that this situation results from the fact that curriculum developers are not expected to be experts in the *CEFR*, and furthermore no specific training is offered to them by the national educational authorities. This does not come as a surprise since the awareness of the *CEFR*'s implications for the methodology of language teaching is extremely low among decision-makers because they are politicians and not necessarily educators, not to mention the fact that they are never experts in language education. Although curriculum developers themselves are language experts, usually they are chosen at random and basically form a mixed group of academics and language teachers. The main criterion that the selection of experts to this group is based on is the variety of backgrounds these experts come from, and not necessarily the complementarity of their expertise. This variety mainly means that the experts represent different languages and different sorts of educational institutions. There is also an element of politics in this selection since it is the minister of education or their deputy who makes the selection of the experts.

The most important single influence was therefore the desire to become more 'European', rather than the wish to imitate other countries or nations, and the impact of international comparisons was thus not a significant factor in decision-making, as it may have been in other countries (see for example, Goullier, Hu, this volume). No research publication, report or debate on the application of the *CEFR* in other nations was commissioned in Poland as preparatory work for the development of the new 2009 national curriculum framework. However, within the Education and Training 2010 programme supporting the Lisbon Strategy, the European

Commission moderated the creation of a platform for sharing experience among the member states of the European Union and for providing examples of good practice. Some of the member states have taken the opportunity to present their initiatives connected with language teaching and the *CEFR*. However, it was very difficult to find examples of valuable initiatives, and this platform did not influence Polish policy-makers to any great extent.

The Curriculum Development Process

The developers of the 2009 national curriculum generally used existing knowledge in Poland about the *CEFR* in the writing process. However, as mentioned earlier, the *CEFR* was not treated deeply and profoundly in this document. During the second stage of the process, the first draft of the curriculum was reviewed by researchers and specialists in the field. One of the reviews concentrated only on the relations between the *CEFR* and the new curriculum. The review informed the curriculum developers of many shortcomings the draft had in reference to the *CEFR*. These were mainly: (i) adoption of terminology different to the one used by the *CEFR*; (ii) lack of reference to the proficiency level in the grades: I – III; (iii) lack of coherence between the *CEFR* descriptors and the curriculum requirements for some of the skills or sub-skills; and (iv) unclear gradation of the development of language proficiency between stage two and three of the education process, which in the Polish context means the second part of primary school, Grades 4-6, and the lower secondary school (Poszytek, 2008).

Although developers warmly welcomed the review, some of its conclusions were not taken into consideration when producing the final version of the document. The process had its time limits, whereas all the exercises connected with the *CEFR* are very time-consuming. In its final stage the curriculum underwent a consultative process that took the form of online consultations on the ministry's website in which everyone could participate. However, these elements did not bring anything new to the final version of the document. Everything was followed up by a familiarisation process in the form of regional meetings with selected teachers. During these meetings the issues connected with the *CEFR* were also raised, but they did not constitute a focal point of this training. It must be stressed that teachers' knowledge about the *CEFR*, if they have any, probably does not originate from curriculum innovation. A general lack of profound knowledge of the *CEFR* on the individual teacher level is also, and probably mainly, caused by the fact that it is only the beginning of a process in which the *CEFR* is gradually finding its proper place in pre-service teacher training curricula.

Influences on Assessment and Teaching

The main area of language education in which the *CEFR* occupies a focal position and is widely debated is assessment. National high-stake language examinations, namely the examination at the end of lower secondary level and especially the examination at the end of upper secondary education – which is a matriculation examination with the function of selecting students for higher education – have both been influenced by the *CEFR*. The former uses the proficiency levels described in the *CEFR* as a reference standard. The latter, which was given a new structure and a new format in 2005, was partially linked to the *CEFR*. The first step in this process was undertaken by the Central Examination Board in Poland, which took part in the pilot exercise organised by the Council of Europe in which various test administrating bodies submitted data on their tests. Since the examination is still quite new, the process of relating the matriculation examination to the *CEFR* levels could not be finalised because of a lack of all the necessary data required by the Council of Europe's *Manual for Relating Language Examinations to the CEFR* (Council of Europe, 2003). Although this pilot exercise resulted in the establishment of a proficiency level, which, according to the Central Examination Board, could be linked to the *CEFR* scale, the final result was not entirely satisfactory and convincing from a scientific point of view. This was because the pilot exercise was undertaken in 2004 on the basis of formal documents describing the format of the new examination and the real examination tasks were not included in the analysis, since the first examination took place in 2005. Consequently, this pilot exercise had its limitations with potentially huge implications for the validity of the results.

Further research analysed the constructs and the proficiency levels of this examination and included analysis of the first examination results. This research (Poszytek, 2008) revealed certain difficulties. For example, the use of different codes, wording and terminology in the descriptive bands of the *CEFR* scales on the one hand and in the assessment criteria and the criteria included in the standards of attainment or the national curriculum framework on the other poses a substantial obstacle to accurate matching of the respective and relevant entries. The lack of descriptors for levels C1 and C2, or having the same descriptors for higher proficiency levels, also blurs the picture of proper proficiency level assignment. The *CEFR* as a matrix for designing, producing or evaluating tests is a useful tool because it helps to analyse them in the context of different parameters of language proficiency. However, the *CEFR*'s limitations and shortcomings make these processes extremely difficult.

In the context of assessment, however, the *CEFR* positively influenced the development of tests in the certification system of Polish as a foreign language, since from the very beginning of creating this system its developers took the *CEFR* as a matrix for the construction of their test (Seretny *et al.*, 2004).

The *CEFR* had far less influence on teaching methods. Although, as previously stated, numerous training events were held on the *CEFR* and issues related to it, this did not affect the local or teacher level to an extent that could form a critical mass in this respect. It is also worth adding here that it was not training for the curriculum, but rather training provided by publishers that had the biggest impact on how teachers teach. However, apart from putting, quite unreflectively, labels with the *CEFR* proficiency levels on their course books, publishers seem not to treat the *CEFR* very profoundly. In most cases they reduce the *CEFR* to a marketing tool only.

Similarly, as regards the issue of the number of languages taught and the starting age of compulsory language education, the *CEFR* did not have significant influence either. Although the starting age for compulsory language education was lowered in 2008 from age ten to age seven, the main driving force behind this was the pressure from parents and the general European trend in this respect, rather than any reference to Council of Europe recommendations or the *CEFR*.

To some extent the *CEFR* has also been debated and negotiated in language education at tertiary level. Yet because of the high-level of autonomy of Polish universities, most of them apply their own approaches to language education and the data concerning these approaches is not gathered centrally. However, within the Council of Europe's initiative to create Language Education Policy Profiles that report on how languages are learnt, taught and approached in individual countries, some examples of good practice were identified in Poland. One of them is the University of Warsaw, which organises language courses for students of all faculties and for all languages on offer on the basis of the *CEFR*. This programme is sanctioned by a number of regulations passed by the rector and the university senate. The university offers 50 languages for which syllabi and examinations are constructed according to some of the guidelines from the *CEFR* (Council of Europe, 2007: 31).

Conclusions

Although the *CEFR* is broadly discussed in Poland on some occasions, and Poland can boast of having some examples of good practice in applying the *CEFR* into the educational system, the *CEFR* is still not well understood, which sometimes even results in misinterpretation of this document on a large scale with huge implications for educational process. This situation may be caused by two main factors. First, the ideas, methodological assumptions and the tools included in the *CEFR* are very difficult to apply in practice. Second, most of the teachers and experts have not undergone thorough training in the *CEFR*, and because of the high degree of complexity of this document, the most suitable training may better be realised within pre-service teacher formation than in-service education. As in the case of every innovation, it will take at least one generation of teachers for the knowledge of the *CEFR* to get rooted for good and find its proper place in the general awareness of all the people involved.

References

Council of Europe (2003) *Relating Language Examinations to the Common European Framework of Reference for Languages: Learning, Teaching, Assessment. Manual. Preliminary Pilot Version*. Strasbourg: Language Policy Division.

Council of Europe (2007) *Language Education Policy Profile. Poland*. Strasbourg: Language Policy Division.

Poszytek, P. (2008) *European Standards of Testing Language Proficiency and the Polish 'Nowa Matura' Examinations in English*. Krakow: Universitas.

Poszytek, P. (2008) Unpublished Review of the Draft of the National Curriculum Framework for Languages. Unpublished report (August). Warszawa: Ministry of National Education.

Seretny, A., Martyniuk, W. and Lipinska, E. (eds) (2004) *Opisywanie, Rozwijanie i Testowanie Znajomości języka Polskiego Jako Obcego*. Krakow: Universitas.

9 Academic Perspectives from Poland

Hanna Komorowska

Historical Context

In the period when the *CEFR* was published, Poland was entering the second decade of transition after the fall of communism. Thinking about language teaching in Poland was at that time undergoing dramatic changes. Formerly it had been shaped by four important stages of the country's social and political history:

- centuries of multilingual and multicultural Poland preceding the loss of independence in the 18th century with a long tradition of learning languages through direct contacts and a need for intercomprehension;
- the period between the loss of independence in the 18th century and the end of World War I when the school systems of the occupying forces, Russia, Prussia and Austria, banned Polish and imposed teaching through the medium of their languages, which led to hatred of schools and the loss of motivation to learn languages;
- the interwar period with a revival of motivation for language education and with a promotion of language teaching methods combining grammar-translation and functional approaches; and
- the communist period with its mandatory grammar-translation teaching of Russian introduced into school curricula as a political message of subordination with little chance of it ever being used for communicative purposes, together with Western European languages taught to a small fraction of upper secondary school students by means of modified audiolingual or communicative methods.

As a consequence, Poland met the fall of communism in 1989 with a huge variety of both positive and negative attitudes to learning languages and with an experience of a vast array of language teaching methods: direct, functional, grammar-translation and communicative. Which aspects of this varied experience would come to the forefront at that significant historical turn depended on the type of educational reforms to be implemented.

The first democratic government installed in the autumn of 1989 almost immediately (i.e. in February 1990) implemented the reform of foreign language teaching in the school system by granting equal status to all the foreign languages taught in the school system, encouraging language choice and lowering the language start to the age of 10. Actual language choice was, however, limited by the acute shortage of qualified teachers of English, German and French (Komorowska, 1991).

In October of the same year there followed the reform of teacher education. The reform established three-year teacher training colleges supervised by universities that recognised their coursework and granted BA degrees to their graduates. In consequence of social expectations, universities, which had formerly given only marginal attention to teacher education and whose diplomas automatically carried teaching qualifications, started offering an optional teaching component of around 300 hours. Language teaching methods promoted in teacher education were fully based on the communicative approach. Yet many unqualified teachers of English, employed in the school system to help replace the 20,000 teachers of Russian, were still using grammar-translation methods either because their lack of proficiency did not permit communication and interaction in the classroom, or because they were replicating their experience of learning a foreign language (Russian at that time) in their school days (Komorowska, 2002).

At the same time, a rapid promotion of secondary and tertiary education took place and a huge market for paid educational services emerged. State and non-state schools faced a pressing demand for language education, while private language schools mushroomed across the country – Poland was open to new ideas in language teaching.

The *CEFR*, published in 2001 and popularised throughout Poland by trainers taking part in teacher education seminars and networks of the Graz European Centre for Modern Languages, met with immense interest. The Polish translation of the *CEFR* was published in November 2003.

The Reception of the *CEFR* into Teaching Practices

To analyse attitudes towards the *CEFR* and decide which of its aspects have been emphasised, accepted, rejected or downplayed in Polish language education, it is worth looking at:

- opinions expressed in articles, papers, debates and teachers' conferences;
- legal acts published after the publication of the *CEFR*; and

- the content of course books and supplementary materials recommended by the Ministry of Education after the publication of the *CEFR*.

Approval and Enthusiasm for the *CEFR*

The aspect of the *CEFR* very strongly emphasised in Poland – as in almost every other country – was the idea of levels. Levels confirmed intuitions on which language school placement procedures had been based with their traditional courses for beginner, intermediate and advanced students. This analogy gave rise to a certain feeling of security, which helped absorb more innovative ideas. Level distinctions were almost immediately used in legal acts referring to new secondary school leaving examinations called *Nowa Matura* and to teaching qualification standards (*Standards of Attainment 2003, Regulation by the Minister of Education on Teaching Qualification Standards 2002, 2004*), as well as in publishers' materials and language schools' course planning. It also formed the main basis for reforms in tertiary language education.

Another aspect that met with immediate approval and was very strongly stressed from the beginning was the concept of descriptors. The roots of this approval can be traced to teachers' disappointment with post-structural objective testing and with their fear of integrated testing, which looked too much like the old grammar-translation essays. What appeared even more attractive was the final shape of descriptors based on the concept of 'can-do' statements. This positive approach proved to be in line with the new democratic context of a country whose historical tradition in education was based on the search for error perceived as guilt, and on efforts to correct every possible deviation from models imposed from above. Strong approval for both 'can-do' descriptors and 'learning to learn' naturally led to emphasis being placed on one more aspect, self-assessment. 'Can-do' statements immediately found their way into final parts of course book units and paved the way for the popularity of five Polish versions of the European Language Portfolio for five age groups: children aged 3–6, 6–10 and 10–15, upper secondary or tertiary learners and adults (*Europejskie Portfolio Językowe*, 2004, 2006a, 2006b, 2006c, 2007), validated by the Council of Europe in the years 2004–2007.

The country's rapid development made educators aware of the speed of the changes and, as a consequence, of the difficulties in attempts to identify contexts in which learners would be functioning in the future. Language teachers, therefore, welcomed another aspect of the *CEFR* – its stress on 'learning to learn', which immediately found its reflection in course book sections entitled 'Learner's corner' or 'Learner training' and in new modules on strategy training introduced into teacher education curricula.

One more aspect of the *CEFR* that was very strongly emphasised in legal documents such as the *Polish Core Curriculum* (*Podstawa Programowa* 2002, 2008) was the intercultural component. What is particularly interesting is that this emphasis, as revealed in examination analysis (Poszytek, 2008), has not been transferred into school leaving examination practice, and found its way into materials development in often superficial forms of basic information about other countries. This aspect of the *CEFR* seems to have been accepted at the level of values and knowledge, though not at the level of competence and skills.

Acceptance of the *CEFR*

Although not all aspects of the *CEFR* were openly discussed, quite a number of those that were less emphasised proved fully acceptable to teachers, curriculum constructors and materials designers. One of the most important that have not made their way into public debate, and yet have been fully accepted with all their consequences, is the idea of reception and production. Course planners in language schools and syllabus designers for schools of all levels immediately accepted not only this idea, but also the concept of domains and topics, which soon became an integral part of every language course, and the determinant of exit competences, as can be seen in national core curricula and in the secondary school leaving examination syllabuses (*Podstawa Programowa*, 2002, 2008; *Standards of Attainment*, 2003) as well as in annual examination guidelines. The reasons for this reaction can be traced back to the discrepancy between the emphasis on speaking skills in the Polish curriculum documents and the omnipresence of multiple choice lexico-grammar tests considered both practical and objective.

This naturally led to the acceptance of the idea of differentiation in educational aims and of individualisation in language education. The *CEFR* was seen as a response to one of the greatest difficulties faced by teachers, namely the combination of mixed ability and the so-called broad-banding caused by the mushrooming of paying language courses for children in preschool and initial education, which resulted in huge differences in the language experience of learners in the same school class. Both pre- and in-service teacher education courses soon started to include modules on individual learner variables and on methods of teaching mixed-ability classes.

The task-based approach also met with the approval of teachers and course writers, though there was significantly more interest in the ways in which it could be practically implemented in teaching languages for specific purposes and in the structure and content of course books for adult professionals.

The concept of error as a learning step was also easily accepted, probably because it caused no cognitive dissonance with the general guidelines accompanying the communicative approach.

Resistance to Theoretical Aspects of the *CEFR*

Apart from the obvious relevance of the document for teachers and teacher educators, its European status played an important part in shaping the initial reactions to its content. As the *CEFR* is an internationally significant document under the aegis of the Council of Europe and has thus been treated as an exponent of European language policy, it is understandable that open criticism addressed the form of the document rather than the approach adopted. Resistance to or rejection of certain aspects would rarely, if ever, be openly presented by authors, most probably for fear of being labelled traditional, outdated or anti-European. The lack of response in educational practice seems to be a more reliable index of resistance, at least for the first years of acquaintance with the document.

The aspect that met with no response whatsoever was the concept of curricular scenarios with varying aims for successive languages offered in the school system. The growing role of English as a lingua franca which raises voices in the international forum of countries with less widely-spoken languages would naturally call for differentiating goals and methods of teaching other languages in the Polish educational system. Yet syllabus designers or materials developers for other languages have never taken this option into consideration, possibly because the second and third foreign languages most commonly taught in the school system are French and German, which are spoken in countries Poles often visit for reasons of work or tourism. The communicative approach and a uniform curricular scenario seemed, therefore, to be the best solution.

In consequence, another aspect of the *CEFR* also met with resistance, the concept of partial competences. Again, nobody openly defied it, but apart from the changes in the approach to error, no conclusions have ever been formulated and no implications of this idea have been sought for the school system. This reaction can be traced back to the influence of the communicative approach, which stressed the value of balancing language skills. As suggested elsewhere (Komorowska, 2003), organisational and financial problems in changing course structure and examination format caused decision-makers, especially in commercial educational services, to ignore the issue.

Among the aspects definitely downplayed and perhaps misunderstood in the Polish reception of the *CEFR*, the descriptive, non-evaluative character of the document is probably the most important. From the very beginning, the document was often considered to be a set of guidelines offered by the Council of Europe to be followed by member states in language teaching and teacher training. This was reflected in common mistakes while quoting the Polish title of the *CEFR*. The text, published under the title of *Europejski System Opisu Kształcenia Językowego* (ESOKJ, 2003), which in translation reads *The European System for the Description of Language Education*, was often erroneously presented as *The European Description of the System of Language Education* in the belief that the right model is at last being presented to the ignorant. It should be noted, however, that the *CEFR* itself contributed to this confusion to a certain degree by openly favouring the communicative approach, while at the same time stressing its non-dogmatic character (Poszytek, 2008).

Another aspect obviously downplayed was that of mediating skills. Although these skills are not presented in the *CEFR* in detail, their role as activities in the *CEFR* terminology is worth much more attention than they have actually received in Poland in comparison with receptive, productive or interactive activities.

Criticisms

The main line of teachers' criticism was connected to the terminology employed in the document (e.g. the term *activities* was used to label four basic language skills with two extras of *interactive activities* and *mediating activities*). Trainees in pre- and in-service education could not understand the reason for that change. What added to their difficulty was the multitude of tables, most of which remained unused by educators and learners (Komorowska, 2004).

Researchers criticised the insufficient dynamics of phonological competence development as presented in the *CEFR* and reflected in descriptors on particular levels (cf. *Phonological Control* table in *CEFR*: 117), which claim that natural pronunciation and intonation can be achieved at B2 level, although it is impossible to speak of natural intonation without finer shades of meaning referred to in *CEFR* only at the C1 level (Sikorski, 2007).

Syllabus designers were unhappy with not being able to find any language content specification in the *CEFR*, due to its lack of lexical and grammatical descriptors within levels – a problem noticed not only in Poland (Keddle, 2004).

Teachers were disappointed because of the lack of clear demarcation lines between levels, and especially because of unequal distances between them – too large between A2 and B1, and too small between B2 and C1. Test constructors and researchers who were engaged in evaluation procedures claimed that it was not easy to treat the *CEFR* as a basis for test comparisons (Poszytek, 2008).

Teachers of languages for specific purposes pointed to the lack of clear and sufficient references for this strand of language education and especially to evaluating proficiency, as the *CEFR* gives no more than a few examples from the *Threshold Level* (*CEFR*: 53–54) and offers some references in the self-assessment grid (*CEFR*: 26–27), though only at B2 – C1 – C2 levels (Gajewska & Sowa, 2007).

Teachers working in the field of special education pointed to the lack of sufficient reference to Specific Linguistic Impairment and particularly to deficits commonly encountered in mainstream education such as dyslexia or attention-deficit hyperactivity disorder (ADHD) (Smuk, 2010).

Reasons for the Differential Reception of the *CEFR* in Poland

Reasons for the positive reception of the *CEFR* in Poland and for the incorporation of various aspects of the document were manifold. At the time of the publication of the *CEFR* in 2001 and of its Polish translation in 2003, Poland was preparing for its access to the European Union, which finally took place in 2004. In the pre-accession period, the question of European identity came to the forefront of educational decisions. As an offer promoting new tendencies in language education and facilitating useful international comparisons the *CEFR* was welcomed enthusiastically.

As in many European countries, a great deal of interest was elicited by *CEFR* scales and levels. Polish needs in this field were immense because at the time the *CEFR* was published Poland was in the process of implementing important school reforms and introducing an external secondary school leaving examination which also largely determined university admissions. Other sectors of Polish education were at that time also waiting for important changes in the language offer, as well as in placement and evaluation procedures. The great practicality of level distinction proved useful not only for language schools, but also for higher education as exemplified by new initiatives in the field of placement, examination and certification at Warsaw University (Urbanikowa, 2007).

In this situation, in the first years after its publication the *CEFR* mainly influenced the structure and content of examinations and testing. Yet due to the role of the so-called washback effect, preparation for examinations involved a considerable change in the teaching methods employed as well as in the materials used. Levels, therefore, proved useful for publishers and designers of course books, supplementary and online materials. Teachers, on the other hand, found 'can-do' descriptors useful for evaluation in the classroom.

The work on new core curricula for all the levels of Polish education which took place in the second half of the decade (*Podstawa programowa*, 2009) formed a social context that was more than ready to absorb a large number of aspects of the *CEFR*'s theoretical basis, and which strengthened the role of this document for the everyday practice of teaching and learning languages in Polish schools.

Restraints on the Influence and Adoption of the *CEFR*

Restraints are mainly connected with the criticism of the *CEFR* discussed above. Yet not all the criticism can be ascribed to characteristics of the *CEFR*; some of it springs from the nature of the Polish educational context. Part of the resistance comes from evaluative traditions in Polish education, where approaches and methods tended to be prioritised into those 'objectively' better and those 'objectively' worse, and where traditions of single right answers are still quite strong.

A more pragmatic factor is the fact that teachers are underpaid and often take extra jobs, which results in their refusal to engage in the analysis of lengthy documentation.

The influence of the *CEFR* is also limited by a pressure for educational outcomes measured by end-of-stage tests and examinations and the annual ranking of schools. Not only the role of individualisation, but even the value of learner-centred education is often forgotten in the drive for high scores on tests.

Tests and examinations assess proficiency across language skills, which hinders work on the differentiation of curricular scenarios. Combined with organisational difficulties, this does not encourage attempts at promoting modularity in course planning.

Conclusion

Although the *CEFR*'s limitations are numerous and the amount of criticism directed at the document in Poland is large, the number of aspects approved of is far greater, and what is more, their significance is immense. All in all, the evaluation of the role of the *CEFR* in Polish education has been more than positive, which explains its sustainable, favourable reception in Poland. It opened many eyes to the complexity of language teaching and learning, restrained the tendency to look for single right answers and positively influenced the structure and content of core curricula for primary and secondary schools as well as speeding up tertiary education reforms. It also paved the way for the promotion of other documents of the Council of Europe, such as the European Language Portfolio (Little, 2000) and the EPOSTL – *European Portfolio for Student Teachers of Languages* (Newby *et al.*, 2007).

References

Europejskie Portfolio językowe dla dzieci od 3 do 6 lat wraz z Poradnikiem dla nauczycieli i rodziców – numer akredytacji Rady Europy 87.2007. (2007). Warsaw: CODN.

Europejskie Portfolio językowe dla dzieci od 6 do 10 lat wraz z Poradnikiem dla nauczycieli i rodziców – numer akredytacji Rady Europy 72.2006. (2006a). Warsaw: CODN.

Europejskie Portfolio językowe dla dzieci od 10 do15 lat wraz z Poradnikiem – numer akredytacji Rady Europy 62.2004. (2004). Warsaw: CODN.

Europejskie Portfolio językowe dla uczniów szkół gimnazjalnych i studentów wraz z Poradnikiem – numer akredytacji Rady Europy 76.2006. (2006b). Warsaw: CODN.

Europejskie Portfolio językowe dla dorosłych – numer akredytacji Rady Europy 6.2006. (2006c) Warsaw: CODN.

Europejski System Opisu Kształcenia Językowego: uczenie się, nauczania, ocenianie. (2003). Warsaw: CODN.

Gajewska, E. and Sowa, M. (2007) Ewaluacja biegłości językowej a nauczanie języka Specjalistycznego. In M. Pawlak and J. Fisiak (eds) *Dokumenty Rady Europy a nauczanie języków w polskim systemie edukacji* (pp. 121–133). Łódź: Wydawnictwo WSHE.

Janowska, I. (2007) Europejski system Opisu Kształcenia Językowego – początek nowej ery w dydaktyce językowej. *Języki obce w szkole 4, 30–37.*

Keddle, J.S. (2004) The CEF and the Secondary School Syllabus. In K. Morrow (ed.) *Insights from the Common European Framework* (pp. 43–45). Oxford: Oxford University Press.

Komorowska, H. (1991) Second Language Teaching in Poland Prior to the Reform of 1990. In G. Alatis (ed.) *Georgetown University Round Table on Languages and Linguistics 1991* (pp. 501–508). Washington, DC: Georgetown University Press.

Komorowska, H. (2002) *The Common European Framework* in Poland. In *Common European Framework of Reference for Languages: Learning, Teaching, Assessment. Case Studies.* Strasbourg: Council of Europe Publications.

Komorowska, H. (2004) *The Common European Framework* in Pre- and In- service Teacher Education. In K. Morrow (ed.) *Insights from the Common European Framework* (pp. 55–64). Oxford: Oxford University Press.

Komorowska, H. (2003) *Europejski System Opisu Kształcenia Językowego* w pracy nauczyciela. *Języki obce w szkole 6, 74–79.*

Little, D. 2002. The European Language Portfolio: Structure, origins, implementation and challenges, *Language Teaching* 35.3: 182–9.

Little, D. (2010) *What does "implementing" the Common European Framework of reference for Languages (CEFR) mean?*, http://www.caslt.org/pdf/ReflexionsMay10.pdf.

Ministry of National Education and Sport (2003) Standards of Attainment – the Basis for Administration of a Matura examination. Annex to the Regulation of the Minister of National Education and Sport (10 April). Warsaw: Ministry of National Education and Sport.

Newby, D., Allan, R., Fenner, A.B., Komorowska, H., Jones, B. and Soghikyan. K (2007) *European Portfolio for Student Teachers of Languages*. European Centre for Modern Languages: Graz. Council of Europe Publishing.
Newby, D. (ed.) (2012) *Insights into the European Portfolio of Student Teachers of Languages (EPOSTL)*. Newcastle: Cambridge Scholars Publishing.
Pawlak, M. and Fisiak, J. (eds) (2007) *Dokumenty Rady Europy a nauczanie języków w polskim systemie edukacji*. Łódź: Wydawnictwo WSHE.
Podstawa Programowa wychowania przedszkolnego i kształcenia ogólnego 2002. Dz. U. nr 51, poz. 458 (Regulation by the Minister of National Education and Sport of 26th February 2002 on Curricular Guidelines for Preschool and General Education in Particular Types of School. Journal of Laws of 2002, no 51, item 458).
Podstawa Programowa 2008. Rozporządzenie Ministra Edukacji Narodowej z dnia 23 grudnia 2008. Dz. U. nr 4, poz. 17 (National Core Curriculum 2008. Act by the Minister of Education from 23 December 2008, Journal of Laws of 2008, no 4, item 17).
Poszytek, P. (2008) European Standards of Testing Language Proficiency and the Polish 'Nowa matura' Examinations in English. Kraków: Universitas.
Regulation by the Minister of National Education and Sport of 26th February 2002 on Teaching Qualification Standards. Journal of Laws of 2002, no 155, item 1288.
Regulation by the Minister of National Education and Sport on Teaching Qualification Standards for Foreign Languages. Journal of Laws of 2004, item 2110.
Sikorski, J. (2007) Ocena aktualnej kompetencji fonetycznej. In Pawlak, M., Fisiak, J. (eds) *Dokumenty Rady Europy a nauczanie języków w polskim systemie edukacji* (pp.145–158). Łódź: Wydawnictwo WSHE.
Smuk, M. (2010) *Wyzwania dla autentyczności w ujęciu glottodydaktycznym*. Unpublished doctoral dissertation. Warsaw University.
Urbanikowa, J. (2007) Europejski Rok Języków. Proces Boloński i polityka językowa na Uniwersytecie Warszawskim. In M. Pawlak and J. Fisiak (eds) *Dokumenty Rady Europy a nauczanie języków w polskim systemie edukacji* (pp. 51–63). Łódź: Wydawnictwo WSHE.

Commentary on the European Cases

Michael Byram and Lynne Parmenter

As a first stage in our consideration of the four European cases, let us identify some commonalities. First, there is what Goullier calls a 'chronological coincidence' of the appearance of the *CEFR* and national curriculum change, although the impulse for change varies from country to country. Another common point is that 'entry' to the *CEFR* is via the scales and 'levels' and in connection with assessment and/or self-assessment and the European Language Portfolio; this also introduces the risk that the *CEFR* is seen only in terms of the levels. Thirdly, there are aspects of the *CEFR* that are *not* influential or accepted – in particular the notion of plurilingualism and its implications for curriculum design. Across the European cases, the difficulty of new terminology is widely noted and may raise problems of translation. Similarly, across the cases, the impact of the *CEFR* on classroom practice may be very limited, and resistance may be manifested not as explicit rejection so much as in the ignoring of innovations and the continuation of existing practices. Finally, the influences of the *CEFR* on assessment systems are substantial, and the attention to levels and scales is a consequence of a general demand, by politicians and others, for measured outcomes from all teaching and learning, and this translates into language competences in the case of foreign language teaching. It is in this assessment dimension that the chronological coincidence is particularly favourable to the *CEFR*, whereas the other two keywords of its subtitle 'learning, teaching' and the ways these are described do not coincide with changes or reforms.

There are also some interesting differences. Two cases, Bulgaria and Poland, are countries that were part of the communist/socialist era in East and Central Europe, and for them there was a generalised urge towards 'Europeanisation', meaning attention to the expectations of the European Union and the Council of Europe. Obviously, in the case of France and Germany this was not an issue, but there too there was in the period around the publication of the *CEFR* a strong tendency to compare themselves with other countries. This was brought to a head in the case of Germany by the

OECD comparison studies and the PISA shock. Europeanisation in France and Germany meant some degree of harmonisation too, but questions of European identity were not present in the same way as in Poland and Bulgaria.

The four cases divide into the same two pairs with respect to criticisms. In both France and Germany, it was argued that the *CEFR* does not give sufficient attention to 'education': to the aspects of language teaching which are not only utilitarian, and which are not necessarily measurable. There was also a fear that Europeanisation would lead to reductionism in language education in so far as it would lead to a focus on certification, as is indeed evident from the example given in North Rhine Westphalia.

It is striking that in both France and Germany the impact of the *CEFR* comes through strong centralisation. In France this is a well-established tradition, but in Germany too, despite there being 16 federal state education systems, the importance attributed to international comparisons led to a centralised and hierarchical structure with the KMK at the apex.

Bulgaria and Poland have not only the history of being under Soviet/Russian influence in common, but also long periods of earlier foreign domination. The influence of this on attitudes to language learning is striking in both cases, although in different ways. In Bulgaria, there was a strong tradition of language learning, but with teaching methods being influenced for each language from the target language country. The importance of the *CEFR* was to offer a basis for a methodology for all languages. In Poland, attitudes were very varied, but there was also a wide variety of inherited teaching methods here too. The *CEFR* was associated with the democratic turn away from Soviet times, and the learner-centred philosophy of *CEFR* was seen as an important element of this reaction against the Soviet period, even if other factors, including pressure to have measurable outputs from the education system, sustained the tradition of teachers making assessments of a holistic and perhaps reductionist kind.

The question of whether the *CEFR* is a normative document was strongly debated in Germany but was present elsewhere too. It is striking that in Poland the Polish title of the *CEFR* was misquoted as 'The European Description of the System of Language Education' by practitioners who were perhaps hoping not just for guidelines but for guidance. On the other hand, criticism by academics of the normative character of the *CEFR* was widespread – as in Germany – even though this criticism should sometimes have been directed not at the *CEFR* but at its use by others, such as assessment authorities.

On the other hand, from the Council of Europe perspective, it might be argued that the normative policy of the values associated with plurilingualism, with 'learning to learn', with learner-centred education, is precisely what has been largely ignored in the four cases. This might be for lack of knowing how to implement such a policy, despite the curriculum scenarios presented in Chapter 8, but it is also a consequence of strong traditions of separation of languages in the curriculum which are assumed to correspond with the psychological separation of languages in learners' minds.

The *CEFR* is, we argued in our introduction, a policy document, and it therefore has normative intentions at the level of general concepts and values, even though it purports to have no preferences at the technical level. The evidence that its 'key values' are 'infecting' the case study countries – to use the medical metaphor – is thus still very limited. There is resistance among practitioners – whether teachers, policymakers or other stakeholders – to the 'virus'. It may have more effect on coming generations whose resistance, hitherto built up by tradition and experience, can be expected to be lower. This remains to be seen.

Part 2

THE *CEFR* BEYOND EUROPE

America

Argentina

The authors:

Melina Porto has the degree of Teacher and Translator of English from Universidad Nacional de La Plata (UNLP) in Argentina. She is a researcher at CONICET (Consejo Nacional de Investigaciones Científicas y Técnicas) in the Instituto de Investigaciones en Humanidades y Ciencias Sociales (Institute of Research in the Social Sciences and the Humanities) from Facultad de Humanidades y Ciencias de la Educación (School of Humanities and Sciences of Education) at the National University of La Plata. She holds an MA ELT from the University of Essex, UK and a PhD Sciences of Education from UNLP. She is Titular Professor in the Chair English Language II at UNLP. She is co-author of the New English Curriculum Design for Primary School in the Province of Buenos Aires in Argentina. She has been involved in research funded by the International Reading Association (IRA), Fundación Antorchas, the National University of La Plata and CONICET. She is currently a member of the Language Diversity Committee of IRA, and of the Grants and Research Committee of IRA. She is involved in research on cultural understanding in EFL reading in Argentina.

Silvana Barboni is an EFL teacher and translator from Universidad Nacional de La Plata (UNLP). She holds an MA in TEFL (University of Reading, UK) and is currently a Doctor in Education International Student at London University (UK). She teaches ELT Didactics at La Plata State University and English Curriculum Design and Teaching Practice at The Catholic University of La Plata. She has several years' experience teaching in both primary and secondary schools and has coordinated English departments at several schools. She coordinates the Programme of Foreign Languages of the Ministry of Education of the Province of Buenos Aires and produces teacher education materials for the ministry. She is co-author of the New English Curriculum Design for Primary School in the Province of Buenos Aires.

10 Policy Perspectives from Argentina

Melina Porto and Silvana Barboni

Introduction

In Argentina, the development of language policies in general, and curricular innovations in ELT in compulsory schooling in particular, have been strongly tied to political decisions at a national level for a number of years. The biggest and most influential province in the country, the Province of Buenos Aires, which has the second largest and most complex system of education in Latin America, is the best exponent of the ways that language policies have been applied in the country. Distinct cultural, political and social needs have guided the decisions made in the province as regards educational policy planning and implementation. Certain features of international educational tendencies have exercised an important influence too, as in the case of the European model for the teaching of languages embodied in the *CEFR*.

This chapter describes how the most recent English language curriculum developed in Buenos Aires is the outcome of the workings of national and provincial life in a complex, culturally-specific setting, and the connections and interrelationships between this unique setting and the *CEFR*. The following questions guide our reflections: what are the particular cultural, political and social needs that have led to policy and curricular change? How has a strongly localized curriculum been developed with an international perspective in mind? In what ways has borrowing from the *CEFR* been possible? What challenges, difficulties and achievements have emerged?

Policy Changes in ELT Education: The Influence of Local Needs

In Argentina, the teaching of English in schools began between the late 1880s and the first decades of the 20th century almost exclusively in the private sector through subtractive bilingualism models based on a monoglossic conception of language learning (García, 2009). Many traditional bilingual schools and private institutions appeared (Banfi & Day, 2005), targeted at the high-income sectors in the main provincial capitals around the country. Also, there were several educational initiatives arising from immigrant communities of the working classes who wanted their children to be taught the language of their ancestors. These institutions were in many cases co-financed or supported by the state. It was not until the 1960s that English was first introduced extensively in the curriculum for secondary school. However, the impact of an education in languages was restricted to a limited population simply because secondary school was not compulsory at that time.

A big change took place in the 1990s: English was incorporated and became compulsory in primary and lower secondary schools (basic level, three years). In this period, English Language Teaching (ELT) was conceived in purely instrumental terms, aimed at providing sufficient linguistic competence to get better chances of employment, and social and economic mobility in a highly competitive market. Teachers were immersed in a narrow system that downgraded the more noble aims of foreign language education (Vior *et al.*, 2008) at the expense of productivity. Curricular prescriptions were product-oriented (i.e. they included competence standards intended to operate as a means of standardization in a highly decentralized educational system). The main rationale behind the Federal Education Act, passed in 1993, was the idea that decentralization would allow schools to decide on their best interests. Concurrently, the neglect of profound inequalities among schools in terms of financial resources, facilities and qualified human capital led the private sector to gain enormous profits while public schools collapsed into an insurmountable deficit, enormously widening the existing gap in education (Vior, 2004).

By 2001, the consequences of a 10-year neo-liberal era deepened, leading to a profound and severe social, political and economic crisis that exploded with the resignation of the elected president. The ongoing polarization in income distribution during the 1990s had generated increasing numbers of impoverished sectors and concomitant social exclusion (Tedesco, 1999, 2000) leading to social conflict (Vior, 2004). In this scenario, educational policies gradually started to be viewed as part of a strategy for social cohesion within a new conceptualization of the role of the state and its regulatory function in society in order to guarantee conscientious and responsible citizenship as well as social welfare (Vior *et al.*, 2008).

In this context of change, educational policies were redefined (Vior *et al.*, 2008), articulating centralized policies with market ones to produce what Whitty (2008: 33) describes as 'the apparent paradox of the "free market and the strong state"', which is also seen in other parts of the world. This was done centrally through curricular prescription and innovation and a focus on the re-professionalization of teachers as agents of social change (Hunt, 2009; Tedesco, 2000). A new professional identity for teachers developed, which brought about tensions between the academic cultures of the existing entrepreneurial communities of practice and the new perspectives on teacher identity in an Argentine context influenced by international reconceptualizations of ELT practices globally (Savignon, 2007; Akbari, 2008).

On the one hand, the role of languages was redefined within the school curriculum, placing an increasing emphasis on the need to foster multiliteracy practices. The state thus began to fulfil a key role in the educational system through curricular and teacher education policies aimed at social inclusion and the democratization of knowledge, or education for all (Tedesco, 1999, 2000). The state acknowledged the centrality of education to achieve social cohesion and build a sense of citizenship (Tesdesco, 1999). For example, the 2008 curricular innovation in ELT in the Province of Buenos Aires stated as one aim 'the strengthening of their [the children's] own cultural identity by enabling the processes of social integration' (Diseño Curricular de Educación Primaria, 2008: 321). This change of focus rested on a political model that transcended the traditional conceptions of underdevelopment toward a view of development based on autonomy, immersed in a global strategy within Latin America (Bruno Bologna *et al.*, 1987). There emerged a growing awareness of the value attached to native languages (Spanish and indigenous languages), with the recognition of the linguistic rights of ethnic minorities throughout Argentina. This acknowledgement was in tune with similar calls in Latin America as voiced by the Organization of American States in its documents and agreements on linguistic diversity from 1999. Simultaneously, English became compulsory in all schools – primary and secondary – within an educational framework that adhered to the 2003 UNESCO documents stressing the need for multilingual education as a core element in all systems of education worldwide (UNESCO, 2003).

These developments contrast sharply with the previous instrumental curricular prescriptions. Now our educational aims are broader: with the National Education Act passed in 2006 (Law 26.206), which makes school compulsory from ages five to 18, English teachers are expected to participate in a comprehensive literacy project that will allow our children and young people to become 'citizens of the world' (Starkey, 2005). English is no longer conceived as purely instrumental for employment, education, health and social and economic mobility, but rather as an important resource to make communication possible worldwide, with an emphasis on common bonds, understanding and peace in a multicultural, highly diversified, globalized world (García, 2009). At the same time, the 21st century has radically modified the linguistic needs of English learners, and Argentina has not escaped this drive (Cassany, 2000). This change has been accompanied by a redefinition of the role of the school given this scenario (Dussel & Finocchio, 2003). With this conception, and set in this framework, English becomes a core subject throughout compulsory primary and secondary schooling.

The agenda of English practitioners has thus broadened and has become more complex in a number of ways, demanding a school curriculum that focuses on two distinct aspects of the role of teachers within this new policy. First, the 2008 curriculum acknowledges that teaching English in the 21st century necessarily involves an 'intercultural dimension' (Byram *et al.*, 2001). ELT is concerned with the development of the necessary knowledge, skills and attitudes that will help children and young people to open up to the Otherness pervading in increasingly diverse contexts (Barboni *et al.*; Diseño Curricular de Educación Primaria, 2008: 323–324; hereafter DCEP). Secondly, the ELT professional faces more complex demands, as Sercu (2006) points out in general terms, among which is the need to cater for diversity in the classroom in all its forms. Considering that diversity on all fronts transmutes our current contexts of work (UNESCO, 2008 Report), the new curriculum was flexible enough to allow for a diversity of practices while strongly enforcing a teaching agenda coherent with an educational policy for social justice (Zeichner, 2009).

The Local Adoption of Cross-National Trends in ELT

In this local context of educational policy development, the *CEFR* served as a theoretical foundation for the development of curricular innovations in ELT. Its influence as a relevant framework of reference has become quite institutionalized in the Argentinean setting – an influence that was heavily dependent on the ideology behind the new curricular policy described above (i.e. a policy anchored in the specific social, political and economic context of the Province of Buenos Aires).

This is clear from a comparison of principles in the *CEFR* and the curriculum policy of the Province of Buenos Aires (DCEP):

- A sociolinguistic description of language. Language is seen as discourse (i.e. as a negotiation of meanings in which interlocutors are involved to produce meaningful interaction). Meaning is at the core of the process of learning and using language. This aspect is coherent with the ideological basis of the curriculum since literacy development, as opposed to the knowledge of English as a system, is the main goal of compulsory schooling (*CEFR*, 2001: 13; DCEP, 2008: 335).

- The recognition of linguistic diversification in a multicultural and multilingual world. Both primary and secondary school curricula prescribe the development of knowledge, skills and attitudes that constitute the basis for intercultural understanding. In both documents, the EFL classroom is conceived as a third space that helps students become conscious of the diversity around them and open up to Otherness. This view of the EFL class as a vehicle for understanding among people of diverse backgrounds is also coherent with an educational policy that embraces diversity as part of the richness of our society and the classroom as an exponent of it (*CEFR*, 2001: 1–2, 4–5, 168–176; DCEP, 2008: 323–24).
- A task-based methodology for the teaching and assessment of language. As the language is used as a genuine means of communication, learning takes place through the use of the language to solve problems and carry out purposeful and meaningful tasks. This is also in line with an overall educational policy that aims at lifelong learning (e.g. learning to learn) in a changing world (*CEFR*, 2001: 15, 157–162; DCEP, 2008: 326; 340–41)
- A *can do* description of students´ competences in the foreign language. This is congruent with an understanding of learning as a lifelong process that enables and empowers students. Descriptions of their competences at different moments of the process are expressed in terms of achievements, not failures (*CEFR*, 2001: 24, 26–29, 58–87, 96, 110, 112, 117–118, 122, 124–125, 129; DCEP, 2008: 336)

The Challenges Presented for Curriculum Developers

The *CEFR* draws on a long-standing applied linguistics tradition in the teaching of languages that forms the basis for the teaching of English in Argentina in academic contexts. In other words, the guidelines in the *CEFR* are a familiar part of existing discourses and practices of English teachers and academics. The *CEFR* is part of the required reading lists in most teacher education institutions (tertiary and university-based) and postgraduate language education. Furthermore, these guidelines are well known to a range of actors in the ELT field in the Province of Buenos Aires such as classroom teachers working in private and public schools, faculty members in private and public institutions, specialized librarians, policy-makers, freelance consultants, materials writers and student teachers. One reason for this may be that the *CEFR* appears in the bibliographies of supporting documents accompanying the last curricular innovation in ELT in the Province of Buenos Aires (including expanded theoretical frameworks, bibliography of literary works, literature projects, lists of linguistic exponents, etc.).

Interestingly enough, the use of the *CEFR* in this specific curriculum development (i.e. process-based) differs from its uses in other contexts in Argentina. Firstly, the private sector uses it as a source of standardized descriptions of linguistic competence as required by the available TESOL international examinations in the country (i.e. for outcome-oriented purposes, almost exclusively to assess students' linguistic competences).

Secondly, a growing and disturbing concern has been recurrently raised regarding the use of the linguistic descriptions provided by the *CEFR*. This concern stems from the cultural and methodological aspects behind the new curriculum, with a focus on how teachers should teach instead of only on what students should learn – a neglected area in our local context. The focus on the levels of the *CEFR* posed a challenging goal to us as curriculum developers, which was to help teachers develop new readings of the guidelines – guidelines they had followed mechanically for years. In the new curriculum, we as members of the authoring group used the *CEFR* not only to describe levels of competence but also to focus on methodological aspects, such as task, theme and project-based methodologies. Because these proposals contrasted so sharply with the instrumental view of ELT that had been dominant for decades, the document encouraged an element of reflexivity and criticality in the evaluation of past and traditional practices, leading to conscientious and responsible professional development. In other words, this curricular document favoured a shift of focus from a conception of student learning as a product to be assessed through international exams to a view that sees English language learning in Argentina as part of a lifelong process with a deeper and long-standing aim: the discovery of what unites human beings, with a focus on commonalities and bonds, in an attempt to be as much at ease as possible with each others' languages, cultures and individualities (DCEP, 2008: 223).

We faced these challenges both during the actual development of the text of the curriculum itself and after it was finished (i.e. while it was being implemented in schools throughout the Province of Buenos Aires). Like the majority of language educators in the country, we had encountered the *CEFR* as student teachers at the National University of La Plata, and later as practitioners. Therefore this contact was mainly through reading lists and competence standards for internal, local and international examinations. In other words, we had ourselves been immersed in the product and linguistic orientation of the *CEFR* in this setting. It was clear to us that we needed to design and implement measures to address the challenges described above on two fronts: curriculum development and teacher education.

Regarding the former, the process of writing the curriculum involved a number of stakeholders with different levels of participation and decision-making chances. We invited other primary and secondary school curriculum writers to offer feedback. Like us, they were faculty members from different universities located in the Province of Buenos Aires, specialized in ELT theory and methodology. To soften the impact of the new uses of the *CEFR* that we were making in this document (beyond levels of competence), we included explicit and thorough descriptions, explanations and exemplifications, tying theory and practice and encouraging teachers to grasp the theoretical principles as applied in practice within classroom contexts. Even though the document was of course prescriptive, these descriptions and explanations were intended to stimulate reflection and criticality so that teachers could exercise their autonomy and discretionary judgement, given the diversity of teaching contexts present in the Province of Buenos Aires.

With respect to the latter, a teacher education programme for primary and secondary school teachers was devised, passed and implemented with the aim of offering free teacher education in a variety of formats. This innovation, called 'Maestros y profesores enseñando inglés' (Primary and secondary school teachers teaching English), was first implemented in 2005 and has been growing significantly to reach a population of more than 6000 teachers, who have accessed the programme through traditional teacher development courses and on-site dialogic assistance in their own schools. These teacher education provisions are based on the analysis of case studies and particular scenarios so as to contribute to the development of a teaching identity in line with the legal regulations of the curriculum, but respecting professional discretionary judgement and fostering enquiry-based practices (Johnson, 2009). This teacher education programme was released before the new curriculum was actually implemented. In this way, teachers had the opportunity to become familiar with, and elaborate on, the content of the document and the new uses of the *CEFR* evidenced in it. In addition, it was also concurrently sustained during and after the curricular innovation itself. In other words, it accompanied teachers as acknowledged key stakeholders in the process and fostered the appreciation of teaching as a rewarding professional activity worth pursuing.

Conclusion

The justification to resort to the experiences of other countries, in this case the *CEFR*, in times of curricular change can be understood as part of a 'global educational reform movement' (Tatto, 2007: 267) that sees quality education 'as an engine of development among virtually all countries and donors' (Iredale, 1996: 12) and 'the teacher as a key actor in the process of educational transformation' (Tedesco, 1997: 23).

In Argentina, this whole process of curricular innovation, accompanied by the combination of teacher professionalization programmes and an accountability document – as a curriculum can be – is part of a global reform strategy related to the regulatory function of the state to develop better educational opportunities for all citizens. The use of the *CEFR* as a reference work for curricular development in the Province of Buenos Aires can be seen as part of the global spread of ideas on how languages need to be taught in this century as a result of the current global scenario. Yet the level of semantic construction that Schriewer and Martinez (2004: 33) point out as 'the construction of world views and reference horizons out of particular sociocultural and national settings and driven by these settings´ internal needs' have determined the ways in which the *CEFR* was appropriated in our context and the extent to which its guidelines were applied in the construction of a new ELT curriculum in the Province of Buenos Aires.

In addition, many barriers exist, and need to be acknowledged here, regarding the borrowing of the *CEFR* in Buenos Aires and in Argentina as a whole. These include a mismatch between theory and reality in many areas (due to many factors, including social, cultural and financial); the educational consequences of the increasing gap between rich and poor; the actual low performance of Argentinean students in standardized international testing; a lack of emphasis on early and adult education; high drop-out rates in primary and secondary schooling; the clouding of the 'equality of access' to education (which all educational policies advocate) by the failure to take account of 'equality of outcome' (McKay & Warshauer Freedman, 1990: 399) or 'equality of opportunity to achieve' (McCarty, 2003: 149) for a variety of reasons; a crisis of recruitment and retention of qualified teachers for the public school sector; consequently, poorly-qualified teachers for public schools (because of low salaries and the low reputation associated with being a schoolteacher in this country); an inflexible and ineffective system of teacher regulation (regarding salaries, compensations, leaves of absence); and a teacher culture in public school contexts that tends to be dominated by a lack of commitment and dedication, absenteeism and strikes.

References

Akbari, R. (2008) Postmethod discourse and practice. *TESOL Quarterly* 42, *641–652*.

Banfi, C. and Day, R. (2005) The Evolution of Bilingual Schools in Argentina. In A. de Mejia (ed.) *Bilingual Education in South America* (pp. 65–78). Clevedon: Multilingual Matters.

Barboni, S., Beacon, G. and Porto, M. (2008) Diseño Curricular de Inglés para EPB (Educación Primaria Básica) de la Provincia de Buenos Aires. *Diseño Curricular para la Educación Primaria. Segundo Ciclo. Volumen 1* (pp. 321–352). Dirección de Currículum, Dirección General de Cultura y Educación de la Provincia de Buenos Aires. 1 Edición.

Bruno Bologna, A., Trevisan, M. and Lechini, G. (1987) *Cuadernos de Política Exterior Argentina. Serie 'Documentos de Trabajo' N° 1*. Rosario: Centro de Estudios en Relaciones Internacionales de Rosario (CERIR) *1–39*.

Byram, M., Nichols, A. and Stevens, D. (2001) *Developing Intercultural Competence in Practice*. Clevedon: Multilingual Matters.

Cassany, D. (2000) De lo analógico a lo digital. El futuro de la enseñanza de la composición. *Lectura y Vida* 21, *6–15*.

Dussel, I. and Finocchio, S. (2003) *Enseñar Hoy. Una introducción a la educación en los tiempos de crisis*. Mexico: Fondo de Cultura Económica.

García, O. (2009) *Bilingual Education in the 21st Century: A Global Perspective*. West Sussex: Wiley Blackwell.

Hunt, B. (2009) *Efectividad del Desempeño Docente. Una reseña de la literatura internacional y su relevancia para mejorar la educación de América Latina*. Chile: PREAL.

Iredale, R. (1996) The Significance of teacher education for international educational development. In C. Brock (ed.) *Global Perspectives on Teacher Education*. Oxford: Triangle.

Johnson, K. (2009) *Second Language Teacher Education: A Sociocultural Perspective*. London: Routledge.

McCarty, T. (2003) Revitalising indigenous languages in homogenising times. *Comparative Education* 39, 147–163.

McKay, S. and Warshauer Freedman, S. (1990) Language minority education in Great Britain: A challenge to current US policy. *TESOL Quarterly* 24, 385–405.

Savignon, S. (2007) Beyond communicative language teaching: What´s ahead¿ *Journal of Pragmatics* 39, 207–220.

Schriewer, J. and Martinez, C. (2004). Constructions of internationality in education. In G. Steiner-Khamsi (ed.) *The Global Politics of Educational Borrowing and Lending* (pp. 29–53). New York: Teachers College Press.

Sercu, L. (2006) The foreign language and intercultural competence teacher: The acquisition of a new professional identity. *Intercultural Education* 17, *55–72*.

Starkey, H. (2005) Language teaching for democratic citizenship. In A. Osler and H. Starkey (eds) *Citizenship and Language Learning: International Perspectives* (pp. 23–39). Staffordshire: Trentham Books.

Tatto, M.T. (ed.) (2007) *Reforming Teaching Globally*. Oxford: Symposium Books.

Tedesco, J.C. (1997) Enhancing the role of teachers. In C.D. Day, van Veen and Wong Kooi Sim (eds) *Teachers and Teaching: International Perspectives on School Reform and Teacher Education*. Arlington: International Council on Education for Teaching.

Tedesco, J. (1999) Educación y sociedad del conocimiento y de la información. Paper presented at *Encuentro Internacional de Educación Media* held in Bogotá, Colombia, 8–12 August 1999.

Tedesco, J. (2000) Los pilares de la educación del futuro. Online at www.iipe-buenosaires.org.ar/system/.../pilares-educacion-futuro.pdf. Accessed on 24 November 2009.

UNESCO (2003) *Education in a Multilingual World*. Education Position Paper. Paris: UNESCO. Online at: http://unesdoc.unesco.org/images/0012/001297/129728e.pdf

UNESCO (2008) *Report 2008 A View Inside Primary Schools*. Online at: www.uis.unesco.org/template/pdf/wei/sps/Report.pdf *Accessed on 24 November 2009.*

Vior, S. (2004) Una visión crítica de las políticas educacionales en la Argentina de los 90. El caso de la enseñanza de la ciencia y la tecnología. *Periodico Do Maestrado em Educacao da UCDB* 17, *11–28.*

Vior, S., Misuraca, M. and Rocha, S. (eds) (2008) *Formación de Docentes: ¿Qué cambió después de los '90 en las políticas, currículos y las instituciones?* Buenos Aires: Jorge Baudiño Ediciones.

Whitty, G. (2008) Changing modes of teacher professionalism: Traditional, managerial, collaborative and democratic. In B. Cunningham (ed.) *Exploring Professionalism* (pp. 28–49). London: Bedford Way Papers, Institute of Education, University of London.

Zeichner, K. (2009) *Teacher Education and the Struggle for Social Justice.* New York: Routledge.

11 Academic Perspectives from Argentina

Melina Porto

Introduction

The purpose of this chapter is to focus on the aspects of the *CEFR* that have been borrowed, as well as those which have been silenced or downgraded in Argentina – and why this should happen – by reference to several of the contexts in the country as a whole. I stress that the spirit and motivation for its adoption here lie in the need for unification in language education regarding objectives, content, assessment and standards, considering the multiplicity of its contexts of use. I explain how a change of focus has taken place, in particular with new curricular developments (one of which we describe in the previous chapter). This leads to a consideration of competing models of education around which such change occurred, and how these models have made possible the appropriation of some aspects of the *CEFR* and the disregard for others at different historical and social periods in the country.

Globalization in Argentina

Argentina has not escaped the penetration of the different forms of globalization that characterize the new millennium. However, it can best be seen as an exemplar of what Tilly (2004:18) calls 'international inequality' in income, schooling, life expectancy and the internet: 'Seen from the centers of influence, it looks as though the entire world is globalizing. Seen from the edges, penetration of global influence is highly selective. At least in the short and medium runs, it increases inequalities' (Tilly, 2004: 20). In addition, Argentina also offers testimony of the many 'darker sides of globalization' (Tilly, 2004: 21) such as deforestation, the displacement of local populations by industrial developments, the strangling of indigenous languages by the widespread domination of Spanish and English and so on. In this framework, the interest in the Argentine case as a peripheral country in this globalization process can be supported by the recurrently stressed need for investigations of how individuals in different parts of the world live their literacy experiences in their native and other languages (Canagarajah, 2006). This chapter seeks to capture this local dimension of globalization in language education policy in a description of how the *CEFR* has been appropriated and used.

This foregrounding of the local experience is important in a description of how Argentina reflects on educational issues while it integrates international knowledge and experience in the particular case of the *CEFR*. The reason for this is that 'externalizations to "foreign examples" or to "world situations" ... involve the discursive interpretation of international phenomena ... [which] filter the reception and description of an international environment according to the changing problem configurations and reflection situations internal to a given system' (Schriewer & Martinez, 2004: 32). Put differently, the process is subject to local, biased interpretations by all the actors involved, including myself as the writer of this chapter. In a sense, there is an inescapable tension here, as Schriewer and Martinez point out, between global processes of diffusion and idiosyncratic processes of reception in culturally-specific settings, of which Argentina is an example. Because this tension also involves inseparability, both aspects of this local-global discourse can be comprised in what Spring (2009: 123) calls 'glocalization' (i.e. the adaptation or appropriation of borrowed policies in specific settings).

The *CEFR* in This Local Context

Within the discourse of education, Argentina has traditionally looked to the United States and Europe as its main sources of influence and reference. Evidence of this can be found in the history of education in Argentina, an example being the process of Europeanization and modernization promoted by the oligarchies in the first half of the 19th century, with the importation of the structure and ideology of the French system of education (Puiggrós, 2003). Regarding language education, the *CEFR* is embedded within this region of reference – i.e. Europe – and therefore in a predominantly Western rationality. This frame of thought is one of the broadest filters involved in the selection and appropriation of the *CEFR* in Argentina, and this and other filters are affected by political and ideological influences, which are internal to the country (Ochs & Phillips, 2004; Puiggrós, 1990, 1996, 2003). It is interesting to note, however, that such influences transcend the boundaries of Argentina with an internal consistency characteristic of this region of the world as a whole. In other words, ideologically there is an overall coherence among countries in the area, which might be worth exploring in the future (Puiggrós, 2003).

Concentrating here on Argentina, it is clear that the *CEFR* has been extensively adopted throughout the country in a variety of contexts and for a multiplicity of purposes. An internet search reveals that the *CEFR* is widely and explicitly referred to as a salient characteristic in varied areas, namely:

- general language courses in Spanish, English, Italian, French, German and Portuguese provided by private and public institutions and schools, both online and on-site;
- language courses for specific purposes in these languages (e.g. English for international aviation, http://www.escuelaflying.com.ar/ingles-aeronautico.htm; www.fhycs.unam.edu.ar/content/view/1273/78/);
- textbooks for the teaching and learning of these languages, published by international publishing companies;
- international examinations and certifications to attest competence in these languages such as the University of London exams, University of Cambridge exams, the Educational Testing Services of Princeton University, CELI (Certificación Internacional de Lengua Italiana, http://www.iunir.edu.ar/info/celi.asp), CELU (Certificado Español Lengua y Uso, http://www.celu.edu.ar/) and many others (http://www.pearsonpte.com/PTEAcademic/Institutions/Pages/home.aspx; http://www.casache.com/e/methodology.php; http://www.eslbase.com/schools/argentina);
- teacher education/development courses and programmes at tertiary and university level. At university level (http://www.fahce.unlp.edu.ar/academica/Areas/lenguasmodernas/Catedras/diccininglesai/dicing12006.pdf); http://www.fahce.unlp.edu.ar/academica/Areas/lenguasmodernas/Catedras/didcticaespecialyprcticasdocentesenlenguainglesai/) and Ministry of Education level (http://abc.gov.ar/lainstitucion/organismos/direcciondecapacitacion/modulos/documentosdedescarga/segundoanio/ingles.pdf).

In all these cases, a strong and explicit emphasis on the framing of these services within the *CEFR* is made, as the language courses and tests offered are matched to its specific levels of linguistic development.

Two reflections concerning the use of the *CEFR* in Argentina can be made given this scenario. First, although Argentina is thought of as a predominantly Spanish-speaking country, there exist several immigrant languages (Italian, German, Levantine Arabic, South Bolivian Quechua, Catalán, Mandarín, Japanese, Korean, Welsh and others) (Gordon, 2005) and as many as sixteen or more living indigenous languages (Censabella,

1999). From this perspective, the political origin of the *CEFR* as a means to achieve mutual understanding and cooperation in a strikingly multilingual and multicultural context such as Europe (*CEFR* 2001: 1–8) resembles the aims for its adoption in this country. This spirit toward unification and common ground prevails in all the contexts in which the *CEFR* is adopted and/or referred to above. In other words, the *CEFR* is used here to describe current practices in different settings, to compare these practices with the status quo internationally, and in so doing to tentatively improve such practice. Furthermore, in congruence with the multiple contexts of use mentioned before, there exist a variety of users in this setting, namely classroom teachers, university teachers, course designers, materials writers, curriculum developers, examination boards and self-directed learners.

Second, a comprehensive common specification of language skills and competences of language learning, as offered by the *CEFR*, is important considering the increasing numbers of non-native speakers of Spanish as well as of non-native speakers of English (given the undeniable status of English here as a language of international communication) and the simultaneous (and also increasing) diversification and specialization of the language skills and competences needed to function effectively in the 21st century (Warschauer, 2000).

Emphasized and Ignored Aspects of the *CEFR* in this Setting

Of the 'theoretically borrowable' aspects of the *CEFR* (Phillips, 2004: 57; Ochs & Phillips, 2004), the following are the most evident, as already described in the case study of the previous chapter: the guiding philosophy or ideology (a sociolinguistic conception of language, plurilingualism and pluriculturalism, the notion of social agent and foreign language learning as a vehicle for intercultural experience), the goals (need for unification and harmonization of linguistic and cultural practices associated with language education in the country), the processes (like the process-based curricular innovation described in the previous chapter) and the techniques (task-based methodologies, the type of linguistic activity generated through those tasks, positive assessment in the form of *can do* statements).

The previous chapter has exemplified the four stages of educational borrowing (attraction, decision-making, implementation, internalization; Ochs & Phillips, 2004) in one specific setting within Argentina. In this process, the *CEFR* has been introduced in Argentina through influence rather than through imposition by local or central governments, or purposeful borrowing by policy-makers, for instance. This influence comes from many sources, one of which is undoubtedly the increasingly dominant trend among the education workforce to pursue postgraduate education abroad. This favours 'brain drain' and 'brain circulation' (Spring, 2009: 177, 185), where these professionals (teachers, policy-makers, curriculum writers, etc.) end up temporarily working and/or living in regions of reference. Another source is the 'importation' of foreign teachers and education experts to fill local demands (particularly in Portuguese and English) – what Spring (2009: 187) calls 'brain gain'. All of the foregoing is important because it allows for discussions (and therefore growing awareness) in the country regarding worldwide educational discourses, processes, institutions and so on, and how these affect local educational policies and practices.

In Argentina, one finds a deliberate reference to the *CEFR* in its contexts of appropriation (i.e. language courses, tests, university syllabi, policy and curricular documents). This contrasts with Ochs and Phillips (2004), who report calculated omissions of such international influence in some local reforms. The reasons here are mainly practical, such as accountability and credibility issues, the need for common definitions of literacy and language competences, as well as common assessments. It is noticeable, however, that there is no explicit intent to reflect the broader philosophical, ideological, and political aspects related to the *CEFR*. This might be tied to the overall performance-oriented foregrounding of the *CEFR* in such contexts. In other words, the emphasis in all cases resides in descriptions of linguistic competence, in particular the levels of linguistic proficiency offered by the *CEFR*.

The focus on the sociocultural dimension of language education as well as on the notions of mutual understanding, cooperation and the individual as a social agent is downplayed in the majority of these settings. Such downgrading can be understood if framed within conceptions of foreign language education in this country which have traditionally tended to embrace an instrumental view, functional and pragmatic, closely tied to training in de-contextualized and isolated linguistic skills and knowledge. Evidence of this comes from the main product-oriented focus of the policy and curricular documents developed in the country during the 1990s. In this context, the *Waystage, Threshold* and *Vantage* series developed in the framework of the Modern Languages Programme of the Council of Europe (prior to the publication of the *CEFR*) were used to make informed decisions about the standards for the teaching of languages at the different levels of education – standards which were accepted internationally and were recognized as solid. Despite some limitations and possible criticisms, from this perspective the *CEFR* has catered for the coherence of linguistic policies not only at the different levels of the education system but also within the same level among different languages.

Winds of Change

The downgrading of everything other than the linguistic in the *CEFR* in Argentina is rooted in a long history of political attempts toward the unification and homogenization of its population through education, especially language education. For example, in the first half of the 19th century, Sarmiento, a key historical figure associated with education in this country, put in motion the imposition of the central culture and language and the elimination of difference (linguistic, social, cultural) represented by the gaucho and the several Indian languages alive in those times (Puiggrós, 1990). The aim of education was to reproduce the dominant culture in the younger generations – a culture that mirrored Europe. The appropriation of the *CEFR* described in the previous paragraph echoes this rationale for homogenization, unification and commonalities in the history of education of the country.

As Puiggrós (1990) explains, the Argentine education system was founded around this paradigm of education for unification and homogenization, which continued to dominate the thought of politicians, pedagogues and intellectuals during the 20th century. Military governments adopted a repressive and overt intent of domination over the thinking and behaviour of the masses in the 1970s. The modern system of education toward the end of the 1990s also kept this intent toward conformity (regarding school routines, methods, accepted versions of disciplinary content, adult-youth relationships, etc.). Language education did not escape this prevailing rationale, and the *CEFR* was initially used mainly following these lines of thought.

Then Freire revolutionized educational conceptions in Latin America as a whole by introducing the notions of transformation, agency, social awareness, citizenship and education as liberation. Within language education in particular in Argentina, Freire's influence offered a fertile milieu for the foregrounding of the sociocultural, agency, intercultural experience and processes (beyond products) involved in the *CEFR*. Recent curricular innovations (Barboni *et al.,* 2008) and policy documents (Thisted *et al.,* 2007) emphasize foreign language teaching as *educational* (i.e. aiming at the learners' *literacy* development, not only *language* development), and view learners as responsible, active and conscientious citizens. The policy documents designed in the Province of Buenos Aires are the results of efforts under a recently created Office of Intercultural Education, framed under the

National Law of Education 26.206 (2006), which promotes 'policies of recognition that are the centre of debates, policies and practices beyond the Argentine provincial and national contexts toward the Latin American context in countries such as Brazil, Ecuador, Chile, Bolivia, Peru and Bolivia' (Thisted *et al.,* 2007: 3, my translation).

Byram (2010: 318) explains that 'The other, and apparently alternative, purpose of foreign language teaching – the educational purpose – suffers beneath the weight of concern to make language learning efficient and effective for the instrumental purpose. Wherever one looks, policymakers are concerned about the level of proficiency attained through language teaching'. What has propelled a change of focus in Argentina is the recognition that educational purposes can coexist with functional-pragmatic goals. At a national level, the curricular document for foreign languages in the capital district of the country also acknowledges this coexistence in these terms: 'To an extent, the instrumental value of a foreign language is an inevitable consequence of its learning. ... Regarding its *formative* sense, this curricular document approaches it from an educational project committed to social and cultural democratization' (Diseño Curricular de Lenguas Extranjeras, 2000: 21, Gobierno de la Ciudad Autónoma de Buenos Aires).

Such a change in conceptualization occurred at a time when two competing world models of education (Spring, 2009) seemed to be walking hand in hand in the country. One is the human capital education model that views (language) education as a tool for learners to open up to the world and have access to knowledge, information, health, education, employability, economic growth and social and economic mobility through different resources and means. In this sense, language education, particularly in English because of its significance as a language of international communication, is seen as empowering and instrumental to development. This view prevails in the programmes of cooperation and development in the region, financed by organizations such as the World Bank and the Inter-American Development Bank.

The influence of this model on intellectual thinking has been significant in Argentina as it is tied to the strong association between economic development and education in the history of education in the country. At the end of the 18th century, historical figures such as Manuel Belgrano represented this view; for instance, he founded navy, mining and mathematics schools, among others. This generated a fracture between the traditional and colonial educational modality of the previous two centuries and the beginning of the modern school system in the first half of the 19th century (Puiggrós, 2003).

These historical antecedents paved the way for the pedagogic neo-liberalism that dominated the scene, especially in the late 20th century, when education was tied to the economic rationale behind international financing organizations like the World Bank. This led to the decentralization and privatization of education, the pyramidization and reduction of the teacher workforce, and to tight control by the national government through the imposition of common and unified curricula, instruction and assessment (Puiggrós, 1996).

With regard to language education, this discussion is pertinent to the *CEFR* because it represents the idea of unification that dominated its adoption in the multiple contexts of the complex linguistic map of Argentina mentioned earlier. In addition, the *CEFR* provided for the coherence of linguistic goals and achievement standards in the midst of decentralization and privatization drives which also affected the provision of foreign language education in the country, as the previous chapter has shown.

The second model of education is Progressive Education, the main tenets of which are education for active citizenship, for social justice and for the protection of local languages, celebrating the students' interests and participation. This model echoes Freire's revolutionary conceptions. Some examples are UNESCO, United Nations for Latin America and the Caribbean, PREAL (Programa de Promoción de la Reforma Educativa en América Latina) and other organizations which have traditionally been influential in educational thinking in Argentina, advocating a more humanistic view of education, centred on lifelong, responsible and conscientious learning, critical thinking and its value for democracy. These tenets have come to dominate language education policy (Thisted *et al.*, 2007) and curricular developments (Barboni *et al.*, 2008) from the beginning of the 21st century. As far as the *CEFR* is concerned, these views have facilitated the adoption of its guiding philosophy or ideology as set out for example by Trim (this volume).

As an example, the following curricular document explicitly recognizes, in its introduction, the role of language as a vehicle, a symbol and a representation of culture, emphasizing intercultural issues as follows:

> From a wider perspective, contact with a foreign language confronts children with difference and allows the approach and the inevitable experience of the other, the different, the foreign, and the diverse. To teach English to a child is to give them opportunities to interact with texts and/or people of other cultures and so enrich their cosmovision, their socio-cultural context and their place in such a context, fortifying their own identity. Confrontation with difference through a foreign

> language helps children to become aware of the principles that make democratic life possible, stressing the common bonds of humanity and every other aspect that joins human beings. (Diseño Curricular de Educación Primaria, 2008: 320 – my translation)

It does so too in the main objectives of ELT in primary school, which are to:

- Promote the development of intercultural competence and the strengthening of their [the children's] own cultural identity by enabling the processes of social integration.
- Develop practices of the language centred on the creation and interpretation of meaning by taking into account the communicative needs of the children.

(Diseño Curricular de Educación Primaria, 2008: 321)

The underlying reality, however, is that within the existence of a possible educational global superstructure (Spring, 2009), complexity is unavoidable, as are the models attempting to capture it. In Argentina, these competing models can, and in fact, do coexist, influencing the borrowing of different aspects of the *CEFR*.

Politically and ideologically, the concurrent operation of these models has been accompanied by recent and renewed views of education centred on a welfare state, a public school system of excellence, the value for children and their education together with a concomitant belief in decentralized practices, the site-based management of schools within a global common policy, a centralized curriculum that nonetheless allows flexibility (as the experience described in the previous chapter shows) and increased teacher autonomy in order to achieve proposed goals.

This complex scenario has facilitated the adoption of the *CEFR* in the ways described here, in the various private sectors which have traditionally provided language education related services (and still do) as well as in policy and curricular efforts at the provincial and national levels.

The *CEFR* has thus been and still is influential in Argentina, in different degrees and in varied areas of reference. Beyond the private sector, at the level of policy, the differences in its uses suggest that policy-makers have appropriated and applied its descriptions and guidelines in the context of wider political decisions and with different understandings of what education in Argentina has encompassed at different historical and social moments.

References

Barboni, S., Beacon, G. and Porto, M. (2008) Diseño Curricular de Inglés para EPB (Educación Primaria Básica) de la Provincia de Buenos Aires. *Diseño Curricular para la Educación Primaria. Segundo Ciclo. Volumen 1* (pp. 321–352). Dirección de Currículum, Dirección General de Cultura y Educación de la Provincia de Buenos Aires. 1 Edición.

Byram, M. (2010) Linguistic and cultural education for *Bildung* and citizenship. *The Modern Language Journal* 94 (ii), 317–21.

Canagarajah, S. (2006) TESOL at Forty: What are the issues? *TESOL Quarterly* 40, 9–34.

Censabella, M. (1999) *Las Lenguas Indígenas de la Argentina. Una Mirada Actual*. Buenos Aires: Eudeba.

Council of Europe (2001) *Common European Framework of Reference for Languages: Learning, teaching, assessment.* Cambridge: Cambridge University Press.

Gordon, R. G., Jr. (ed.) (2005) *Ethnologue: Languages of the World* (15th edn). Dallas, TX: SIL International. Online at http://www.ethnologue.com. Accessed on 17 February 2010.

Morrow, K. (ed.) (2004) *Insights from the Common European Framework.* Oxford: Oxford University Press.

Ochs, K. and Phillips, D. (2004) Processes of educational borrowing in historical context. In D. Phillps and K. Ochs (eds) *Educational Policy Borrowing: Historical Perspectives* (pp. 1–6). Oxford: Symposium Books.

Phillips, D. (2004) Toward a Theory of Policy Attraction in Education. In G. Steiner-Khamsi (ed.) *The Global Politics of Educational Borrowing and Lending* (pp. 54–69). New York: Teachers College Press.

Puiggrós, A. (1990) *Imaginación y Crisis en la Educación Latinoamericana.* México, DF: Consejo Nacional para la Cultura y las Artes.

Puiggrós, A. (1996) Educación neoliberal y quiebre educativo. *Nueva Sociedad* 146, 90–101.

Puiggrós, A. (2003) *Qué pasó en la Educación Argentina. Breve Historia desde la Conquista Hasta el Presente.* Buenos Aires: Galerna.

Schriewer, J. and Martinez, C. (2004) Constructions of internationality in education. In G. Steiner-Khamsi (ed.) *The Global Politics of Educational Borrowing and Lending* (pp. 29–53). New York: Teachers College Press.

Spring, J. (2009) *Globalization of Education. An Introduction.* New York: Routledge.

Steiner-Khamsi, G. (ed.) (2004). *The Global Politics of Educational Borrowing and Lending.* New York: Teachers College Press.

Thisted, S., Diez, M.L., Martínez, M.E. and Villa, A. (2007) Interculturalidad como perspectiva política, social y educativa. Dirección de Modalidad de Educación Intercultural. Dirección General de Cultura y Educación, Gobierno de la Provincia de Buenos Aires.

Tilly, C. (2004) Past, present, and future globalizations. In G. Steiner-Khamsi (ed.) *The Global Politics of Educational Borrowing and Lending* (pp. 13–28). New York: Teachers College Press.

Warschauer, M. (2000) The changing global economy and the future of English teaching. *TESOL Quarterly* 34, 511–535.

Colombia

The authors:

Beatriz Peña Dix is Assistant Professor in Foreign Language Teaching and Foreign Language Pedagogy at the Universidad de los Andes (Bogota, Colombia), where she has been teaching since 1999 in the department of Languages and Socio-Cultural Studies. Some of her main academic concerns are foreign language methodologies, didactics and teacher training strategies, in addition to other related topics like intercultural language teaching and learning, bilingualism and bilingual education in contexts where the second language has no official status.

Anne-Marie de Mejía is Associate Professor at the Centre for Research and Teacher Education at Universidad de los Andes, Bogotá, Colombia. Her research interests include bilingual classroom interaction, the construction of bilingual curricula and processes of empowerment, and bilingual teacher development. She coordinated a research project sponsored by the National Ministry of Education into the state of the art of bilingual education in different regions in Colombia, as well as a diagnostic study about the conditions and needs of three bilingual public (state) schools in Bogotá in their transition towards bilingualism. She is the author of a number of books and articles in the area of bilingualism and bilingual education both in Spanish and English.

12 Policy Perspectives from Colombia

Beatriz Peña Dix and Anne-Marie de Mejía[1]

In Colombia, the Ministry of Education has officially adopted the Common European Framework of Reference (*CEFR*) (Decree 3870, Article 2, 2006) to guide developments in the sphere of education to ensure the quality of labour and human development in the field of languages, decreeing that:

> *The Common European Framework of References for Languages: Learning, Teaching, Assessment* will be adopted in order to provide an internationally acknowledged system of reference for learning, teaching and assessing processes in Colombia. Every educational institution offering programmes for qualified labour and human development in the field of languages must align their programmes with the pre-established levels in the *CEFR*. (Our translation.)

The main purpose of the Colombian Ministry of Education (MEN in the Spanish acronym) in measuring language skill levels and the progress of learning with reference to international standards is to respond to the changes associated with economic globalization. The idea is to educate competitive individuals to perform in demanding labour markets and to create committed citizens within a framework of tolerance and intercultural understanding. As a result, successive Colombian governments have maintained that education, 'is the key to addressing two of the country's biggest challenges: (a) the concern for social peace, inclusion, and social integration; and (b) the need for economic development in an era of competitiveness and globalization' (Light *et al.*, 2009: 91). Thus, learning foreign languages in Colombia means enhancing possibilities and the country's competitiveness to build on the nation's goals, and there is a general agreement that English has a predominant position in Colombia's social and economic advancement. According to Velez-Rendon (2003), this is evidenced in the educational policies and programmes in which English has a prominent position in the national curriculum, as well as in the unprecedented boom of the English language teaching industry in the country.

Some Background to Understand Why the *CEFR* was Adopted

Colombia can be described as a middle-range developing country with a centralized government, 1170 municipalities, four special districts and 32 departments (provinces). The Colombian public education system is one of the largest components of the public sector in terms of size, share of public expenditure, and geographic coverage (Borjas & Acosta, 2000). In order to increase accountability and participation in decision-making processes, educational reform in Colombia has been fuelled by the idea of *decentralization*, which originated in the late 1980s. The central government has promoted a reorganization of the state administration to give the different regions of the country more responsibility with respect to finances and the administration of most public services (Borjas & Acosta, 2000).

Decentralization was enshrined within the Colombian Political Constitution of 1991 and aimed at the redistribution of functions and the delegation of responsibilities to guarantee a better service and ensure a policy of participatory democracy. This explains the three levels of the administration of public education in the country: (1) the central level, which includes the Ministry of Education and other relatively autonomous agencies in charge of higher education, science and technology; (2) the departmental level (provinces) which includes the Departmental Secretaries of Education and the Regional Education Fund, which administers resources transferred by the central level; and (3) the municipal level represented by the Municipal Secretaries of Education (Borjas & Acosta, 2000). However, these two levels sometimes overlap in so far as the departmental level is responsible primarily for non-certified secretaries, whereas those who have been certified have greater autonomy. This tripartite model governs Colombian education at present, and it attempts to represent the voices of and include participation from all educational stakeholders and promote decentralization and autonomy (see Table 12.1).

At all three levels, English is seen as an important component of the curriculum and as essential for an interdisciplinary education. For this reason, the General Law of Education (1994) made the learning of a foreign language compulsory from primary school onwards. The Programme of Bilingualism and Information Technology followed in 1997, aiming to improve English language teaching integrated with technology in public

Table 12.1 Distribution of education functions according to the Constitution of 1991 (Law 60, 1993 and Law115, 1994). (Adapted from Borjas & Acosta, 2000: 4)

Sector	Functions
Nation	To establish technical, curricular and pedagogical norms that will be used by the territorial entities as an orientation.
Department	To plan, administer, and coordinate the teaching service and to decentralize it in the municipalities. To assume the functions of the technical development of the pilot centres. To prepare teachers. To administer the funds of co-financing with own resources and to take care of the infrastructure and investments in the educational establishments.
Municipalities	To administer the preschool, primary and secondary service on the terms that the department delegates. To make the necessary investments in infrastructure and maintenance of educational establishments. To inspect and supervise the provision of educational services.

education (Velez-Rendon, 2003), but it was not until 2004 that the Colombian government transformed English language teaching and learning into an official state policy through the nationwide initiative *Bilingual Colombia Programme* (Colombia Bilingüe, 2004–2019). This initiative aims at educating 'citizens capable of communicating in English by using internationally comparable standards, enabling the country to facilitate processes of universal communication within the global economy and the promotion of cultural openness' (our translation) (www.colombiaaprende.edu.co).

The goal of improving English language at all educational levels requires that the students' school-exit level should be B1, or intermediate, and their English teachers should at least reach a B2 level by 2019 (Cárdenas, 2006). The following table displays the proficiency levels expected by the year 2019:

Table 12.2 Levels expected in the target populations of the *Bilingual Colombia Programme* (Adapted from Cárdenas, 2006)

Population	Level expected in 2019
Teachers of English in levels 1–11	B2
Primary teachers and teachers of other areas	A2
Students who finish high school (11th grade)	B1
Graduate language teachers	B2–C1
Students who finish higher education	B2

In order to achieve these proficiency targets and regulate the achievements of the *Bilingual Colombia Programme*, in 2006 the Ministry of Education designed and published a document regulating national standards, *Basic Standards for Foreign Language Proficiency: English* ('Estándares Básicos de Competencias en Lenguas Extranjeras: Inglés', see Appendix 12.1) based on the *CEFR*. In this way, the *CEFR* became an important part of Colombian foreign language education policy.

The Adoption of the *CEFR*: Onset and Further Considerations

The introduction of the *CEFR* into the Colombian foreign language public education system was framed within a series of national needs and circumstances. Firstly, in addition to pursuing world competitiveness and free trade agreements, Colombia had earlier set up a *National Development Plan* (Plan Nacional de Desarrollo, PND, 1994), designed to increase the country's productivity through educational advances, an improved labour force and technological development (Light *et al.*, 2009). In this context, the need to manage English as a means of communication, knowledge and to create opportunities for competitiveness increasingly became a priority validated by the above mentioned decree after the Ministry of Education recognized the low levels of English language teaching and learning in the country. Secondly, and as a consequence of the need to improve the quality of language education, the *Bilingual Colombia Programme* has been seen as one of the most important language education policy initiatives in the country. In order to get an idea of the importance of this, we will provide a brief historical overview of language and education policy developments over the past 50 years.

From the 1960s to the 1980s, the *Language Electronic Institute* (Instituto Electrónico de Idiomas), which depended on the Ministry of Education, acted as a regulating agent in setting language curricular content and training teachers. However, in the 1990s, the principle of autonomy, upheld in the General Law of Education (1994), gave each region in the country the freedom to design and implement language curricula based on national guidelines established by the ministry. Therefore, schools had to design their own *Institutional Educational Project* (Proyecto Educativo Institucional, PEI) taking into account both local needs and national policies.

In 1999 the Ministry of Education produced a theoretical document, *National Curricular Guidelines,* to orientate English language teaching and the development of communicative competence. Although there were no unified national standards, the guidelines provided a set of theoretical descriptors, disseminated through workshops, to help teachers implement foreign language programmes throughout the country.

The *CEFR* was initially introduced in Colombia by some private and state universities and bilingual schools. Later, the local secretary of education for Bogotá decided that, as this was the capital city, it was important to foster foreign language proficiency in the public education sector to help increase productivity Therefore, the local secretary of education together with the British Council started a project to define language levels with a needs analysis which included a diagnostic stage, where English teachers' and learners' English language proficiency was measured by using the Quick Placement Test designed by the University of Cambridge ESOL Examinations and aligned with the *CEFR*. This computerized test enabled a large number of students to be tested quickly and the results analysed rapidly. In addition, it was within the budgetary constraints of the local authorities.

As a result of the success of this local initiative and due to the growing popularity and increasing importance of English in the country, the Ministry of Education, now headed by the former secretary of education from Bogotá, started a process that sought to systematically improve the English language teaching (ELT) curriculum. The government of the time, led by Alvaro Uribe, was focused on competitiveness, and bilingualism, understood as ELT, was one of the key aspects involved in this endeavour.

A committee involving representatives from both public and private Colombian universities was set up under the coordination of the British Council, which was selected as an educational advisory partner due to its positive reputation in educational matters in Colombia over the last 70 years, and its academic credibility and 'neutrality', in the search to redefine the Colombian language curriculum and aiming at greater clarity about language proficiency level achievements and assessment.[2]

The Ministry of Education, which was working on 'Standards' for other content areas based on the 'Quality Assurance Model' that had been adopted, felt that as the Bilingual Colombia programme was becoming increasingly important, 'Standards' should also be produced for this content area. They therefore commissioned the British Council to organize and manage the production of these standards by the educational community. The *CEFR* seemed to provide a good option to regulate common national language learning and teaching outcomes for various reasons. First of all, it takes into account contexts of development and implications of use, as well as leading to the generation of reflection and discussion rather than prescription. Furthermore, the *CEFR* gives a clear direction as to the levels of proficiency in English that students can reach, as well as providing a common language with which to communicate with different agencies, such as the universities and the local education authorities.

However, there were difficulties, chief of which was the fact that the *CEFR* levels were designed for adults rather than children and that the *CEFR* was developed for a different (European) context. It was therefore decided to create the Colombian Standards for English, adapting the *CEFR* language levels to reflect the context of local teachers. The challenge was how to ensure that the levels in the Standards represented international standards while reflecting the realities of the Colombian context.

The steering committee carefully reviewed other international standards from Australia, Britain, the United States, Ireland, Canada and Spain. However, it was considered that the Australian framework was designed specifically for immigrants and, while it provided a practical description of language levels, it did not generate academic discussion. The US ACTFL guidelines had the advantage (as did the *CEFR*) of being 'language-neutral', and did not involve one specific foreign language, as in the case of the Australian example. Some of the disadvantages of ACTFL included: no widespread recognition (beyond the United States); difficulty in access to documentation (everything had to be 'bought'); and the fact that it was not supported by a wide range of examination bodies (at that time only ACTFL itself seemed to have a battery of tests, which could only be 'bought' from them).

The committee thought that the *CEFR* was richer and was not curriculum-specific. Most importantly, the *CEFR* presents a contextualized, integral vision of foreign languages, taking into account the importance of competencies and sociocultural contexts where descriptors refer to more than one language. Additional advantages adduced were that the *CEFR* is extensively used in many countries throughout the world, and most of the supporting documentation and a substantial body of academic analysis surrounding its implementation are freely available for consultation.

Analysis of similar experiences with the *CEFR* contributed to its implementation. There were two countries in Latin America using the *CEFR*: Chile and, later, Mexico, which provided reassurance to the ministry that Colombia was not isolated in this effort. The case of Chile, for instance, and its project 'English Opens Doors', which started in 2003, gave some insight about the *CEFR* used in a similar context. With an important budgetary investment advantage (with an approximate ratio of 10:1 US dollars in one specific year), Chile was a year ahead of Colombia in using the *CEFR* proficiency levels. In Mexico, various local educational authorities later used the *CEFR* to set goals for local internal exams. The *CEFR* provided the structure, proficiency levels and a common language that helped consolidate a foreign language educational community targeting common outcomes and competencies aimed at ensuring equal education opportunities. The clarity of the *CEFR* in setting clear guidelines for the competencies students should achieve and the possibilities provided for self-assessment made it a unanimous choice for the Colombian Ministry of Education.

Once the *CEFR* was firmly chosen as a feasible model in 2004 and became an official part of national foreign language education policy, the *Foreign Language Proficiency Basic Standards: English* ('Estándares Básicos de Competencias en Lenguas Extranjeras: Inglés', http://www.colombiaaprende.edu.co/html/mediateca/1607/articles-115375_archivo.pdf) were launched in 2006 (see Table 12.3). After this, there was a period of dissemination of the Standards in order to introduce them to teachers and other education stakeholders. In this context, guest speakers and experts shared with the academic community and with practising teachers their knowledge and vision of the *CEFR* and its influence and alignment with the new foreign language national standards by means of workshops and lectures.

In Colombia, the *CEFR* has been used almost exclusively for the learning of English, which may seem strange if we remember that it was originally created to increase plurilingualism in the European context. However, from the outset the Colombian Ministry of Education was clear that they were not developing programmes only for English. There had to be room for other languages. While the priority was English, because of its importance in studies abroad, better work opportunities and access to international scholarships and funding, there was also interest in French and Chinese.

Table 12.3 Colombian Foreign Language Proficiency Basic Standards: English (Estándares Básicos de Competencias en Lenguas Extranjeras: Inglés (2006: 6))

Levels according to the *CEFR*	**Common name of this level in Colombia**	**Educational level expected to be developed at each level**	**Goals for the educational field by 2019**
A1	Beginner	Grades 1 to 3	
A2	Basic	Grades 4 to 7	
B1	Pre-Intermediate	Grades 8 to 11	• Minimum level for 100% high school graduates.
B2	Intermediate	Higher Education	• Minimum level for English teachers. • Minimum level for other field professionals.
C1	Pre-Advanced		• Minimum level for newly undergraduates from teaching programmes.
C2	Advanced		

The decision to start with English was never intended to exclude other languages, but as there was limited funding available, it was a case of prioritizing. In fact, over the last two years, for example, French has regained its position within the school curriculum, with the support of the Ministry of Education, the French Embassy and the *Alliance Colombo-Française* as part of an agreement between the French and the Colombian governments.

The *CEFR* in Colombia: Tensions and Debates

Initial debates and highly contested topics involving the use of the *CEFR* in Colombia (2005–2007) were mainly political in nature and centred on the use of an alien model. There was pressure from some academics to develop a separate framework for Colombia. Furthermore, there was the argument that as the *CEFR* was used as reference for levels of English in countries with well-resourced educational systems, it was felt that inequity would be generated in rural and indigenous communities. The question asked was how far it was fair to push teachers towards standards used in developed countries. The setting of targets would place Colombia in the international community and it was felt by some that the fact that Columbia is a small country meant that it should measure itself with other small communities.

However, the MEN wanted results to challenge and promote change. It was felt necessary to create standards that were sufficiently wide so that the different regions could adapt them to the particularities of their own contexts. Nonetheless, there is a perception among some of the policy-makers that were consulted that many of the teachers who went to congresses and events were rather confused about the lack of concrete information provided about the *CEFR*. Instead, they were subjected to heated political debates about the wisdom of basing the Standards on the *CEFR*, conducted mainly by Colombian academics, and this eclipsed pedagogical considerations about its implementation and use.

All in all, however, the results of the interviews conducted as the basis for this chapter lead us to understand that the policy-makers involved in the decision to use the *CEFR* as a guiding framework for the National Bilingual Programme have been satisfied with developments, in that they believe that the *CEFR* has been successful in organizing discussion around ELT and in identifying key issues. It has been useful in helping with the development of a common language, unifying, clarifying and providing an ongoing discussion around curriculum development. It has also been a powerful motivator of change. However, there is also a feeling that the *CEFR* is not being used at its full potential, particularly by schools, and that there is still a lot of work to be done.

Notes

(1) The authors would like to thank Rosa Maria Cely, Ricardo Romero, Aida Salamanca and Jan Van de Putte for their valuable contributions to the interviews which formed the basis of this chapter.

(2) The alliance of the Ministry of Education with the British Council started in 1991 with an agreement to improve English language teaching through better training of language teachers and through appropriation of resources. The COFE (Colombian Framework for English) project emerged from this agreement and implemented a survey to establish the state of the art of language teacher education in Colombia with the participation of 29 of the 31 universities running teacher programmes (Velez-Rendon, 2003). The British Council was the body which administered the COFE project with the help of a steering committee in which key Colombian universities, such as Universidad de los Andes, Universidad Javeriana, Universidad Nacional and Universidad Pedagógica participated.

References

Borjas, G.J. and Acosta, O.L. (2000) *Education Reform in Colombia*. Bogota, FEDESARROLLO: Working Papers Series 19.

Cárdenas, M.L. (2006) Bilingual Colombia: Are we ready for it¿ What is needed¿ 19th Annual EA Education Conference 2006, Australia. Online at http://www.englishaustralia.com.au/index.cgi¿E=hcatfuncs&PT=sl&X=getdoc&Lev1=pub_c07_07&Lev2=c06_carde.

Colombia, Ministerio de Educación Nacional (2006) *Estándares Básicos de Competencias en Lenguas Extranjeras: Inglés*. Bogotá: MEN. Online at http://www.colombiaaprende.edu.co/html/mediateca/1607/articles-115375_archivo.pdf and http://www.mineducacion.gov.co/1621/article-115174.html.

Colombia (1991) Constitución Política. Online at http://www.cna.gov.co/cont/documentos/legislacion/constitucion.pdf. Accessed on 24 April 2011.

Colombia. Ministerio de Educación Nacional [MEN]. (1994) Ley General de Educación (Ley 115 8 February 1994). Online at http://www.mineducacion.gov.co/1621/articles-85906_archivo_pdf.pdf. Accessed on 15 April 2011.

Colombia. Ministerio de Educación Nacional [MEN]. (1999) Lineamientos curriculares idiomas extranjeros. Online at http://www.mineducacion.gov.co/cvn/1665/articles-89869_archivo_pdf4.pdf. Accessed on 22 April 2011.

Colombia. Ministerio de Educación Nacional [MEN]. (2002) Revolución educativa: Plan sectorial 2002–2006. Online at http://www.mineducacion.gov.co. Accessed on 17 April 2011.

Colombia. Ministerio de Educación Nacional [MEN]. Decreto 3870, 2 de noviembre de 2006. Programas de educación para el trabajo y el desarrollo humano en el área de idiomas. Online at http://www.mineducacion.gov.co/1621/articles-112277_archivo_pdf.pdf. Accessed on 15 April 2011.

COLOMBIAPRENDE, La red del conocimiento. Online at http://www.colombiaaprende.edu.co/html/productos/1685/article-158720.html. Accessed on 26 April 2011.

Light, D., Manso, M. and Noguera, T. (2009) An educational revolution to support change in the classroom: Colombia and the educational challenges of the twenty-first century. *Policy Futures in Education* 7 (1), 88–101.

Velez-Rendón, G. (2003) English in Colombia: A sociolinguistic profile. *World Englishes* 22, 185–198.

13 Academic Perspectives from Colombia

Anne-Marie de Mejía

Introduction

While bilingualism and multilingualism have characterised the existence of Colombia both prior to and following the arrival of Columbus in the 15th century, it was only in the Political Constitution of 1991 that the multilingual and pluricultural nature of the country was officially recognised. Spanish was designated the official language of Colombia in this landmark legal document, but it was also stated that, 'The languages and dialects of the ethnic groups are also official in their territories. The teaching in communities which have their own linguistic traditions will be bilingual' (Title 1, Article 10) (author's translation – all subsequent Spanish quotations in this chapter have also been translated by the author).

The official policy of 'Ethnoeducation' for minority communities, ratified by the Education Law of 1994, thus recognises the importance of designing curricula which take into account the type of educational provision that reflects the visions of the indigenous communities themselves, as well as respect for their cultural and linguistic heritage. However, in spite of these efforts, bilingualism or multilingualism in minority Amerindian or Creole languages is often not recognised as such and is still undervalued (de Mejía, 2005).

In 2006, the Colombian Ministry of Education (MEN) published a consultative document 'Education: Vision 2019' (MEN, 2006a) as part of the National Bilingual Programme (2004–2019), in which a section was devoted to proficiency in English as a foreign language. Here, the case was made for the importance of all school leavers reaching an intermediate level of English proficiency, as this would constitute a comparative advantage, increasing both individual and national competence and competitiveness. The document also made reference to the use of the *Common European Framework of Reference for Languages* (*CEFR*) as a point of reference for the formulation of the differing levels which characterised the 'Basic Standards of

Competencies in Foreign Languages: English', also published in 2006. The reasons given in these documents for adopting the *CEFR* were the fact that it was the result of ten years of research, and that it provided a common language to establish foreign language performance levels throughout the Colombian educational system, particularly in relation to international standards, as the following quotation shows: 'The adoption of a common referent with other countries will allow Colombia to examine advances in relation to other nations and introduce international parameters at local level' (MEN, 2006a: 57).

In November 2006 the Ministry of Education issued Decree No. 3870 which:

> Adopted the *Common European Framework of Reference for Languages: Learning, teaching and assessment* as the system of reference for the processes of learning, teaching and evaluation carried out in Colombia (MEN 2006c: Article 2).

The educational body responsible for the Colombian Baccalaureate examinations, the *Instituto Colombiano para el Fomento de la Educación Superior* (ICFES), welcomed this development, claiming that the use of the *CEFR* will:

> [a]ct as a source of information in the construction of assessment indicators in the service of the educational sector, so as to encourage the evaluation of institutional processes, policy formulation and facilitate the decision making process in all levels of the educational system (ICFES, 2008 cited in López, 2009: 2).

Right from the beginning, however, the adoption of the *CEFR* has generated a series of criticisms and complaints by academics from some of the leading universities in the country, as well as defensive statements by the Ministry of Education and by the British Council, the agency that coordinated the development of the 'Standards' document. In the following sections, I will attempt to account for these differing stances in the light of some of the academic and political factors that have been discussed within Colombia over the past five years.

Criticism of the *CEFR* by Colombian Academics

In the 'Vision 2019' (MEN, 2006a) document it was explicitly stated that school leavers would be expected to have reached an intermediate level of both spoken and written English, enabling them to demonstrate oral and written comprehension, write simple texts and participate in simple conversations. At university level it is expected that graduates should be able to understand complex texts in their field, to communicate fluently with native speakers, to produce detailed texts on different topics and argue their points of view, although, as López (2009) has pointed out, no standards have been produced to guide the teaching and learning of English in higher education in the country.

This emphasis on communicative language competence in line with the theoretical approach adopted in the *CEFR* is not new in Columbia, at least in theory, though Valencia (2005: 13) notes in this respect that 'Previous research has demonstrated how despite language policy reforms, traditional pedagogical orientations in ELT (e.g. Grammar Translation) still prevail'. What is new is the official adoption of the notions of linguistic, sociolinguistic and pragmatic competence to characterise each specific standard at the different grade levels from Grade 1 (primary) to Grade 11 (secondary) (MEN, 2006b). Furthermore, there is a description and exemplification of each of these sub-aspects of communicative competence in terms of their situated nature in relation to specific contexts of interaction, ending with the observation, 'More than the knowledge of an isolated code, it is important to offer children and young people real possibilities to understand and interpret their reality' (MEN, 2006b: 12).

To my knowledge, this emphasis on contextualised communicative language teaching and learning has not been questioned directly as a desirable goal. Colombian academics, teachers and learners have lived for the past 20 years or so with the discourse of language as communication within a vision of inclusion, efficiency and quality in education at all levels (MEN, 2000). What has been hotly disputed have been the socio-political and cultural implications of adopting the *CEFR* in the Colombian context. I will outline some of the arguments put forward by Colombian academics and will try to provide some explanations for these positions.

One of the most cited objections is that of adopting a framework that has been developed in a foreign context (Europe) for use in a very different scenario (Colombia) (Ayala & Alvarez, 2005; Cárdenas, 2006; Gonzalez Moncada, 2007). For example, Ayala and Alvarez (2005: 12) maintain, 'We consider that if we are to propose standards, they should be based on a Colombian context, informed perspectives and methodologies', while Gonzalez Moncada (2007: 312) notes:

> Although this analysis has focused on the use of the CEF, the adoption of any foreign language framework for teaching and learning English is an inadequate approach to promote bilingualism in Colombia. There is

> no one single model that fits our reality regarding the diversity of settings, achievement of standards, resources, teacher preparation, student motivation, and curricula.

This objection has been incorporated within a wider externalisation vision where, according to Usma Wilches (2009: 131 citing Steiner Khamsi, 2004), in order to make local school systems appear competitive, 'national governments adopt different discourses and models accepted by an imaginary international community or a concrete other, which is evoked as a source of external authority'. In this case, the international model accepted is, of course, the *CEFR*. Usma Wilches maintains that the whole process has been highly contested, particularly by local scholars, while teachers and students are often caught in the middle of the debate, as described in the previous chapter on policy perspectives.

Another important focus of dissent is the role of foreign agencies in the implementation of the official language and education policies relating to the teaching and learning of English. The universities in Colombia, particularly the influential state (public) universities in the large cities of Bogotá, Medellín and Cali, have traditionally been responsible for the training and educating of foreign language teachers. However, the adoption of the *CEFR* as the point of reference for policies relating to the National Bilingual Programme, as explained in more detail in the preceding chapter, has meant that private agencies, such as the British Council, have assumed a dominant role in many of these processes, such as the initial use of both the Teaching Knowledge Test (TKT), designed by the University of Cambridge, and the implementation of the In-service Certificate in English Language Teaching (ICELT) model of professional development, which has been criticised as inadequate because of context insensitivity and being top-down in character (González Moncada, 2007). This researcher also maintains that local research knowledge produced by Colombian universities has not been sufficiently valued in the implementation of these international standards. This criticism has been specifically related to the actions of the British Council by Torres Martínez (2009: 62–63), who claims, 'The intervention of the British Council, for its part, presupposes a delegitimisation of the development of the local communities involved in the process, casting great shadows on the criteria used by the Ministry of Education in leaving the future of the teaching of English in Colombia in the hands of a foreign organization'.

A similar stance has been advanced by Usma Wilches (2009) who has condemned an increasing tendency towards the standardisation of language teaching and learning in the country based on the introduction of international models as a move in the direction of 'uniformity through stringent normalization and control' (Usma Wilches, 2009: 136). He sees the adoption of models such as the *CEFR* as evidence that international organisations are driving definition of local standards within the context of language and education reform in Colombia at the expense of local expertise, generating 'inequality, exclusion and stratification' (Usma Wilches, 2009: 137).

A final group of arguments against the adoption of the *CEFR* has to do with the particular nature of the socio-cultural conditions pertaining currently in the country. Cárdenas (2006: 3) postulates that 'The reality established in the *CEFR* would have to be contrasted with the conditions of Colombian educational institutions, namely infrastructure, curriculum organization, use of foreign languages in the academic and cultural domains of the country, working hours and competences of language teachers'. She also goes on to argue that English is not a priority in much of the country, particularly in remote rural areas and in areas of population displacement due to the ongoing internal conflict. In other words, in order to work effectively, the *CEFR* would need to be modified to fit the particularities of the Colombian context. In this type of situation, the expectations that all school leavers will reach a B1 level are seen as unrealistic.

As has been noted in the previous policy chapter, the *CEFR* has, up to now, only been applied with reference to teaching English in Colombia, and many of the criticisms cited above have to do with the fact that the reality of language in education use is not adequately represented in the National Bilingual Programme as it stands. These criticisms would appear to be justified in so far as a full understanding of the notion of plurilingualism as developed by the *CEFR* to represent the multilingual nature of Europe where bilingual programmes are also present would allow a quite different use of the *CEFR* to take account of all language present in the national language ecology. However, as is made clear by the policy-makers involved in this initiative, the priority was to start with English and later add other languages within the framework of the Standards document.

Motivations for Incorporating Aspects of the Framework in Educational Policy and Practice

Now that we have examined some of the criticisms of the use of the *CEFR* in the country, I would like to turn to the motivations for incorporating aspects of the framework in educational policy and practice. In November 2007, Rosa María Cely, academic consultant to the National Bilingual Programme at the Ministry of Education, was interviewed in relation to the implementation of the 'Standards for English' (MEN, 2006b) and asked specifically why the *CEFR* had been adopted. She explained that there was no such document in existence in Colombia, and although other possible frameworks had been considered, such as those in force in the United States, Ireland, Spain, Australia and Canada, the ministry considered that the *CEFR* was the framework that could best guide some of the policies for English in the country. She noted specifically that:

> The Ministry found the *CEFR* to be a guiding document, which is flexible, adaptable to our Colombian context, complete, sufficiently researched, used throughout the world in general and in the Latin American context in particular, which has finally been accepted as the referent for the Bilingual Programme. (Cely, 2007: para. 12)

According to Jan Van de Putte (2009), coordinator of the joint programme of the Ministry of Education and the British Council for the National Bilingual Programme at the time of the publication of the National Standards for English (2006b) based on the *CEFR*, there are a number of factors which influenced the incorporation of aspects of the framework within the National Bilingual Programme. The first of these is the fact that language is seen as centred in social action and language users as social actors who carry out tasks in specific social contexts. Van de Putte also refers to what has also been mentioned earlier in this chapter, the inclusion of competences not traditionally associated with language use in Colombia (sociolinguistic and pragmatic competence) as well as the general competences associated with knowing, knowing how to do, knowing how to be and knowing how to learn.

Van de Putte also highlights the fact that the action-based approach which characterises the *CEFR* includes a series of descriptors that help to determine exactly what someone is capable of doing at each particular level. These have been adapted to the Colombian context and appear as part of what is expected at each of the five different levels associated with the *CEFR* scales: A1, A 2.1, A2.2, B1.1 and B1.2 (which students are expected to reach at the end of Grade 11). A final point emphasised by Van de Putte is that the *CEFR* does not distinguish between language learning and use; instead, learning is accomplished through use of the language in new situations.

Factors Limiting the Influence of the *CEFR* in the Colombian Context

One of the great difficulties found by teacher educators and advisors sent by the Ministry of Education to help teachers and institutions understand the implications of adopting the 'Standards' based on the *CEFR* through a series of regional workshops in 2007 and 2008 was the absence of stable working groups of teachers set up to study the documents produced by the Ministry of Education, particularly in the remote rural areas of the country. Furthermore, Lucia Estrada from Universidad Nacional noted in 2008 that in the Department of Antioquia (in the west of the country) there were few schools that had adopted the 'Standards' as referents for the curricular design of English, in line with the requirements of the Ministry of Education. López (2009: 12) also claims that '[t]he new language education policy has not been fully explicated and therefore there is a lot of confusion and lack of trust in what the government is trying to accomplish'.

Silvia Valencia (2007) observed that there were a series of tensions among teachers which she maintains has limited the influence of the National Bilingual Programme. One of these is a widespread perception among teachers in the state (public) sector that the bilingual policy has been imposed on them from above and that many were unprepared to assume these 'impositions'. This has resulted in more hours of work for teachers at schools, as attested also by those who initially undertook ICELT certification processes who had no reduction of their teaching load. Thus many practitioners felt 'overwhelmed by their work demands and those of the ICELT course' (Hernández Peña, 2007: 34).

The Balance of Influence

While a vision of language as action, a focus on contextual appropriateness and intercultural awareness, as well as grammatical accuracy, have strongly influenced the descriptors which characterise each of the five levels of foreign language competence expected of pupils at different points of the educational process, as explained in the preceding chapter, there have also been a series of difficulties associated with the design and implementation of this policy. Thus while the terms A1, B2 and so on are commonly used by educators in Colombia to refer to language proficiency levels, what is not clear is how far the thinking behind these labels has actually influenced classroom practice, as there is relatively little explanation given of the approach adopted in the 'Standards' (2006b), even though the original policy document produced by the committee did in fact contain an extensive rationale and explanation of the thinking behind the decisions made (Aida Salamanca, 2010: personal communication). Therefore, as López (2009) found in a recent study carried out in thirty-eight Colombian universities, there have been few attempts by foreign language departments to align their programmes to the *CEFR*, due to the general lack of knowledge of what these levels actually mean or how they could guide language programmes.

In this respect it is important to take into account an observation made in the Intergovernmental Forum of the Council of Europe in 2007, which warned of the possible dangers of the implementation of the *CEFR* in cases where understanding of the nature and status of the framework have not been sufficiently understood. As Martyniuk and Noijons (2007: 13) have observed:

> There are consistent signs that the *CEFR* is susceptible to being misused in a number of ways: an imbalance in the implementation of the *CEFR*´s various components, entailing a significant risk that their substance will be depleted; misunderstandings regarding the *CEFR*´s status, which where no contextualization takes place, may result in a homogeneity contrary to this instrument's goals; shortcomings in the training process and in the explanations given to ... users, which may result in superficial use and even poor understanding of the tool, sometimes leading to its rejection.

In other words, adapting rather than adopting is very much part of the ongoing debate both in Colombia and other parts of the world.

In order that the introduction of the *CEFR* may serve as an effective orienting framework for the teaching, learning and evaluation of foreign languages in Colombia, it is necessary for policy-makers and practitioners to bridge the wide gap that currently exists between them.

Acknowledgement

I am very grateful for the observations of Beatriz Peña on a previous draft of this chapter.

References

Ayala J. and Álvarez, J.A. (2005) A perspective of the implications of the Common European Framework implementation in the Colombian socio-cultural context. *Colombian Journal of Applied Linguistics* 7, 7–26.

Cárdenas, M.L. (2006) Bilingual Colombia: Are we ready for it¿ What is needed¿ Presentation at the 19th Annual EA Education Conference 2006, *English Australia.*

Cely, R.M. (2007) Una Colombia bilingüe. Entrevista con Rosa María Cely. *El Educador.*

de Mejía, A.M. (2005) Bilingual education in Colombia: Towards an integrated perspective. In A.M. de Mejía (ed.) *Bilingual Education in South America* (pp. 48–64). Clevedon: Multilingual Matters.

González Moncada, A. (2007) Professional development of EFL teachers in Colombia: Between colonial and local practices. *Íkala, Revista de Lenguaje y Cultura* 12 (18), 309–32.

Hernández Peña, L.J. (2007) Pertinencia de un modelo de metodología del inglés certificado internacionalmente. *Revista Internacional Magisterio*, 25, Febrero – Marzo 2007, 32–35.

López, A.A. (2009) Impact of a policy-driven test effort on foreign language programs in Colombian universities. Paper presented at *Pensando Educación*. Universidad de los Andes: Bogotá, Colombia.

Martyniuk, W. and Noijons, J. (2007) Executive summary of results of a survey on the use of *CEFR* at national level in Council of Europe member states. Intergovernmental Forum: The Common European Framework of Reference for languages (*CEFR*) and the development of language policies: Challenges and responsibilities. Strasbourg: Council of Europe, 6–8 February 2007, Report of the Forum.

Ministerio de Educación Nacional (2000) *La Revolución Educativa*. Plan Sectorial 2002–2006. Bogotá: Editorial MEN.

Ministerio de Educación Nacional (2006a) *Educación: Visión 2019*. Bogotá: MEN.

Ministerio de Educación Nacional (2006b) *Estándares Básicos de Competencias en Lenguas Extranjeras: Inglés*. Bogotá: MEN.

Ministerio de Educación Nacional (2006c) *Decreto No. 3870*. Bogotá, Colombia.

Torres Martínez, S. (2009) Las vicisitudes de la enseñanza de lenguas en Colombia, *Diálogos Latinoamericanos* 15, LACUA, Latin American Center, University of Aarhus, Denmark, 56–75.

Usma Wilches, J. (2009) Education and language policy in Colombia. Exploring processes of inclusion, exclusion and stratification in times of global reform. *Profile* 11, 123–142.

Valencia Giraldo, S. (2005) Bilingualism and English Language Teaching in Colombia: A critical outlook. Presentation at the *Conference on English Language Teaching in Colombia*, Universidad del Quindío, October 2005.

Valencia Giraldo, S. (2007) Empowerment and English language teaching (ELT) in public education in Colombia. Presentation in the symposium *Language, Education and Diversity*, University of Waikato, Hamilton, 21–25 November 2007.

Van de Putte, J. (2009) Un bilingüismo de calidad para Colombia. *Palabra Maestra*, 6–8.

USA

The authors:

Jacqueline Bott Van Houten is the World Languages & International Education Consultant at the Kentucky Department of Education, where she is responsible for directing world language policy, teacher professional development and agreements with foreign ministries of education. She holds a PhD in Educational Leadership from Miami University of Ohio. She has several years' teaching experience in French and teacher training in secondary schools and universities. A past president of the National Council of State Supervisors for Languages (NCSSFL), she is currently president of the National Network for Early Language Learning (NNELL) and serves on the board of directors for the Joint National Committee for Languages (JNCL) and the National Council for Languages and International Studies (NCLIS). She is actively involved in The College Board's Chinese Initiative, the National Security Language Initiative STARTALK program and has played a leading role in the development of LinguaFolio in the United States.

Heidi Byrnes is George M. Roth Distinguished Professor of German at Georgetown University. Her research focuses on the acquisition of academic literacy in a second language by adult instructed learners from curricular, pedagogical, and assessment perspectives.

In 2010, she was president of the American Association for Applied Linguistics, and has in the last three decades participated in major language education policy efforts in the United States, such as through the American Association of Teachers of German (AATG; standards for teacher education), the American Council on the Teaching of Languages (proficiency- and *Standards*-related initiatives), the Modern Language Association (MLA, linking language and literature teaching in an integrated curriculum). She has played a leading role in a curriculum project in her own department that has gained national and international attention. As Associate Editor of a twice-yearly column, *Perspectives*, in the *Modern Language Journal*,, she has frequently addressed language education policy issues, including the role of the *CEFR*.

14 Policy Perspectives from the USA

Jacqueline Bott van Houten

A cohort of American state education agency consultants followed the course of action of educational borrowing when they were introduced to the *Common European Framework of Reference for Languages* (*CEFR*), embraced its principles, and incorporated them in the development of LinguaFolio, an American version of the European Language Portfolio (ELP). These consultants, or state supervisors, as they are sometimes called, are charged with addressing priorities of their state boards of education, developing standards, providing service to primary and secondary schools, collaborating with universities, embassies and foreign ministries of education and crafting or reviewing legislation. They belong to an organization, the National Council of State Supervisors for Languages (NCSSFL), the mission of which is to provide leadership in facilitating and promoting policies that support language education. While not traditional policy-makers, the members of the National Council of State Supervisors for Languages (NCSSFL) acted as catalysts for change in creating LinguaFolio, which has affected curriculum and assessment and provided them and their creation with legitimacy. In essence, they constructed a context that resulted in policy outcomes because of the effects on practice (Rizvi & Lingard, 2010).

In the United States, broad educational policies are formulated and funded at the federal level, but because the American public education system is decentralized, decisions for their implementation become the responsibility of the states or institutions. The development of curriculum and assessment are prime examples, being left to state education agencies only when their legislature approves it, and more often to local school districts and universities. When there are few policies and little or no guidance or funding (silent policies), as is the case with languages with the exception of English, then policies often come into existence through the actions of groups with legitimate status advocating for change and using official means to enact it. Such groups include professional organizations, like the American Council for the Teaching of Foreign Languages (ACTFL), the

Modern Language Association (MLA), the Goethe Institute, the American Association of Teachers of French (AATF) and NCSSFL.

Each of the above organizations played some role in furthering the influence of the *CEFR* in the United States. Every year since 2003, when NCSSFL members introduced the *CEFR* at the Delegate Assembly, ACTFL's annual conferences have provided a vehicle for workshops, presentations and discussions around the *CEFR* and ELP. The Modern Language Association's conventions have also addressed the topics, but with fewer offerings. In 2007, the winter edition of the National Federation of Modern Language Teachers Associations' *Modern Language Journal* focused on the *CEFR* with several scholarly articles. Closely following the evolving policies in Europe, the Goethe Institute and the American Association of Teachers of German (AATG) began sponsoring myriad workshops and seminars to introduce the tools to showcase their use in textbooks and train German teachers to implement them. Some university German departments, such as that at Cornell University, used the *CEFR* and the ELP for total curriculum redesign. In 2008, AATF offered its members use of an electronic Global Portfolio, modeled on the ELP and developed by Dr Patricia Cummins of Virginia Commonwealth University. While different groups contributed significantly to the influence of the *CEFR* on foreign language curriculum and assessment in the United States, it is NCSSFL's work – through the development and promotion of LinguaFolio – that has brought about the greatest impact on policy.

In 2002, foreign language consultants from ten state education agencies (California, Indiana, Georgia, Kentucky, Maryland, Maine, Nebraska, South Carolina, Texas and Virginia), travelled to Düsseldorf, Germany, to learn about new European language policies. The *Goethe Institut Inter Nationes* sponsored the seminar on Foreign Language Education in Germany and Europe in that and two subsequent years to introduce participants to the *CEFR* and the ELP in the context of the German schooling system. Organizers linked the policy development to European educational change in general by citing new demographics and mobility trends, and, perhaps more relevant to the American audience, reactions to high-stakes testing, specifically the Programme for International Student Assessment (PISA) study and the German English Student Assessment International (DESI) results (see also Hu, this volume). Introducing the *CEFR* by linking new policies to high-stakes testing struck a cord with the state supervisors, who were still reeling from the negative impact of the No Child Left Behind Act on foreign language programs and enrolment (Rhodes & Pufahl, 2009).[1]

Within two months of their return from Europe, the NCSSFL team organized a meeting to discuss adapting the *CEFR* to the needs of American language learners. Not long after, LinguaFolio, an ELP-inspired tool, had been developed and evolved into policy when its use became required by the National Security Language Initiative (NSLI) STARTALK programs. Phillips (2004) provides a framework for understanding this cross-national policy attraction and the transfer process. Using this theory and its four stages: cross-national attraction, decision, implementation and internalization (Phillips, 2004) can help explain why the *CEFR* appealed so strongly to NCSSFL members, and how, in a nation practically void of formal foreign language education policies, NCSSFL was able to adapt the *CEFR* to the US context, legitimize the LinguaFolio reflective learning tool and create an imaginary of new American language policies.

The Attraction of the *CEFR*

It is important to understand that the National Council of State Supervisors for Languages (NCSSFL) members did not intentionally seek out international trends, ideas or standards to stimulate change, which Phillips (2004) suggests is a trend in global borrowing. However, when they were presented with concepts, which aligned with their language learning philosophies, and tools that answered emerging needs to strengthen independent learning, chart continuous progress, and make the language learning process more comprehensible to stakeholders, their decision to import policies was almost spontaneous. They experienced an immediate realization of the potential of 'borrowing' certain elements of the *CEFR*. Several contextual factors led to this attraction, such as compatibility with educational movements, in particular the growing focus on formative assessment and the use of backward planning that emphasized identifying desired results first, then determining acceptable evidence of learning and, finally, planning instruction.

The state supervisors found the *CEFR*'s efforts to make language learning transparent appealing. The Common Reference Levels offered a clear explanation of the progression of the learning process, bridging the knowledge gap of what language proficiency looks like from a learner perspective and how to align a language program. Supervisors believed that seeing language learning as it was presented in the *CEFR* would inform school administrators and help them vertically align K-12 languages programs. It also suggested a proficiency approach to developing state standards and frameworks supporting multiple entry points.

The American language profession has tools of its own, such as *The Standards for Foreign Language Learning in the 21st Century* (1996), which nearly every state has adopted and most teachers can identify. The *ACTFL*

Proficiency Guidelines (1986, 1999, & 2001), intended for use in academia, identify functional competency in four subdivided levels (Novice, Intermediate, Advanced and Superior) are used to report scores from assessments such as the Oral Proficiency Interviews (OPI), Written Proficiency Tests (WPT) and the Standards-Based Measure of Proficiency Test (STAMP). The *ACTFL Performance Guidelines for K-12 Learners* (1998) describe at the Novice, Intermediate and Pre-Advanced levels the proficiency of younger learners whose language learning has taken place in the classroom. Nowhere was there a self-assessment that aligned to proficiency scales. What the state supervisors found in the *CEFR* was an original next step, a user-friendly set of checklists for learners to self-assess. It was this innovative concept of providing learners positive, motivating, can-do descriptors and enabling them to self-assess what they could do with language, to understand and direct their own learning, which hit home with American educators, who were steeped in the tenets of Dewey's (1916) pragmatic, hands-on approach to self-activated learning, but had no tools to facilitate it.

The can-do statements provided a starting point for school district supervisors and teachers to develop benchmarks and indicators, aligned to a local curriculum, and then to deconstruct them into learning targets for lessons and units. The positive tone of the can-do statements contrasted with the academic language and deficiency-oriented Proficiency Guidelines, which were intended for sorting and gatekeeping purposes, but which made it difficult for teachers to use in rubric design, especially if the students were the intended users. Neither the Proficiency nor Performance Guidelines offered the motivational, self-empowerment of the can-dos.

Additional elements of the *CEFR* piqued state supervisors' interest, such as the 'commonness' of the document for use across languages and borders. The push for international benchmarking[2] supports shared criteria and, with the escalating number of foreign language teachers hired through states' memoranda of agreement to hire native speakers from other countries, common tools offered a way to facilitate both the hiring and the classroom acculturation processes. The emphasis on building independent learners drew interest in light of the increasing opportunities for online learning and proficiency credit granting. The suggestion that teachers' pedagogy would improve with use of the *CEFR* stirred excitement among supervisors, who were already promoting student-centered classrooms, total use of the target language, reflective learning and formative assessment, and believed that tools like the European Language Portfolio could lead to positive changes in classroom instruction.

Also appealing were the *CEFR*'s recognition of heritage language learners and the new concept of interculturality. Both offered hope for countering weaknesses in the No Child Left Behind Act, which perceived English language learners from a deficiency perspective as Limited English Proficient (LEP) students. During the development of LinguaFolio, national initiatives to strengthen proficiency in critical need languages and to recruit heritage speakers to the teaching corps increased the potential for successful adaptation of the borrowed policies by claiming goals compatible with the high value the *CEFR* placed on linguistic and cultural background.

The Implementation Phase

The integration of elements of the *CEFR* into foreign language teaching and learning in America through LinguaFolio occurred swiftly, involved adaptation from the original, encountered some barriers and achieved policy status from the bottom-up and top-down. The LinguaFolio journey began for a team of NCSSFL members at a three-day meeting in Kentucky in February 2003. The European Association of Quality Language Services (EAQUALS) director, Frank Heyworth, whom the group had met in Germany, was invited to provide details about the *CEFR* and ELP. As a result of their collaboration, a 30-minute interview with Heyworth about the *CEFR* was conducted and filmed, and was subsequently distributed to language associations in several states. Soon after, Kentucky assembled a team of teachers to adapt the Centre for Information on Language Teaching ELP for young learners (http://www.cilt.org.uk/shop/product.aspx?id=37) and to create LinguaFolio Junior, while Virginia and Indiana followed suit by developing secondary versions of the ELP. All three states piloted the portfolios in 2004–2005. At the same time, Nebraska developed both versions and began a grant-supported professional development effort, which, through Ali Moeller at the University of Nebraska Lincoln, resulted in a five-year longitudinal research project and several graduate student dissertations focusing on goal setting, teacher beliefs, classroom practices and other topics. Their model two-week immersion workshop involves teachers using a personal LinguaFolio to evaluate their own language proficiency and set goals while studying a target language novel. Ongoing face-to-face and web-based follow-up provides support, while teachers apply what they learned in the classroom. One lesson learned from years of NCSSFL training is that teachers have more buy-in and are more prepared to guide student use of the tool, when they, themselves, experience the self-assessment, goal-setting process. The goal-setting process, when teamed with backwards planning, has had the greatest impact on curriculum and instruction.

After developing and piloting LinguaFolio versions in individual states, four states banded together under a memorandum of agreement, and were later joined by a fifth to create and pilot, from 2005–2007, a common web-based tool hosted on the Virginia Department of Education website. They developed descriptors and attempted to align them to the *CEFR* and ACTFL scales, a process that involved numerous revisions. A final product was posted on NCSSFL's website in 2009, but not before users were clamoring for an interactive online version.

The early paper version of LinguaFolio was problematic, so NCSSFL collaborated with the Center for Second Language Acquisition Studies (CASLS) at the University of Oregon to design LinguaFolio Online, an e-portfolio that allows learners to self-assess, upload and store evidence – text, MP3 files, videos, and so on – and decide with whom to share it. CASLS and NCSSFL created a first iteration to an online version for STARTALK's critical need summer language camps and found that the number of uploads far exceeded that which was anticipated. Currently, LinguaFolio Online is available only to select groups in a few states as a beta version, but teachers are so eager for the online vehicle that some school districts and states, like North Carolina, have built their own platforms.

The content of LinguaFolio also evolved. At first, the Global Scale and many of the *CEFR*'s descriptors were used, but modified as time went on. British wording (i.e. Threshold, Waystage) was not familiar to American learners. Using the Proficiency Guideline terminology (i.e. novice low) was preferable because American teachers are familiar with it and most national assessments (i.e. STAMP, OPI) use it to report scores. Numerous teams met over the years to write, pilot and revise the can-do statements until a final version was posted on the NCSSFL website (www.ncssfl.org) in 2009. Initially, an alignment of the two scales was suggested on the grid, but that has since been removed due to the controversial nature of such an alignment. Questions about the feasibility of aligning the *CEFR* and ACTFL Proficiency scales prompted European and American language experts to organize the first ACTFL-CEFR Conference, in Leipzig, Germany, in 2010, where the outcome was a clearer theoretical and empirical understanding of the two scales. A second conference, titled 'The Elements of Proficiency: An Emerging Consensus for Language Assessment and Instruction', continued the discussion in Provo, Utah, in August 2011, and focused on the elements of proficiency, their application to testing and their implications for teaching and learning. There were general conclusions that a crosswalk bridging the two scales is more feasible than any alignment; that both the United States and the EU face similar education policy challenges, and that, ultimately, continued dialogue will reap benefits for the proficiency of learners and international benchmarking. LinguaFolio pilot groups found the A1 level lacked enough descriptors to show progress and motivate American students, so these were expanded under Novice Low, Mid and High categories. Also, the Passports for young and adult learners were adjusted to fit the US elementary and secondary/post-secondary schema.

From the beginning, NCSSFL disseminated information about LinguaFolio through workshops and presentations at national, regional and state foreign language conferences. Their members presented at embassy-sponsored Teach Europe seminars, universities and school districts, regional and national conferences and meetings for the MLA, Asia Society, Center for Applied Linguistics, National Capital Resource Center, Center for Educational Resources in Culture, Language and Literacy (CERCLL), STARTALK and so on. Workshops in north and south-eastern states were sponsored by the National Network for Early Language Learning (NNELL) in 2006 and in the mid-west and west by state and local Foreign Language Assistant Program (FLAP) federal grant recipients. There was a concerted effort to organize all training from a LinguaFolio perspective with participants actively involved in goal setting, reflection and self-assessment on the topics they were learning. When more teachers started to use LinguaFolio, NCSSFL members produced 'train the trainer' workshops and posted on their website a five-module Power Point presentation for self-instruction. In 2005, LinguaFolio was NCSSFL's project for ACTFL's Year of Language. Publications in professional practitioner journals, such as NNELL's *Learning Languages*, also spread the word about LinguaFolio.

Becoming 'Policy'

The swiftness in implementing borrowed policies from Europe was facilitated by NCSSFL's focused efforts as well as supportive national education trends that were being promoted by state education agencies. These included Wiggins and McTighe's Understanding by Design, a backwards instruction design model; formative assessment, of which self-assessment is an example; and the communication, collaboration and global competence skills emphasized by the national Partnership for 21st Century Skills and EdSteps, both of which are influential education policy-making organizations. The timing and financial conditions under which most of the development and dissemination of Linguafolio occurred were favorable. Were it to happen today, under the current economic restraints of education agencies and with many supervisors' roles being redefined to meet new state and national priorities, it is doubtful that LinguaFolio's policy impact would have been as great.

The borrowed elements of the *CEFR* became policy, not through government regulation, but through process, involving actions, texts and changes

Table 14.1 Milestones in processes of implementation

Top-Down	*Bottom-Up*
• School and district use of LinguaFolio for curriculum design and formative assessment. • LinguaFolio theme-based state language conferences. • Organized state-wide training. • Use of LinguaFolio as a reporting requirement for local education agency federal grant proposals. • State standards and benchmarks documents using LinguaFolio descriptors, developed by teacher teams under state direction.	• Creation of Concordia Language Villages Visa based on LinguaFolio. • Inclusion of LinguaFolio in Curtain and Dahlberg Languages and Children Making the Match textbook widely used for teacher training and professional development. • Inclusion of LinguaFolio in Chinese Guest Teachers training by The College Board. • Required use of LinguaFolio by participants in the US Department of Defense's STARTALK program.

in practices. Phillips (2004) refers to an internalization stage during which there are milestone manifestations of the process. In the case of LinguaFolio, these milestones occurred in a top-down and bottom-up manner (see Table 14.1). NCSSFL, as the agent of change, represented neither grass roots nor the federal government, yet had effects on both. Its team of state agency employees had no official power to enact change, but did yield influence to do so because of a perceived authority that lent legitimacy. Because of a lack of national curricula, similar instances have tended to occur in other content areas and are particularly common today in those areas that are not nationally funded or assessed.

Conclusions

Because the development of the foreign languages curriculum and assessment in the United States occurs most frequently at the local level, it is nearly impossible to determine the extent of influence the *CEFR* or LinguaFolio have had. Therefore, the focus of this case study has been on LinguaFolio's effect on education policy. What is known is that LinguaFolio training has been widespread, in at least 38 states and in venues that draw from national participants, and that NCSSFL-sponsored training, publications and related websites have always been aimed at promoting the use of LinguaFolio for the improvement of teaching and learning. Most of the training has been closely linked to backwards design, which leads teachers to think first of outcomes, goals and assessment, and then to plan instruction strategically and incrementally to help students achieve the goals. LinguaFolio is the students' companion piece, empowering learners to follow a similar path of goal setting, evaluation and reflection on their own learning journey.

Specific incidents of effects on curriculum can certainly be noted, but with the understanding that they cannot be generalized. Ali Moeller's research (2010) with teachers who were trained in and used LinguaFolio reported a significant correlation between goal setting and achievement, showing that LinguaFolio is being implemented in the curriculum and that it is having a positive effect. Teachers in Jefferson County Public Schools, the 28th largest district in the United States, used LinguaFolio descriptors to develop learning targets that guide their curriculum. In 2009, Kentucky used the LinguaFolio can-do statements as the benchmarks in the state's world languages standard document. Florida and Ohio are also utilizing them to a lesser degree in their framework. North Carolina produced an English language learners version aligned to high-stakes assessment, modeled standards for their core subjects on the can-do format and created their own LinguaFolio online site with space for the uploading of evidence.

Allowing students to provide pieces of evidence that demonstrate the LinguaFolio can-do descriptors, along with outside validations such as performance assessments or standardized proficiency tests, will offer a flexible way to address granting credit for proficiency, rather than for time spent in a classroom. The potential is there, too, for 2.0 LinguaFolio applications for personal use on phones, iPads or other technologies to provide new opportunities for autonomous learning. NCSSFL has plans for the revision and expansion of its LinguaFolio Junior, while Utah, Louisiana and South Carolina are adapting the can-dos for maximum use in content-based immersion schools. Concerns linger over the relationship between *CEFR* and ACTFL Proficiency scales, but hope remains through continued dialogue begun in Leipzig that a common understanding will bridge this divide as a true example of international benchmarking.

Notes

(1) NCLB was the education act passed under President George Bush that focused on standards-based education reform and was based on the belief that setting high standards and establishing measurable goals can improve individual outcomes in education. The Act required states to develop tests in basic skills and administer them to all students in certain grades. If schools did not live up to their accountability standards, schools faced decreased funding and students were permitted to move to different schools. As a result, in many cases the core content areas (i.e. reading and mathematics) were emphasized and foreign language and arts programs were

diminished or dropped. In a survey conducted by the Center for Applied Linguistics, nearly one-third of public schools with language programs reported having been negatively affected by NCLB, suggesting resources from their programs were cut to serve mathematics, language arts and other core subjects.

(2) Since the 1999 TIMMS report and subsequent PISA results, government and independent educational policy-makers have increasingly focused on American students' achievement in comparison to their international peers. Recently, the National Governors Association's and the Council of Chief State School Officers organization's initiative for benchmarking standards against those of other countries, led to the development of Common Core State Standards in mathematics and language arts, currently adopted by 35 states. Work has begun on developing common standards for the science and the arts and interest has also been expressed in addressing foreign languages (http://www.corestandards.org/about-the-standards).

References

American Council on the Teaching of Foreign Languages (1986) *ACTFL Proficiency Guidelines for Reading and Listening*. Yonkers, NY: American Council on the Teaching of Foreign Languages.

American Council on the Teaching of Foreign Languages (1998) *Performance Guidelines for K-12 Learners*. Yonkers, NY: American Council on the Teaching of Foreign Languages.

American Council on the Teaching of Foreign Languages (1999) *ACTFL Proficiency Guidelines: Speaking*. Yonkers, NY: American Council on the Teaching of Foreign Languages.

American Council on the Teaching of Foreign Languages (2001) *ACTFL proficiency Guidelines: Writing*. Yonkers, NY: American Council on the Teaching of Foreign Languages.

Dewey, J. (1916) *Democracy and education: An Introduction to the Philosophy of Education*. New York: The McMillan Company.

LinguaFolio. Online at http://www.ncssfl.org/LinguaFolio/index.php?linguafolio_index. Accessed on 1 May 2010.

LinguaFolio Nebraska. Online at http://www.nde.state.ne.us/forlg/LinguaFolio/Lingua Folio.htm. Accessed on 2 April 2010.

LinguaFolio Online. Online at http:/casls.uoregon.edu/lfo.php. Accessed on 15 May 2010.

Moeller, A., Theiler, J.M. and Wu, C. (2010) Goal setting and student achievement: A Longitudinal study. Manuscript under review.

National Standards in Foreign Language Learning Education Project (1999) *Standards for Foreign Language Learning in the 21st Century*. Yonkers, NY: National Standards in Foreign Language Learning Education Project.

Ochs, K. and Phillips, D. (2003a) *Toward a Structural Typology of Cross National Attraction in Education*. Lisbon, Portugal: Educa.

Phillips, D. (2004) Toward a structural typology of cross national attraction in education. In G. Steiner-Khamsi (ed.) *The global politics of educational borrowing and lending* (pp. 54–67). New York: Teachers College Press.

Rhodes, N.C. and Pufahl, I. (2009) *Report from the National K-12 Foreign Language Survey*. Washington, DC: Center for Applied Linguistics.

Rizvi, F. and Lingard, B. (2010) *Globalizing Educational Policy*. New York, NY: Routledge.

15 Academic Perspectives from the USA

Heidi Byrnes

Framing the Reflection

Inclusion of the United States as a site for investigating the impact of the *Common European Framework of Reference* (*CEFR*) on language education policies might initially be unexpected. After all, entities closely associated with the *CEFR* that actively 'lend' aspects of a *CEFR*-inspired educational policy to the United States seem few; likewise, educational policy-makers and actors who advocate 'borrowing' *CEFR*-inspired ideas are not readily apparent. But precisely because the *CEFR* has otherwise had considerable influence around the globe, limited impact in this particular instance itself becomes a phenomenon of interest in the study of language education policy development and implementation in an international context.

To make that argument, this chapter adopts a micro case studies approach. In relation to its companion piece (van Houten, this volume), it identifies broad policy-related intellectual-academic dynamics in the American educational landscape in light of theoretical approaches to comparative international education research (see Alderson (2009), Popkewitz & Rizvi (2009), Rizvi & Lingard (2009), Schriewer (2009), and Steiner-Khamsi (2004)). My interpretation is informed by my experience as a faculty member in a PhD-granting cultural studies department (German at Georgetown University) known for its innovative curricular work (Byrnes *et al.*, 2010), by my participation in influential language professional organizations and key initiatives in language education policy formation in the United States for close to three decades, and by my being closely attuned, as President of the American Association for Applied Linguistics, to the US applied linguistics research community.

I highlight three theoretical positions that shed light on the process of educational borrowing by the United States from the *CEFR*. Following Schriewer and Martinez, I find insightful a 'socio-logical' understanding of the process of internationalization and educational knowledge, with its assumption that 'educational knowledge, reform policies, and developmental models elaborated and disseminated at a transnational level are refracted by each society's internal selection thresholds and needs for interpretation, which are the outcome of cultural traditions and collective mentality, as well as political forces and dominant ideologies' (2004: 50). The papers in Alderson (2009) are also evocative because of their emphasis on the role of individuals and institutional stakeholders in relation to the macropolitics of policy and planning. Finally, the assertion by May and Hornberger that 'policies and educational practices are always situated in relation to wider issues of power, access, opportunity, inequality and, at times, discrimination and disadvantage' (2008: 5) seemingly applies to the observable borrowing practices within the perennially charged atmosphere of language education in an immigrant country like the United States.

Traditions and Beliefs in Language Education Policy and Educational Practice

The US language education landscape is fundamentally shaped by the formal absence of a federal language education policy. This fact is a source of pride in the US education system due to its imputed freedom to act on the part of presumably 'more competent' agents 'closer to the ground'. The resultant veritable jungle of seemingly endless incongruities in educational praxes is at the same time a source of considerable frustration (cf. Byrnes, 2007c, 2008; Jackson & Malone, 2009; Jensen, 2007) and a policy scandal in need of 'fixing' (O'Connell & Norwood, 2007).

But the terrain of language educational policy-making has many more fault lines. Three internal dynamics include the shift towards proficiency and standards-based education; the impact of the federal No Child Left Behind (NCLB) legislation; and differentially manifested notions of learner-based teaching and learning. They are bolstered by the ever-present influence of testing and societal ambivalence toward immigrants and their language use. All share the drive toward proven 'outcomes' within the powerful demands for 'accountability', which is so much a part of contemporary institutional thinking. Inasmuch as acceptable 'proof' requires assessment, testing becomes a tool for often quite disparate intentions and engenders the need for various actors to position themselves in relation to applicable testing regimes. I will argue that it is here that the *CEFR* finds its most prominent link to the US educational scene.

Proficiency and standards-based language education

The Standards movement of the last two decades, which focused on improving the quality of education across the domains of language arts (including reading and writing), math and the social sciences, ultimately became so powerful as to both compel and make it desirable for the foreign language community to align its notions of language education with this ideology. Remarkably, this effort created perhaps the most successful instance of bottom-up professional consensus-building in US language education (cf. *Standards for Foreign Language Learning* 1996/2006; also Phillips, 2003), something akin to a nationwide, though formally non-binding, policy-like environment.

With its unmistakable performance orientation ('what students know and are able to do') the Standards project built on the 'proficiency movement' of the 1980s. Despite the proficiency construct's much-discussed limitations (cf. Bachman & Savignon, 1986; Liskin-Gasparro, 2003; van Lier, 1989), the oral proficiency interview (OPI) according to the rating scales developed under the auspices of the American Council on the Teaching of Foreign Languages (ACTFL, cf. Breiner-Sanders *et al.*, 1999), was *the* central player in the shift toward communicative language teaching in the United States at the primary and secondary levels of schooling, from kindergarten to 12th grade. Indeed, the very nature of speaking ability was expressed in the language of the OPI rating scale: the rating scale, from Novice to Superior, was equated with developmental stages in FL learning; learning goals and outcomes statements were aligned to the scale; curricula, pedagogical recommendations, and materials, including commercial textbooks, followed its construct; and OPI-derived proficiency levels entered guidelines for teacher education and licensure.

The subsequent Standards initiative of the 1990s included a conceptual expansion, inasmuch as the so-called five C's – *Communication, Cultures, Connections, Comparisons*, and *Communities* – made 'culture' and intercultural communication in multilingual environments central constructs. Recent discussion (e.g. Byrnes, 2006a, 2008a, 2010) shows this shift to engender continued debate. However, there is little doubt that the *Standards* took on the role of a substitute national educational policy with repercussions for every aspect of language education, particularly at the K-12 level. Even with a considerably reduced presence at the college level, the tantalizing promise of bridging the formidable divide between secondary and collegiate FL education is associated with the *Standards*, particularly when they are coupled with a genre-based approach (cf. Arens, 2008, 2009; Byrnes, 2008; Scott 2010).

It goes without saying that standards-setting goes hand in hand with 'assessment', even if it enters stealthily through 'good' institutional practices like 'benchmarking' or determining educational goals and outcomes and translating these into curricula and pedagogical practices. In other words, through the *Standards,* the language education community gained a much-needed conceptual focus as well as practical tools for its work while being channeled into narrower ways of imagining and realizing language education that are open to challenge.

The No Child Left Behind legislation: Promulgating language policy through outcomes assessment

But the force of testing is anything but covert in the case of the NCLB legislation, which has dominated educational thinking since its promulgation in 2003 (see Byrnes, 2005, particularly the position paper by Rosenbusch, 2005; for a recent take, see Menken, 2009). Here, the meritorious goals of raising student achievement levels were yoked to extraordinarily punitive assessment practices with severe consequences for schools, school districts and even entire states. More insidious, because assessment was limited to reading/language arts, mathematics, and science, educational decision-makers shifted resources to those domains, thereby further threatening an already vulnerable language education sector (Rosenbusch & Jensen, 2005). The current fiscal situation has only exacerbated these negative consequences. Taken as a whole, the language education community has responded with ambivalence. Some of its sectors have acceded to the demands regarding 'high standards' and 'excellence', a kind of buy-in under duress, and have sought to position themselves favorably within this overall climate. By contrast, others have engaged in variant forms of rejection, subversion or complete disregard. This is true particularly of higher education faculties that still arrogate to themselves the option of 'opting-out' – only to remove themselves from the dominant public discourse about language teaching and learning and creating their own peculiar forms of marginalization.

The ideology of learner-centered teaching and learning

The dynamic of learner-centeredness is securely anchored in the ideological privileging in American culture of the autonomous and 'free' individual. Recently, its cachet has been bolstered by claims that it is the activist, self-regulated, flexible individual who is best able to handle the challenges and opportunities of globalization and global competitiveness. In an increasingly multicultural and multilingual US society, learner-centeredness can also be linked to diversity and identity construction.

To illustrate its extraordinary grip on the imagination, I mention only a few terms regularly used for proposing and authorizing courses of educative action, justifying decisions, reporting educational approaches and outcomes and infusing educational discourse and educational praxes, all the way down to the daily goings-on in specific classrooms: autonomous learning, constructivist learning and reflexive learning as a way of setting personal goals and objectives; the engaged learner, the self-directed and self-motivated learner whose learning activities are scaffolded by an attentive teacher; and the life-long learner. Such constructs flood the discursive self-representation of the language education field, shore up its claims to participation in overall larger educational conversations, and stake out its desire to be accepted as a forward-looking contributor to the contemporary US and global educational enterprise.

The power of tests as enforceable and enforced reporting frameworks

While I have repeatedly pointed to an implicit presence of assessment-like dynamics in contemporary foreign language education, the power of explicit assessment rubrics and regimes to become not so hidden forms of language policy deserves separate attention (cf. Shohamy, 2001, 2008). Ironically, the power of testing mechanisms and routines seems to increase when a country does *not* possess an explicitly formulated language education policy. The following dynamic would seem to apply: unable to appeal to the 'higher authority' of an existing policy, the foreign language community is left with little choice but to surrender to the pressures of high-stakes testing. This is the case particularly when language educators lack the necessary intellectual and procedural resources to counter the typically positivist, decontextualized notions of testing regimes (but see the efforts described in Byrnes, 2006 and Norris, 2006). McNamara (2007) specifically identified assessment as a highly effective approach taken by governments around the world to control the curriculum through the constructs underlying tests inasmuch as tests alone fulfill the reporting requirements enforced by the government, while also specifying and controlling the resource stream.

Societal ambivalence toward multilingualism

Despite its ritually invoked multilingual heritage, the United States has been unable to develop a consensus regarding the educational value of language learning for all citizens that would assure its place in all K-12 curricula. A pointed way to summarize why this is so might be to note that a population's multilingual heritage is connected to immigrants as people, immigrants as workers and migration and immigration as potentially undermining the nation state. Of course, these grounds are just as operative elsewhere. In the United States, however, this ideological/political nexus continues to infuse the calculus of language education policy with a highly volatile factor that is subject to intense manipulation and contentious maneuvering. Among its most consequential manifestations is the English Only Movement (see http://www.massenglishplus.org/content/Language_Rights/English Only_Movement/EngOnly.html), which has already led to the cancellation of long-standing federal approaches to bilingual education in the United States. Quite tellingly, Evans and Hornberger (2005) trace a movement in education policy from viewing language as a resource to language as a right, to language as a problem.

Exploring the Cultural Politics of Educational Borrowing in the US Context

On the basis of this background I now probe the role of the *CEFR* in the United States in terms of areas accepted, criticized, adapted and emphasized; the motivations for incorporating *CEFR* components; constraints for influence and adoption; and the possible areas of resistance.

Adopting, adapting and affirming the CEFR

As an educational approach approximating language policy status in many European countries, the *CEFR* accords well with the communicative language teaching paradigm that is characteristic of US language education. One can argue that the *CEFR*'s strong functional/notional thrust is less developed than the relatively detailed proficiency and *Standards* work put forward by US language professionals. But such differences disappear in light of their largely overlapping interest in 'communication' and 'language performance' and may, somewhat ironically, even favor the *CEFR* (van Houten, 2007). Either way, the very presentation of language abilities in terms of a rating scale (in the *CEFR* from A to C levels), carries a high recognition and acceptance value for US language professionals familiar with the ACTFL rating scale. For these professionals the *CEFR* presents at the very least a non-challenge, that is, a non-threat; more positively, it engenders a sense of self-affirmation and simultaneous other-acceptance. Finally, its learner-focus, prominently set forth in the learner-driven language portfolio, can be understood as well-trodden educational terrain. Its 'can-do' approach has a familiar proficiency scales ring to it, while perhaps being a bit more 'gentle on the mind', inasmuch as statements of deficiency ('L2 user cannot do x'), which pervade the OPI guidelines, are absent. In that sense, the portfolio assessment regime arguably fits well with a pervasively uncritical learner focus in much US educational discourse.

These considerable commonalities combine to account for the fact that the *CEFR* has been duly 'noted' by US language professionals and judged as an interesting, worthy, perhaps even admirable, though very 'European', phenomenon (Byrnes, 2007c), but has found no more than a highly circumscribed echo. However, in an environment that can be likened to an echo chamber – and I take the assessment context to be such an environment – relatively muted responses can become insistent nudges and urges for educational borrowing.

Specifically, it appears that *CEFR* appropriation in the United States illustrates what Schriewer has called 'externalization' (2003) and authorization. Here educational actors justify desired internal action in light of what others, to whom prestige and authority is discursively attributed, have done. This need for 'supplementary meaning' as determined by distinct cultural, political or ideological settings (Schriewer & Martinez, 2004: 51) characterizes the particularities of acceptance and borrowing of the *CEFR*.

To begin with the imputed prestige aspect of European language-related phenomena: the highly vulnerable and fragmented (if not to say fractured) position of language education in the United States, as contrasted with the multilingual exuberance of the imaginary construct 'Europe', with its strong tradition of language education in school curricula, now bolstered by the much-touted 'one plus two' policy of the European Union, cannot but leave US educators envious and covetous. Since creating such a comprehensively favorable context for language education continues to be beyond their reach, it is sensible to make the individual learner the focus for borrowing, particularly when such borrowing can be framed as learner empowerment and the creation of personal goals and objectives, rather than other-imposed standards. The ingenious point of leveraging borrowing is therefore through adapting the European Language Portfolio with its self-assessment aura into a distinctively American version, an e-portfolio that leaves control in the hands of learners and administrators and teachers (Cummins, 2007; Theiler, 2005).

As a point of contact, 'the learner' provides subtle and overt, short-term and long-term benefits. Among the subtle benefits is the potential to recognize the capacities in several languages that many students enrolled in US schools have, although neither the society as a whole nor the school system are able to provide a sanctioned environment for their multilingualism, much less for instructional support. Among the more overt benefits is the obvious 'performativity' of self-assessment and its ability to yield demonstrable 'results' for reporting purposes. Among short-term consequences we find the immediate 'reflexive feedback' quality for the learner who determines his/her 'can-do' levels of performance. Among the long-term benefits are its potential for enhancing learner motivation, a much-touted ingredient of any learning and an assumed and much-bemoaned void for the majority of US instructed language learners, bolstered by its 'path-way' conceptualization of ever better language performance. Taking such information to higher policy levels, teachers and administrators can use the results of self-assessment regimes to build a longitudinally articulated curriculum, an attractive response to the endless calls for articulated curricula (Barrette & Paesani, 2005). Finally, the relatively painless and low-cost nature of electronically managed and locally controlled forms of assessment that seemingly dispense with the rigorous demands of test reliability and validity associated with standardized testing meted out by powerful authorities like the Educational Testing Service, state education agencies, even ACTFL itself, provides yet another adoption incentive.

Motivating the acceptance of the CEFR in the preceding article

The previous discussion of the influence of the *CEFR* implicitly included aspects of what might have motivated such an acceptance. If 'motivation' includes financial support translated into worthwhile professional events, then the initiatives taken by the Goethe Institute (see the description provided by van Houten in the preceding article) that explicitly targeted state foreign language supervisors but also influenced some college faculty members, turned out to be absolutely critical.

Though the *CEFR*'s presence in higher education is sporadic at best, it is created and sustained by the enormous good will US German language professionals extend to the Goethe Institute (see Byrnes, 2008d), itself inherently a link to European language policy discussion. Beyond that, the German profession has managed to carve out for itself the favorable aura among US foreign language professionals of being proactive, innovative and relatively nimble in its ability to respond to new opportunities and challenges. For collegiate faculty, primarily in German, awareness of the *CEFR* is further nourished by long-standing professional links to projects undertaken by the American Teachers of German (AATG) and the ACTFL-directed proficiency and Standards movement, and by insistent calls for curriculum reform in US undergraduate education, most recently formulated by the MLA (2007). These environments, of course, deal with issues across the spectrum of language instruction in the United States, not merely German. The *CEFR* can therefore turn into a useful 'reference frame' for teacher education, curriculum reform and reconfigured assessment practices used by activist and engaged professionals who wish to create – and in their circumscribed environments are able to create – a better world for language education in light of the assumed 'better world' in Europe. There can be little doubt that such convictions are strengthened by a certain novelty, an implicit quality of 'shaming' the US system, the need for a positive response against the negative influences in one's own sphere of work, a not to be discounted professional profile-building and long-standing mutually beneficial forms of engagement with professional organizations.

Even more diffuse, but revealing nonetheless, is that faculty members in higher education can find the *CEFR'* s focus on a 'plurilingualism' that is removed from negative judgments about actual ability levels in different languages particularly desirable. Such a stance can be used to affirm their own interest in a more sociologically rather than linguistically-oriented notion of 'culture' and multilingualism in the contemporary world, as is exemplified in the MLA's chosen educational goals of translingual and transcultural competence (MLA, 2007; also Byrnes, 2008c; Byrnes *et al.*, 2010). Collegiate language program coordinators in charge of the first two years of instruction are keenly aware of the post-structuralist intellectual preferences of their faculty colleagues in literary-cultural departments. As a consequence, they tend to make that connection to bolster the intellectual merits of their often-undervalued language programs, even to the point of denying its underlying dilemmas (Levine *et al.*, 2008).

Constraints for influence and adoption

In light of the previous discussion, constraints on the influence of the *CEFR* are essentially attributable to the 'saturated' educational practice dominated by the *Standards* project. This means that the *CEFR* is not perceived as sufficiently different from already existing work. On the contrary, it might amount to needlessly muddying the waters to introduce yet another system of reference, given the existing dominance and complete infusion of educational practice with *Standards*-related intellectual arguments and practices. This reluctance would seem to apply particularly to teacher education (Glisan, 2005; Donato, 2009). Caution in anything that might be perceived as distancing one's work from the mainstream is indicated all the more as, subsequent to 9/11, language education has gained a certain public presence, conflicted though that is because of its compromised link to defense and security-related interests (Byrnes, 2007b; Jackson & Malone, 2009). However, with funding strongly tied to such concerns and long-overdue federal legislative proposals for improving the lot of language education in the United States thoroughly depending on arguments of defense, security, and global competitiveness, it would be unwise to change course and use completely unfamiliar vocabulary for one's self-representation and public argumentation – and wise to admire the *CEFR* at a distance.

Resistance to the CEFR

All of which does not, by any means, translate into ignoring the *CEFR* – on the contrary! At a meeting at the Herder Institute in Leipzig, Germany, in June 2010, the focus quite unsurprisingly was on assessment issues, specifically the commensurability between the two assessment scales in play, the ACTFL OPI and the *CEFR* scales. From the standpoint of assessment specialists, both suffer from serious shortcomings as assessment frameworks. However, from the standpoint of players on the ground – from teachers, to state supervisors, to government agencies, to, first and foremost, ACTFL itself, which is heavily invested in the multiple meanings of that word in OPI-based assessment – there exists an urgent need to find some sort of compatibility and translatability because of the increasing demand for cross-border test score recognition.

Coda

On that realization, one can look forward to observing the continued unfolding of a dynamic interplay between personal and institutional players, with their respective goals and interests; between academic and quite practical considerations, with their at times disparate viewpoints and discursive practices and interpretations; between testing and language policy formation, with their conflicting and also symbiotic relationships; between the role of governments and their key councils and legislative mechanisms; and the joys and challenges of language and teaching and learning in actual classrooms.

References

American Council on the Teaching of Foreign Languages (2006) *Standards for Foreign Language Learning in the 21st Century* (3rd edn). Lawrence, KS: Allen Press.

Alderson, J.C. (ed.) (2009) *The Politics of Language Education: Individuals and Institutions*. Bristol: Multilingual Matters.
Arens, K. (2008) Genres and the *Standards*: Teaching the 5 C's through texts. *German Quarterly* 81 (1), 35–48.
Arens, K. (2009) Teaching culture. The *Standards* as an optic on curriculum development. In V.M. Scott (ed.) *Principles and Practices of the* Standards *in College Foreign Language Education* (pp. 160–180). Boston: Heinle Cengage Learning.
Bachman, L.F. and Savignon, S.J. (1986) The evaluation of communicative language proficiency: A critique of the ACTFL oral interview. *Modern Language Journal* 70, 380–390.
Barrette, C. and Paesani, K. (eds) (2005) *Language Program articulation: Developing a Theoretical Foundation*. Boston: Heinle Thomson.
Breiner-Sanders, K.E., Lowe, Jr. P., Miles, J. and Swender, E. (2000) ACTFL Proficiency Guidelines - Speaking. Revised 1999. *Foreign Language Annals* 33 (1), 13–18.
Byrnes, H. (ed.) (2005) Perspectives. The No Child Left Behind Act and teaching and learning languages in U.S. schools. *Modern Language Journal* 89 (2), 248–282.
Byrnes, H. (ed.) (2006a) Perspectives: Interrogating communicative competence as a framework for collegiate foreign language study. *Modern Language Journal* 90 (2), 244–266.
Byrnes, H. (ed.) (2006b) Perspectives: The outcomes of collegiate FL programs: Specifications, assessment, evaluation. *Modern Language Journal* 90 (4), 574–601.
Byrnes, H. (2007a) Developing national language education policies: Reflections on the *CEFR*. *Modern Language Journal* 91 (4), 679–685.
Byrnes, H. (ed.) (2007b) Perspectives: National language education policy (R. Blake and C. Kramsch, guest editors). *Modern Language Journal* 91 (2), 247–283.
Byrnes, H. (ed.) (2007c) Perspectives: The Common European Framework of Reference: Perspectives on the making of supranational language education policy. *Modern Language Journal* 91 (4), 540–584.
Byrnes, H. (2008a) Articulating a foreign language sequence through content: A look at the culture *Standards*. *Language Teaching* 41 (1), 97–113.
Byrnes, H. (2008b) Perspectives: From representation at the federal/national level to creating a foreign language education framework. *Modern Language Journal* 92 (4), 614–631.
Byrnes, H. (2008c) Perspectives: Transforming collegiate foreign language departments: A proposal. *Modern Language Journal* 92 (2), 641–685.
Byrnes, H. (2008d) Wer hat Angst vor Englisch? Nachdenken über Deutschlehren und -lernen in den USA. In J. Limbach and K. von Ruckteschell (eds) *Die Macht der Sprache. Teil II: On-line Publikation* (pp. 132–139). Munich: Goethe-Institut. Online at http://www.goethe.de/lhr/pro/mac/Online-Publikation.pdf. Accessed on 23 July 2010.
Byrnes, H. (2009) Perspectives: The role of foreign language departments in internationalizing the curriculum. *Modern Language Journal* 93 (4), 607–627.
Byrnes, H. (2010) Perspectives: Revisiting the role of culture in the foreign language curriculum. *Modern Language Journal* 94 (2), 315–336.
Byrnes, H., Maxim, H.H. and Norris, J.M. (2010) Realizing advanced FL writing development in collegiate education: Curricular design, pedagogy, assessment. *Modern Language Journal* 94, S-1, i–ii.
Cummins, P.W. (2007) LinguaFolio: American model for the European Language Portfolio. *Modern Language Journal* 91 (1), 117–121.

Donato, R. (2009) Teacher education in the age of standards of professional practice. *Modern Language Journal* 93 (2), 267–270.
Evans, B. and Hornberger, N. (2005) No Child Left Behind: Repealing and unpeeling language education policy in the United States. *Language Policy* 4, 87–106.
Glisan, E.W. (2005) Leaving no foreign language teachers behind: A grassroots response. *Modern Language Journal* 89 (2), 268–272.
Jackson, F.H. and Malone, M.E. (2009) Building the foreign language capacity we need: Toward a comprehensive strategy for a national language framework. Online at http://www.languagepolicy.org/documents/synthesis%20and%20summaryfinal040509_combined.pdf. Accessed on 23 July 2010.
Jensen, J. (2007) National foreign language policy: A state language coordinator's perspective. *Modern Language Journal* 91 (2), 261–264.
Levine, G.S., Melin, C., Crane, C., Chavez, M. and Lovik, T.S. (2008) The language program director in curricular and departmental reform. *Profession 2008*, 240–254.
Liskin-Gasparro, J.E. (2003) The ACTFL Proficiency Guidelines and the Oral Proficiency Interview: A brief history and analysis of their survival. *Foreign Language Annals* 36 (4), 483–497.
May, S., and Hornberger, N. (eds) (2008) *Encyclopaedia of Language and Education* (2nd edn, Vol. 1: Language policy and political issues in education). New York: Springer.
McNamara, T. (2007) Language assessment in foreign language education: The struggle over constructs. *Modern Language Journal* 91 (2), 280–282.
Menken, K. (2009) No Child Left Behind and its effects on language policy. *Annual Review of Applied Linguistics* 29, 103–117.
MLA Ad Hoc Committee on Foreign Languages (2007) Foreign languages and higher education: New structures for a changed world. *Profession 2007*, 234–245.
Norris, J.M. (2006) Assessing advanced foreign language learning and learners: From measurement constructs to educational uses. In H. Byrnes, H. Weger-Guntharp and K.A. Sprang (eds) *Educating for Advanced Foreign Language Capacities: Constructs, Curriculum, Instruction, Assessment* (pp. 167–187). Washington, DC: Georgetown University Press.
O'Connell, M.E. and Norwood, J.L. (eds) (2007) *International education and foreign languages: Keys to securing America's future. Committee to review the Title VI and Fulbright-Hays International Education Programs.* Washington, DC: Center for Education, Division of Behavioral and Social Sciences and Education. The National Academy Press.
Phillips, J.K. (2003) Implications of language education policies for language study in schools and universities. *Modern Language Journal* 87 (4), 579–586.
Popkewitz, T.S. and Rizvi, F. (eds) (2009) *Globalization and the Study of Education (Yearbook of the National Society For The Study of Education).* 108 (2). Malden, MA: Wiley-Blackwell.
Rizvi, F. and Lingard, B. (2009) *Globalizing Education Policy.* New York: Routledge.
Rosenbusch, M.H. (2005) The No Child Left Behind Act and teaching and learning languages in U.S. schools. *Modern Language Journal* 89 (2), 250–261.
Rosenbusch, M.H. and Jensen, J. (2005) Status of foreign language programs in the NECTFL states. *Northeast Conference Review* 56, 24–37.
Schriewer, J. (2003) Globalisation in education: Process and discourse. *Policy Futures in Education* 1 (2), 271–283.
Schriewer, J. (ed.) (2009) *Discourse Formation in Comparative Education.* Frankfurt: Peter Lang.

Schriewer, J. and Martinez, C. (2004) Constructions of internationality in education. In G. Steiner-Khamsi (ed.) *The Global Politics of Educational Borrowing and Lending* (pp. 29–63). New York: Teachers College Press.
Scott, V.M. (ed.) (2010) *Principles and Practices of the* Standards *in College Foreign Language Education*. Boston: Heinle Cengage Learning.
Shohamy, E. (2001) *The Power of Tests: A Critical Perspective on the Uses of Language Tests.* New York: Longman.
Shohamy, E. (2008) Language policy and language assessment: The relationship. *Current Issues in Language Planning* 9 (3), 363–373.
Steiner-Khamsi, G. (ed.) (2004) *The Global Politics of Educational Borrowing and Lending.* New York: Teachers College Press.
Theiler, J. (2005) The LinguaFolio USA! initiative. *Modern Language Journal* 89 (4), 622–624.
van Houten, J. (2007) The current and potential impact of the European language portfolio on language learning in the United States. *ADFL Bulletin* 38/3 and 39/1, 15–19.
van Lier, L. (1989) Reeling, writhing, drawling, stretching, and fainting in coils: Oral proficiency interviews as conversation. *TESOL Quarterly* 23 (3), 489–508.

Asia-Pacific

China

The author:

Zou Weicheng is a professor at the Foreign Language School at East China Normal University in Shanghai China. His major fields include classroom research, acquisition issues of Chinese learners, social problems in foreign langue education, course design, development of language curriculum standards and teaching materials and language teacher preparation. He has visited and participated in programmes at universities in New Zealand, Australia, Canada, the United States and France. He was also editor-in-chief (2003–2010) of the Chinese journal *Foreign Language Learning: Theory and Practice*. In recent years he has been involved in consulting on language policies for administrators in both local and central governments, and evaluating current textbooks and foreign language curriculum standards for K-12 students. He has also participated in the organisation, course design and implementation of the K-12 in-service teacher training programmes across China.

16 Perspectives from China

Zou Weicheng

Introduction

Although China and the Chinese education system is not averse to seeking out, analysing and borrowing education policies from other countries where applicable, the impact of the *CEFR* has not been as evident as in some of the other countries represented in this volume. There is no evidence of influence at school education level and our focus is therefore on higher education. Here too the evidence is not to be found in documentation of policy change and curriculum development, and it was therefore necessary to turn directly to those involved in developing the crucial document for higher education: the Chinese College English Curriculum Requirements (CECR). The author interviewed four experts[1] involved in developing the CECR and policymaking:

Table 16.1 Interviewee information

No.	*Interviewees*	*Basic information*
1	Speaker A (SPA)	A university professor, member of the MOE College English Teaching Committee (CETC), involved in the CECR development since the 1980s.
2	Speaker B (SPB)	A university professor, member of the MOE CETC, one of the chief designers and authors of the CECR documents.
3	Speaker C (SPC)	A university professor, involved in the previous versions of the CECR before the end of the last century; a former member of the MOE CETC; a chief designer and developer for the CECR Testing system in the last 30 years.
4	Speaker D (SPD)	A university professor, one of the chief experts who advised policymakers in the MOE on the CECR; member of the MOE CETC. She was also one of the experts who first introduced the *CEFR* to the attention of policy-makers in the MOE.

The Chinese College English Curriculum Requirements (CECR)

'Chinese College English Curriculum Requirements' is a policy document for guiding college (i.e. university-level) English teaching for non-majors in terms of curriculum, pedagogy and evaluation. Since all university students have to study English, and because English is the most important foreign language taught, the course is one of the largest in scale in terms of learners, teachers and programme management in China. Each year, millions of students have to take the tests based on these curriculum requirements. The results of the test have a significant influence on students' chances for further study or employment. Because of this particular social function, no other course in Chinese education has been so much debated or has influenced the lives of so many people, learners, teachers and administrators at various levels.

The origins of the CECR system can be traced back to the early 1960s when the Ministry of Education (MOE) organised a committee of experts in English to supervise the teaching and learning of English in Chinese higher education institutions. According to SPA, 'the original purpose (of this committee) was solely for guiding textbook writing, and tests for evaluation purposes. The requirements were set for only six top universities... In 1987, the MOE began to implement CET (College English Tests, Band 4 and Band 6) for non- English majors in Chinese higher educational institutes'. It was not until the late 1980s that the committee began to look into the issues of the national curricula from which the CECR (draft) was developed in 2003, and its final version was officially put into effect in 2007, after much deliberation and revision. The interviews suggest that the influence of the *CEFR* in China is mainly reflected in the 2008 version of the CECR.

The earlier versions of the CECR, since the 1960s, were almost entirely quantitative in nature. The curriculum developers were mostly concerned with how many words a college student should learn within a given quota of teaching hours. Invariably, each version of the curriculum paid a great deal of attention to the number of words required for the students to learn within the given levels:

> Our concern was how many words you need to learn in each level [grade] at college. So the committee conducted a national survey, and found out that a high school graduate would learn about 2000 words on average. Several studies pointed to about 2000 and 2200 words. (SPC)

Skills such as reading comprehension were also defined and measured quantitatively, as SPA stated:

> Originally we thought students should reach the reading proficiency of 70 words per minute. Later on we raised the requirement to 115 per minute. The quantitative measures were very convenient to both material writers, and test designers.

However convenient the quantitative measures were for materials writers and test designers, criticisms have continued to be made by teachers and students, and the debate eventually effected a change in perspective in policy-makers from the MOE because the arguments over college English increasingly became social and political issues (Cai, 2000). As one interviewee puts it, the response was radical:

> In 2002, the policy-makers in the MOE suggested a change be made by removing the wordlist from the curriculum. (SPA)

The wordlist was found to be playing a misleading role for two reasons. First, there is a great difference in terms of what each university can achieve in language learning, given vast differences in resources and types of learners. One wordlist appropriate for one institution may be totally unachievable for another. Secondly, a wordlist together with one or two meanings in translation as a reference for each entry often gave teachers and learners a misguided understanding. Material developers and teachers would limit the materials or teaching to the few meanings given in the wordlist:

> Teachers and students would only learn those meanings of the words given in the wordlist. For example, students would learn 'school' in a sense of an educational organisation because it was translated in the wordlist in this meaning. However they had trouble when they read 'a particular school of economists' because the second sense was not given in the wordlist and therefore was not set as an objective of teaching for both material developers, and teachers. (SPB)

However, despite their criticisms, teachers and students did not in fact like the idea of removing the wordlist from the curriculum, and finally a compromise was reached to keep the wordlist but remove the translations in the current version of the CECR. This means that both materials developers and teachers have to make their own decision of what to teach according to their own teaching objectives.

The CECR and Traditions of Education and Learning

The quantitative nature of the Chinese curriculum reflects a deeply rooted Chinese belief about what constitutes language competence and how this competence is developed in learners. Although no one has ever developed a formal theory to define language competence in foreign language learning from a Chinese perspective, a widely held belief is that one first needs to know a sufficient number of words and grammatical rules for use in the future. Not only the quantity counts, but also the accuracy of such knowledge is important. It considerably facilitates communication, it is believed, if people have enough accurate knowledge in the first place, and then, when they meet the actual situations, they mobilise such knowledge for communication (Li, 1995). The underlying assumption is that one cannot develop communicative competence or language proficiency unless one has learned enough words and rules accurately.

The Chinese belief, which, in the context of language development in learners, contrasts knowledge itself with the use of such knowledge, has influenced the way to teach in the classroom, and the way to evaluate teaching and learning. With the learning of linguistic knowledge taking precedence over the use of such knowledge, teachers attach great importance to the teaching of linguistic knowledge, considering it to be the most important thing with which learners should be equipped. What a teacher should focus on is the value of such knowledge for the future use of language. SPC put this idea most succinctly in his views regarding the quantity of vocabulary for the future needs of the students:

> We calculated the frequency of the words that appeared in scientific texts that our students will read in their future academic studies. We found out that the top 6800 words in the word frequency count accounts for 99.5% of coverage in our text bank. So this means that the knowledge of these words will enable the students to meet their future needs to read books of any subject or discipline.

The underlying point in this view is that vocabulary and grammar are not universal because they are unique in each language, whereas pragmatics and sociocultural aspects are not only difficult to describe and hence to teach, but are also common to many languages. As a consequence, needless to say, they should not constitute the focus of the foreign language education in the limited hours of classroom instruction.

The severance of linguistic knowledge from its use and context has had serious consequences for Chinese college English teaching. In the first place, students were directed towards the learning of language knowledge in the belief that hard work in language knowledge would lay a solid ground for their future development. The outcomes of such a style of learning are a large number of learners who are not able to use the language for speaking or listening after a decade of learning. This phenomenon is widely criticised by the public in China as 'deaf and dumb English'. SPC criticised this 'disintegration' of language and the exclusion of pragmatics:

> Our students have focused only onto two things: vocabulary and grammar, since they began to learn English in the middle school. Vocabulary and grammar are only two parts of many things in the language. Language is somehow disintegrated if we teach two of them only. For example, there are aspects of language use, like those of pragmatics. Our teaching has excluded these aspects [of pragmatics] from [the curriculum].

The propensity toward the teaching of knowledge and ignoring the use of language has also resulted in the second consequence of the test-driven teaching style prevalent in Chinese English classrooms. It is generally thought that our current knowledge is not enough to provide us with a means to measure communicative competence in a foreign language, especially in large-scale high-stakes tests. The College English Test system is designed on the rationale of word frequency counting as SPB said above, and no matter how much the test developers improve their tests, they are criticised as 'only testing what can be tested' by SPB, and thus ignoring the differences in 'the needs, cognitive abilities, resources, locations of the students across thousands of tertiary institutions. Four or five thousand words may be a piece of cake for students in universities like XXX and YYY, yet they may be unachievable for the students in other schools or disciplines. Even if you gave them ten years, they might not achieve this goal'.

In order to help their learners to pass the CET, teachers in many universities quickly learned the most efficient way of teaching, and spent days and months helping students to prepare for the tests at the expense of applying sound pedagogical principles. Encouraged by administrators, almost all the tertiary institutes took the CET very seriously and many even made it mandatory for students to pass (60 points out of 100) before they could be awarded their degree. This policy plunged students and teachers in many institutions into an educational disaster. The CET was criticised as a harmful subject by many for poisoning the general atmosphere of education. One university president complained that 'many students spent too much time learning English in order to pass the CET. Some did nothing but take the test again and again. As there are two occasions of testing each year, some students begin from the first year, and take eight tests in a row by the time they graduate from the university' (SPA). The criticism and debate over the role of the CET reached such a political height that the MOE eventually ordered a reform of the college English teaching system in 2003. The reform movement tried to address the two problems, which laid a foundation for the CECR, the new form of the traditional Chinese College English Curriculum (CCEC), and the attempt to draw on thoughts and inspirations from the *CEFR*.

The *CEFR* and the Development of the CECR

Although the *CEFR* is a project developed over 40 years (Trim, this volume; Morrow, 2004: 3), it has only a relatively short history in China, first coming to the notice of Chinese scholars in the mid-1990s:

> I may be one of the few who came to know the *CEFR* quite early in China, in around 1996 or 1997 when I was preparing for some research in testing. The things on my mind then were how to conceptualise scales and grades of proficiency so that the new system could address our problems in describing language competence in an integrated and comprehensive way. This system should be consistent in scaling different language abilities from the low end up to the high end. I was trying to search for existing studies, looking for something like 'standards' of language abilities or proficiency skills. What came out of my search was the first draft of the European *CEFR*. Later, I introduced this document to XXXX XXXX (who was one of the chief advisors to the policymaker in the MOE). (SPB)

To address the problems discussed above, Chinese scholars felt an urgent need to construct a system that would change the traditional assessment in the much-debated CET, and SPB was impressed by the internally consistent descriptions of the global scales represented in Table 1, and the self-assessment grid in Table 2 (*CEFR*, 2001). For the first time, Chinese scholars noticed that language competence can be evaluated qualitatively in 'can-do' statements in addition to the quantitative methods.

However, the qualitative description in 'can-do' statements was not well received at the beginning for several reasons. SPA talked about the debate:

> In about 2002, XXX [the policy-maker from the MOE] made some suggestions to the committee [the CETC] about how the assessment should be reformed. He tried to simplify the issue by recommending a qualitative description in assessment. For example, he pointed out, why not say 'be able to understand the English programme in the CCTV [China Central Television] Channel 9 [an English channel] as a way to evaluate a learner's English ability'. ... I realised that he must have been advised by some scholars because it was impossible that he would have invented this 'can-do' statement for us developers. ... at that time, very few people had ever heard of the *CEFR*, and knew about the 'can-do' statements. So at the beginning, the recommendation was a bit surprising. Professor XXX [referring to SPC] strongly opposed this idea as ridiculous while others seemed to like this suggestion. Now, I can see that XXX must have been tipped off about the *CEFR* by the scholars from YYY [a place name].

The discussion of the early debate by SPA seems to confirm the fact that SPB was the person to recommend the *CEFR* to the policy-maker through his associates in research in the mid-1990s, and that initially at least there was a mixture of responses, positive and negative. The advisors and policymakers seemed to welcome the qualitative approach adopted by the *CEFR* and hoped that the CECR developers would borrow and apply it in China. However, this recommendation met considerable opposition at the beginning from the test developers (such as SPC) who considered it impractical from the testing point of view. In spite of the initial controversy, the strong support from the policy-maker played a decisive role in shaping the document of the CECR, which draws on some important thoughts and inspirations from the *CEFR*.

A general pattern emerges from the interview data in so far as all four scholars agree about the value of the *Common reference levels: global scales* and the *Self-assessment grid*. SPB first emphasised what the developers drew from the *CEFR* for the Chinese curriculum:

> Look, the *CEFR* is designed [as reference] for learning, teaching, and assessment with a comprehensive description of scales. Its principle is well defined, you see, ... action-based approach which means it is concerned with language use ... This perspective is very useful for us if we are working on the testing system. (SPB)

It is important to notice, however, that he also emphasises the underlying rationale of an action-orientation in the *CEFR*. SPA further described what elements drawn from the *CEFR* are realised in a concrete form in the CECR document whilst also referring to the action orientation:

> Our CECR is a bit like the *CEFR* now. It has something like a chart for requirements, with the statements such as 'I can apply for studies in a foreign university; I can read advertisements' – things like this. This is something new in our CECR. That means I can understand what I can do with the foreign language, that is, a general requirement for my learning. There is another new element in our CECR, i.e. the description of action, which can tell me what I can do with the language. This is something new in our requirements. (SPA)

SPA and SPB thus echoed each other on what is valued and integrated into the Chinese documents, including: (a) a global description of language abilities; (b) *can-do* statements for self-assessment for the learners; and (c) the *can-do* statements as a guide for action taken to define one's learning objectives and strategies.

SPD also emphasised the positive influence of the *CEFR* on Chinese college English teaching in that the global description helps the learners to find a point of reference for their language ability:

> In the past, people talked about scores of the TOEFL, say you got 500 in the TOEFL. The score means very little to our Chinese students if they take the test because the score won't tell you what your language ability is like. ... With this framework (of the *CEFR*), you can find out what you can do at a particular level of language scales. I think this idea has solved our biggest challenge in our assessment system.

It is this global scaling process which addresses one of the major problems with the Chinese college English teaching which we described earlier (i.e. the separation of knowledge and use in teaching, learning and assessment). The global perspective of language abilities provides an inspiration for Chinese scholars to address this issue. Instead of thinking quantitatively in terms of the number of vocabulary items or grammatical rules, now the global description of the scales enables the developers to see both wood and trees in describing language competence. The contrast is made explicit by SPB as he described what he thought to be the change in the new mentality of language learning, and contrasts the traditional approach with 'the international trend', which seems to be represented by the *CEFR*:

> Ability is not measured by how many words you have learned, or how many grammatical rules you have learned [in the *CEFR*]. They [the

> words/grammatical rules] are in fact incorporated into the description of competence ... we used to describe language knowledge like rules or words as competence. ... We split words and rules from language, as if we cut a cylinder from top to bottom, and then hand them to the students, say, here is what you need for developing your language ability ... in doing this, we had a lot of things in language missing. Now, in my opinion, our concept of language competence based on quantitative description is out of date. It has fallen behind the international trend.

SPD further confirmed this contrast of the quantitative with the 'can-do' perspective of the *CEFR* when she remarked:

> Our past practice was to focus on something quantitative in assessment. For instance, what is your reading speed? How much is your vocabulary? How many words can you write each minute? Now we think this practice is out of date, so we borrowed something from the *CEFR*, specially the can-do statements. I hoped to see more of them.

Another important concept is that of the redefinition of the four skills into understanding, speaking and writing (*CEFR*, 2001: 26) and the focus upon range, accuracy, fluency, interaction and coherence in language teaching (*CEFR*, 2001: 28–29). The CECR developers were inspired to recognise the new relationship in language skills. SPB discussed the importance of seeing language ability in terms of different aspects, and each of them should be taken into account in teaching and assessment:

> Learners need many things in language besides words and grammatical rules ... In those can-do statements, you will see different aspects of language, such as skills like speaking, listening, and speaking and listening with other people, i.e. the interactive listening and speaking. This is a solution to our problem of seeing language competence as separate skills.

As a result of this perspective, the CECR recommends the following principle to approach the curriculum, pedagogy and evaluation:

> The objective of College English is to develop students' ability to use English in a well-rounded way, especially in listening and speaking, so that in their future studies and careers as well as social interactions they will be able to communicate effectively, and at the same time enhance their ability to study independently and improve their general cultural

> awareness so as to meet the needs of China's social development and international exchange. (MOE, 2008: 9)

SPA also mentioned the importance of meeting the different needs of learners in the approach to the development of the CECR, an echo of the focus on needs analysis in earlier stages of the work of the Council of Europe team (Richterich & Chancerel, 1977):

> We're not just teaching for the examinations like the CET. ... Our requirements should allow the students to do different things according to their needs, ... like someone aiming at the high end of the goals, ... but someone maybe, says, we don't want to learn English so much. I need something practical, like learn to read, read those good articles. ... So I think the ideas in the *CEFR* are really good things for China if they can be introduced to here because it is not test-driven in nature in the first place.

Strong evidence of the impact the *CEFR* has had on the CECR is the liberation of thousands of college students from the rigid system of CET assessment in recognition of the variety, differences, and gaps in needs, resources and cultures in which millions of Chinese college students are situated. The current CECR, implemented in 2008, for the first time forsook the administrative power to require every university to use the CET, and to require that their students pass it in order be awarded a degree (MOE, 2008: 5). Instead, it proposes three levels of requirements (equivalents of *CEFR* levels of scale) based on the global descriptions together with some quantitative information as a compromise in the conflict between the old system and the new one. The three levels of requirements are: (a) basic requirements, a minimum guide for all undergraduate students; (b) intermediate requirements, a selective guide for those who opt to aim higher than basic requirements; and (c) advanced requirements, a selective guide for those who have ambitious goals of teaching and learning.

Critiques of the *CEFR*

In spite of its influence on the CECR, the *CEFR* is not taken without critique by Chinese scholars, even within the group of the CECR developers. In a comment on the theory of language teaching in the *CEFR*, SPA remarked:

> The thoughts conveyed in the *CEFR* about language teaching reflect the general theory of language learning, and many of those ideas in fact had

> already been introduced to China well before we knew about the *CEFR*.

The interviewees also criticised the readability of the text of the *CEFR*. For example, SPA said that this has consequences for its dissemination:

> The *CEFR* is not easy to understand, and very few people know about this document, even within our group [referring to the group of developers of the CECR].

He also expressed his doubts on the value of a qualitative or global approach to defining descriptors:

> Besides it is hard to design a test based on 'can-do' statements, and you still need something quantitative for testing. Our teaching is now still very much test-driven, and therefore, they (descriptors) don't have much practical use for us now. In our CECR there are still quantitative elements, which may be a fundamental difference from the spirit of the *CEFR*.

Similarly, SPD argued that quantification is necessary in a high-stakes testing system for millions of students. She took the views of one critic of the CET seriously but thought that they were impractical:

> One scholar from XXX [a place name] criticised the CET system, … 'you worked out this fancy system for measuring only a tiny portion in one's language competence. I can work out a clear description of a student's language ability within ten minutes' talk with him'. … I must say, this scholar is a real scholar as a linguist. However, he did not study language education. Anyone working in language education would know a high- stakes testing system like the CET is very special … each year there are over ten million students to sit this exam. Where can we find enough scholars like him to talk to each student for ten minutes? That's not the only problem, even though you can find enough specialists, how can you guarantee each specialist would faithfully apply your standards when they measure the students? So you can't avoid the quantitative measures in the standards.

In short, the interviewees unanimously agreed on the need to value the *CEFR* as a reference, rather than as a model to be copied as a whole in the face of challenges in China:

> I know that our current situation does not allow us to transfer all the ideas and proposals from the *CEFR* to China. Like what I said just now, our system is different from the situation in Europe. Our teaching is still very much based on reading textbooks, learning vocabulary and working on grammatical rules in the classroom. As complementary measures, some teachers may design task-based activities for the learners. This is because of our teachers' beliefs about language, language development and language teaching. Besides, we need to consider the environment in which our students are learning, including our traditions of learning. That is, we are accustomed to cutting language into numerous discrete points, and then passing them one by one to our learners. For this reason Chinese education was once criticised for killing the critical spirit in the students. ... We are in a dilemma. ... If we introduce the concepts behind the 'can-do' statements and the *CEFR*, and promote them in our teacher development, our teachers would not accept this because they grew up from a culture that does not emphasise these [skills, use of language]. On the other hand, there is a very strong testing culture in our education. This testing system, frankly speaking, can only test what can be tested. And it directed our teaching in the classroom in the wrong direction, a direction away from developing ability in the learners. ... Our system has a lot to be improved, ... it is not that we don't understand those ideas from Europe, but we are more concerned with their applicability to solve our problems. Good concepts as they are, they will be adopted only if they can be useful in solving our problems. So we are not so much concerned with the theoretical value of the framework, as its practical value to address our problem. (SPB)

SPA also pointed out that learning from another culture may sometimes be superficial. For example, with regard to the European Language Portfolio – a tool for developing autonomous learning and plurilingualism (*CEFR*, 2001: 4) – Chinese curriculum developers were much inspired by it at the beginning. Borrowing this idea, together with the tools such as the self-assessment grid, language passports, language biography and dossiers, they designed an instrument called 'Self-Assessment / Peer Assessment Form for Student's English Competence' as an important tool recommended to the teachers and learners. However, according to SPA:

> They don't have much use in fact as a guide for the teacher or learners. The [self-assessment] forms were designed to encourage learners' autonomous learning, especially when the large-scale intranet is introduced into our language classrooms. Students were encouraged to

> work on their own on the network with computers. If they use this form to manage their learning experience, they may know how much they have learned. However, reality tells us that these forms are just forms in the appendix, having little value in real use.

Although the conflict between global descriptors and quantitative measures for defining language levels is hard to resolve in China, as these scholars have pointed out, new efforts are now underway to soften the conflict. Interestingly enough, SPC, who was a most vehement opponent to the concept of 'can-do' at the beginning, is now actively involved in a project with a group of young scholars to test various descriptors borrowed from the *CEFR* in order to adapt them to describe Chinese learners' global language competence. In describing his recent project, he remarked:

> Now I'm working with a group of young scholars and also many experienced teachers to test those descriptors. Our goal is to test how truthfully they can reflect different scales of language proficiency of Chinese learners. Our ultimate goal is to establish a Chinese framework like the *CEFR* for teaching, learning, and assessing our language learning, ... not just English, but also second languages such as dialects, languages of national minorities.

Conclusions

The interviews suggest that Chinese scholars came to notice the value of the *CEFR* because they were troubled by the issues that are common in many countries. In other words, what influenced Chinese scholars is actually a result of a selective learning process. Students learn what they need instead of what is intended by the original designers of the system. Indeed, the global description and the 'can-do' statements are not intended in the *CEFR* as an antidote to quantitative measures, and quantitative measures are indeed not harmful if they are used properly. In fact, the *CEFR* is an instrument for working at the macro level of supporting language teaching, learning and assessment in member states within the Council of Europe, and it is the rigour of the work on global description, levels of scales, presentation of theories of language and language development that really helped Chinese scholars to understand the complexity of language teaching. The best thing about the global description of language ability and the can-do statements in the *CEFR* is its convenience for teachers, administrators, materials writers, programme managers, employers who may be interested in assessing language proficiency and the general public who do not understand the technical jargon in language issues, to compare language ability of learners with diverse learning, social and cultural backgrounds. On the other hand, in most of the interview data, the scholars dwelled upon the technical aspects of description, and especially the accuracy and comprehensiveness of the work, and for this reason they did not recommend the *CEFR* as an important source of thoughts to be made known to the teachers for whom the CECR is developed.

Our investigation thus indicates that the *CEFR* has had a substantial influence in China, especially in the process of college English curriculum development. Motivated by the pressing issues at home for a new conceptual framework for language proficiency and language development, the CECR developers paid special attention to the global descriptions of levels and the self-assessment grid. The qualitative method to define language competence in 'can-do' statements has thus provided an important inspiration for the development of the CECR released in 2008. However, as many ideas of language learning had already been introduced into China well before scholars discovered the work of the *CEFR*, they seemed to be more influenced by the technical aspects of the work, especially the rigour and the systematic method to describe the levels of proficiency. Anyone who is familiar with the *CEFR* would immediately find its influence in the new document of the CECR, which is a very important beginning for the *CEFR* in making its influence known to more teachers and scholars in China in the years to come.

Notes

(1) The author would like to thank the four scholars for the interviews, and Mr Cen Haibing and Ms Ouyang Fengzhi for assistance with interviews, transcription and data processing.

References

Cai, J.G. (2000) *ELT at Tertiary Level in China: Review, Reflection and Research.* Shanghai: Fudan University Press.

Council of Europe (2001) *Common European Framework of Reference for Languages: Learning, Teaching, Assessment*. Oxford: Oxford University Press.

Li, G.Y. (1995) Adopting useful elements from different schools to address our problems. In G.Y. Li (ed.) *ELT with Chinese Characteristics*. Shanghai: Shanghai Foreign Language Education Press.

MOE (2008) *College English Curriculum Requirements* (CECR). Beijing: Tsing Hua University Press.

Morrow, K. (2004) Background to the CEF. In K. Morrow (ed.) *Insights from the Common European Framework*. Oxford: Oxford University Press.

Richterich, R. and Chancerel, J-L. (1977) *Identifying the Needs of Adults Learning a Foreign Language*. Oxford: Pergamon Press.

Japan

The authors:

Masako Sugitani is a professor in the Faculty of Foreign Language Studies at Kansai University in Osaka. She studied German Language and Culture at Kyushu National University in Fukuoka, in the south of Japan, and, after a period as research assistant at Hiroshima National University, she has taught German language and culture at Kansai University.

Since the 1990s she has been involved in the organisation of in-service courses in teaching methodology at regional and national level, often with the support of the Goethe Institute and the DAAD because there are few opportunities in Japan for teacher development except for English. She has been Vice President of the Japan Association for Language Policy since 2008.

At Kansai University she is concerned with trans-language teacher training. Students of English, French, Spanish, Chinese, Korean or Japanese as a foreign language take courses in the language teaching theory of the 'other' languages, and thereby gain 'foreign perspectives' beyond the boundaries of national languages, carrying their insights over into their 'own' language. This approach is new but has proved to be effective, especially because, in the age of globalisation, and despite a strong influence from the United States, Japan can act as a meeting place for concepts from Asia and Europe.

Yuichi Tomita worked as a high school teacher of English in Tokyo for 11 years before moving to teach at Fukushima University for 11 years, then Daito Bunka University for ten years until March 2011. He is now teaching Japanese at Manchester University in the UK. He is interested in elementary school foreign language/intercultural education, and has been actively involved in teacher training, materials creation and other initiatives in this area for many years, including ongoing involvement with NHK (the national TV broadcaster) educational programmes in the field. He is an advocate of foreign language education *not* being equated with English in Japan, and thinks that the *CEFR* could help to break some of the fixed ideas about language education in Japan.

17 Perspectives from Japan

Masako Sugitani and Yuichi Tomita

Introduction

The *Common European Framework of Reference for Languages* (*CEFR*) was translated into Japanese by foreign language education specialists Shigeru Yoshijima (a specialist in German), Rie Ohashi (a specialist in English) and other members of a multilingual team in 2004, and was published with the support of the Goethe-Institut Japan.[1] The translation was received with interest in foreign language education circles in Japan, and was the subject of discussion at a number of national conferences, including the Japan Association of College English Teachers (2005), the Asociación Japonesa de Hispanistas (2007), the Japanische Gesellschaft für Germanistik (2008), the Société Japonaise de Didactique du Français (2009) and the Japan Association for Language Policy (2009). Specialists on the *CEFR*, including a representative of the secretariat of the Council of Europe, were invited to several of these conferences.

As in the rest of the world, the rise of globalization has sparked increased interest in foreign language education in Japan, and this has led to debates about the *CEFR* in high school, university and college foreign language education circles, as well as attempts to apply it in some areas. As described later in this chapter, many of these efforts have involved the creation of can-do statements and their assessment, and the predominant target language is English. At the same time, 'plurilingualism' and 'pluriculturalism', two of the main tenets of the *CEFR*, are referred to very obliquely if at all in official documents related to foreign language education in Japan, and are not part of the prevalent discourse of society or culture in Japan.

Furthermore, there is a significant gap in the influence of the *CEFR* between school education and university education. In school education, which is very tightly controlled by central government, reference to the *CEFR* is scarcely evident, and there is little general interest at present in appropriating the *CEFR* in national policy for compulsory education, although awareness of the *CEFR* is growing among policy-makers and teachers. In university education, on the other hand, there is a great deal more freedom, and this has facilitated much greater interest and influence, as will be described in this chapter.

The first section of this chapter provides a broad overview of the characteristics of foreign language education in Japan. The situation of 'multilingual education' in university education will then be considered, followed by discussion of the *CEFR* in relation to English education in Japan. Finally, 'Japanese as a foreign language' and 'Chinese/Korean' will be discussed as areas in which initiatives to incorporate the *CEFR* are more widely apparent, and in which there is potential to pursue measures for real learning guidelines.

The Dominance of English and its Social Function

As far as education policy in the area of foreign language education in Japan is concerned, the only foreign language that really exists is English. This was evident, for example, in the publication of the 'Action Plan to Cultivate Japanese with English abilities' in 2003. This fact needs to be set within the historical context of foreign language education in Japan. From the time Japan opened up to the world at the beginning of the Meiji era in the 1860s, foreign language education has been an important means of modernization. In the education reforms implemented during the post-war US occupation period, it was compulsory to study one foreign language during the three years of junior high school, which was part of compulsory education, and in 1947 provisional teaching guidelines for English were published. In policy terms, therefore, everyone in this stage of education in Japan was provided with the opportunity to study a foreign language, but in real terms there were very few opportunities to study the languages of neighbouring countries; students opting to study these languages were a small minority, and almost all schools offered only English. The equation 'Foreign language = English' is still alive and well today, an example being that almost all national and public universities, together with most private universities, assume that students will have studied English before they arrive at university. According to statistics from the National Centre for University Entrance Examinations, which runs the central university entrance examination taken by the majority of high school students wanting to obtain university places, 513,898 examinees out of a total of 553,368 took one of the five foreign language examinations provided by the centre in 2010. However, as can be seen from the following breakdown of languages chosen by applicants, almost 100% took English:

> English 99.84%, German 0.02%, French 0.03%, Chinese 0.07%, Korean 0.03% (National Centre for University Entrance Examinations, 2010).

The percentage of all examinees opting for the foreign language examination was 98.7%, exceeding Japanese (the national language) at 95.7%, and the foreign language examination generally has more applicants than any of the other examination subjects. The choice of subjects taken in the national centre examination is determined by criteria laid down by universities, which set their own subject admission requirements, and this is reflected in the situation of English – the stated educational aim of which is to 'develop communicative competence' – being the subject of choice in senior high school.

On the other hand, with the progress of globalization, there has been an increase in recent years in the number of schools offering foreign languages other than English as an optional subject alongside the formal curriculum of 'Foreign Language (English)'. The number of such schools rose from 947 senior high schools in 1999 to 2027 of the total 5242 senior high schools nationwide in 2008. However, the Ministry of Education, Culture, Sports, Science and Technology (MEXT) only issues 'Courses of Study for English', and there are no measures to produce 'Courses of Study' for other languages, with the only provision made being that other languages should 'be in line with guidelines for English', regardless of differences in the number of hours available for study or differences in the nature of the language, such as in the case of Chinese (MEXT, undated).

Influence of the *CEFR* on University Foreign Language Education

The impact of the *CEFR* in Japan has been seen predominantly in universities, where students usually follow a liberal arts curriculum for the first 18 months to two years, which includes the study of a number of languages. As a criterion of establishment, universities must have one compulsory foreign language, but two foreign languages are common and, although this is a minority, there are examples of students having to take three or more foreign languages. In the case of two foreign languages, provision may be in the form of completely optional or semi-optional (e.g. students must take a language but can choose which one), but the general situation is that students start learning one foreign language *ab initio* at university. The most common languages offered as options are Chinese, Korean, German, French, Spanish and Russian.[2]

As an example of the influence of the *CEFR*, Ibaraki University introduced an English education reform programme in 2002, and by 2008 it had set up a university-wide 'General English programme' using the CEFR.

Foreign language education reforms at many other universities, such as Keio University, Kansai University of Foreign Studies, Meijo University, Osaka University of Foreign Studies and Kokugakuin University have also made reference to methods proposed in the *CEFR* and have introduced it to a greater or lesser extent. In the 'foreign language centres' or the corresponding facilities of a number of traditional national universities, such as Tsukuba University, Kyoto University, Kobe University, Kanazawa University and Hiroshima University, symposia and applications of the *CEFR* are being implemented.

The following features are apparent in such applications. Even though the *CEFR* was designed to provide a common European framework for language learning, teaching and assessment regardless of language and country, almost all universities in Japan, from Ibaraki University onwards, have focused predominantly on the can-do statements in the *CEFR* and have applied them to only one language, which in the majority of cases is English. As described earlier, the reason for this is the high social interest in English ability, combined with the perceived lack of students' ability to use English even after six years of English education at secondary school level. Another reason is that many students see as problematic the fact that the aims and assessment of English, which they are obliged to study once or twice a week for one or two years or more after entering university, are so diverse. In this context, the introduction of a common assessment framework based on the *CEFR*, together with the development of can-do statements, primarily served to provide transparency and a focus of mutual collaboration in the provision and assessment of more effective English education among those responsible for providing it. There are also suggestions that reform of understanding about 'teaching and learning foreign languages' is important, in that the development and application of can-do statements is in itself insufficient for the overarching aim of 'foreign language education reform', both for educators and students (Fukuda, 2009). In introducing the can-do statements, basic debate on the aims and evaluation of 'English education and learning' is a prerequisite for educators and learners, and this highlights the problem of higher education institutions providing 'general foreign language education', when they are naturally founded on the principle of 'specialism'. The contradiction between general education and specialist education becomes even starker when the foreign language is being studied *ab initio*, and it becomes even more difficult to trial effective foreign language education reforms based on the *CEFR* at a university-wide level.

An example of *CEFR* assessment being introduced across all languages is the reform programme undertaken by Osaka University of Foreign Studies (which merged with Osaka University from 2007) from 2004 to 2006. At this university the initiative was confined to the 25 languages taught as majors, and did not encompass languages taught as part of general education. In this case, the *CEFR* served the function of meta-narrative in establishing achievement targets based on the *CEFR* can-do list (the American Standards for Foreign Language Learning in the 21st century (SFLL) were considered to be difficult to refer to, and a measure of students' language ability was necessary), providing transparency for the creation of achievement objectives and assessment over four years. The initiative continued through the merger with Osaka University, and was effective in changing awareness among faculty members specializing in fields such as literature or economics who had refused to acknowledge foreign language education as a specialist area.

The reforms also included use of the self-assessment checklist produced in Switzerland for English, the language previously studied by students, as well as development of a Russian curriculum in line with the standard national examination in Russia, and employment of can-do statements as a common index for 'Japanese as a foreign language' in the provision of information to learners of Japanese outside Japan. In this way the initial initiative, which focused exclusively on the assessment of foreign language education within Japan, is beginning to cross national borders and develop potential for mutual comparison and exchange (Osaka University of Foreign Studies Committee for Educational Improvement, 2006).

As this example shows, the *CEFR* is gradually exerting greater influence on the world of foreign language education at university level in Japan, but most initiatives involving the *CEFR* tend to focus on creating transparency in terms of achievement objectives and assessment through development and use of can-do statements, or on quality assurance of foreign language education through such measures. In most cases, the application of can-do statements precedes discussion of the concept of the *CEFR* as a whole. The reason for this, as explained in the previous section, is criticism of the achievement objectives and assessment of general foreign language education as being arbitrary. Criticism of English is particularly severe, with a major factor here being the needs of society, including the business world. In response to this high-level of social interest, there is a tendency for the focus in English to be on 'assessment transparency' and 'common achievement objectives'. In contrast, although their prevalence is much lower, languages other than English tend to focus on the promotion of independent learning, motivation and lifelong learning when they refer to the *CEFR*, with use of the language portfolio for the purposes of self-assessment and the internalization of learning strategies.

The difference between English and other languages can be exemplified by two quotations. The former President of the Japan Association of College English Teachers, Ikuo Koike, emphasizes how the systematic consistency of the *CEFR* levels can be used to improve efficiency in English education:

> In Japan, which has no choice but to go with the worldwide tide of increasing globalization, the level of communicative competence in English, a communication tool and an international language, has to improve dramatically compared to now. The effort of individuals is necessary for this purpose, but it is also a national policy problem. The realization of this requires a coherent system covering all stages of school education to measure effectiveness. Our proposal is to make the *CEFR* Japanese version the mainstay of this system (Koike, 2008).

In contrast, Kazumi Sakai, a German specialist, rings warning bells about the danger of over-emphasizing the levels alone:

> If we do not understand the principles embodied in the *CEFR*, and merely transplant part of it, specifically the 'common levels', wholesale into the context of language education in Japan, surely it will be nothing more than continuation of the bad habit of recasting western civilization, a path we have followed on and on since the Meiji era (Sakai, 2009).

Finally, the approach emphasizing the *CEFR* as a structure for intercultural communicative competence for intercultural encounters and intercultural adaptation is apparent in the language portfolio developed by the Japan Association for Language Teachers (JALT). JALT is an association that transcends the boundaries of language groups within Japan, with Japanese and native speakers of English and other languages working together to improve language education. One of its special interest groups, the Framework & Language Portfolio (FLP) Group, has developed a language portfolio for use with university students in Japan. The main aim of the language portfolio is stated as being 'to motivate students to take responsibility for their own learning by facilitating self-assessment and the setting of clear language leaning goals', and it aims to lay the grounds for lifelong learning by emphasizing agency and awareness in language learning. The publication edited by the FLP-SIG (Schmidt *et al.,* 2010) provides theoretical and practical consideration of the applications of the *CEFR* in Japan at the present time, and is a rich source of information on the current situation.

The *CEFR* and English

In examining the influence of the *CEFR* on English as a foreign language in Japan, the two aspects that need to be considered are the influence on English education in formal education institutions and the influence on English proficiency examinations in general society.

The growing influence of the *CEFR* on university education was described in the previous section, but what is particularly notable in the field of English education is the way in which the clarity and scales of the *CEFR* have become the overriding focus of attention. In this sense, the *CEFR* is highly attractive because it provides the transparency, progression and coherence that are seen to be lacking in many university curricula. This is in contrast to schools, where detailed Courses of Study furnished by the government provide a clear structure for language education, including grammatical structures to be mastered, the number of vocabulary items to be memorized and the language functions and situations to be covered.[3]

The structure provided by the Courses of Study, together with authorized textbooks and Teacher Manuals corresponding to the Course of Study, lead to a situation where teachers and students throughout Japan are all following a common, organized curriculum, but it also means that teachers themselves have little flexibility in deciding the content or structure of education in schools. This probably explains why the *CEFR* has had little impact so far on schools in general in Japan, and indeed is unlikely to do so unless it is promoted top-down from national government level. This will be a long process, and there are no signs at present that the government is particularly interested in using the *CEFR* in the next cycle of reforms of the Course of Study, although this may happen. While some junior and senior high schools and teachers do experiment with their own curricula, and may be aware of the *CEFR*, they are still very much the exception rather than the rule.

The main category of these exceptions in the field of English education has been the Super English Language High Schools (SELHi), which were established through the 'Action Plan' mentioned above. Unlike regular high schools, the remit of SELHi was to go beyond the Course of Study to offer extended and enriched English education. In order to do this, it was obviously necessary to look for examples of foreign language education beyond the status quo in Japan, and some schools, such as Kochi-Minami High School, Fukiai High School and Izumi High School, decided to use the *CEFR* in their SELHi initiatives. The main aspects of the *CEFR* used by these schools were 'independent English learning' and 'establishment of achievement objectives for classes'. However, it must be stressed that awareness and use of the *CEFR* among English teachers in Japanese schools is still very limited, and these SELHi are not representative of the general situation in Japan.

Perhaps because of the lack of potential for flexibility in school education, or perhaps because of greater insularity and lack of networking outside Japan in the field of English education compared to other foreign language education circles in Japan, it is probably fair to say that English lagged behind other languages in Japan in terms of research on the implications and application of the *CEFR* for language education. As mentioned in the previous section, the main research project so far on the application of the *CEFR* to English education in Japan has been the project led by Ikuo Koike, which was carried out by a group of 24 researchers engaged in English education in Japan. However, as the title of the project ('Pioneering basic research using second language acquisition research to ensure coherent, linked English education from elementary school through junior high and senior high school to university') clearly states, the initial aim of the project, which began in 2004, had nothing to do with the *CEFR*, but was intended to apply Second Language Acquisition research to English education in Japan. It is for this reason that most members of the project team were specialists in second language acquisition. It was only during the course of the project that some members of the project group mentioned the *CEFR*. A visit to the Council of Europe in Strasbourg was scheduled into a tour of Europe to study language education in various countries, and the main focus of the project subsequently shifted drastically to application of the *CEFR* to English education in Japan. As a result, the final report contains a considerable amount of content related to research on the *CEFR*. However, most of this research is concerned with issues such as the validity of the six levels and application of the standards to Japan; there has been very little attention to the wider issues raised in the *CEFR*. In particular, the research project was conceived and organized as a project to research English education, members of the project group are exclusively from the field of English education, and the key issue of plurilingualism has not featured as being of any relevance to application of the *CEFR* to Japan in this project. On the positive side, members of the project group have conducted a considerable amount of research on aspects of the application of the *CEFR* in English education in Japan (e.g. Negishi, 2006, 2011), which has added to research already being conducted by others (e.g. Naganuma, 2007, 2009).

Although there may not have been many active initiatives from researchers in English education to engage with researchers in other language fields in Japan, the plurilingual emphasis of the *CEFR* means that it has acted as a catalyst to bring together researchers and educators engaged in different languages in Japan. This is no small feat. There is a historical barrier in Japan between the academic field of English education and those of other languages, and many researchers and educators in English education in Japan have surprisingly little knowledge of and almost no contact with other language education fields. As mentioned above, the *CEFR* has brought people from English education together with people from other language fields in symposia and publications, often for the first time, and this is proving to be an extremely rich experience for those in the English education field, as they find out more about Japanese language education, Chinese language education or other areas they were previously unaware of. This new knowledge is then being reflected back into publications directed at English education researchers and teachers. For example, an October 2010 special issue of *English Education*, the national professional journal for English teachers in Japan, focused on the impact of the *CEFR* on language education in Japan, and included an article by Masako Sugitani (a German specialist) on 'Understanding the foundations of the *CEFR*' and an article by Tomoko Kaneda on 'An initiative applying the *CEFR* to Japanese language education'.

Besides research and education, there is now also interest in Japan in the alignment of existing English language proficiency tests to *CEFR* levels. For example, considerable effort has been expended in aligning the most widely used English proficiency examination in Japan, the STEP (Society for Testing English Proficiency) or 'Eiken' test, established in 1963, to *CEFR* levels, and this has been recognized, with the UK Border Agency, for example, allowing STEP Grade 1 as C1, Grade Pre-1 as B2, Grade 2 as B1, Grade Pre-2 as A2 and Grade 3 as A1.[4] Similarly, scores for the four skills in the Global Test of English Communication (GTEC), administered by the Bennesse Corporation, are aligned to A2, B1, B2 and C1. The majority of school and university students, as well as many adults, take these tests at least once in their lifetime, and often much more frequently. For example, 2.3 million people took Eiken (STEP) tests in the 2010 academic year alone. While the majority of these test-takers are not consciously aware of the alignment of English tests in Japan with international standards, specifically the *CEFR*, it cannot be denied that the *CEFR* is exerting a growing influence over language testing and, consequently, language education in Japan.

The *CEFR* and 'Japanese as a Foreign Language'

The area in which the *CEFR* has had the greatest impact in Japan has probably been Japanese as a foreign language (JFL). There were demands in Japanese language education circles in Europe for the establishment of a curriculum adapted to the *CEFR* can-do statements in order to promote Japanese language education at the secondary level. The Japan Foundation, which works to promote the spread of Japanese language education abroad, published *Japanese language education in Europe and the Common European Framework of Reference for Languages* by the Association of Japanese Language

Teachers in Europe in 2005. Building on its experience of the 1980s and 1990s, when the number of Japanese language learners rose exponentially internationally, an initiative to develop criteria that could be shared internationally in the teaching of Japanese and were in line with the *CEFR* was undertaken, a trial version was published in 2009, and the Japan Foundation Standards for Japanese Language Education were published in March 2010. The debate surrounding this initiative also took into account the establishment of National Standards in various countries and, as the title indicates, this was developed as a 'Standard' rather than as a 'Framework of Reference'.

With the increase in the number of learners of Japanese in many areas of the world, especially in Asia, can-do statements are being developed for the evaluation of Japanese language competence, using the Profil Deutsch as a point of reference. They are categorized into: (1) Can-do language activities; (2) Can-do communication strategies; (3) Can-do texts; and (4) Can-do language competences (linguistic competence, sociolinguistic competence, pragmatic competence), and it is expected they will be used as 'Japanese language education standards for mutual understanding'. In examples of the can-do statements currently published, personal interaction, language learning, daily life, professional life and environmental issues seem to dominate. The socio-cultural contents characteristic of the *CEFR* and the field of political and social systems of the linguacultural region found in the Profil Deutsch, as well as the organization of language activities and domains made with reference to issues such as intercultural coexistence and participation in social decision-making, are not clearly evident at present. In the future, it can be predicted that 'Japanese standards', based on the *CEFR*, will be actualized within the context of language interaction in East Asia.

'Learning Targets' in Chinese and Korean

Chinese and Korean are the most popular foreign languages learned after English. These are the languages of neighbouring countries and major minority groups in Japan, and interest in them is high among Japanese students because of the media and opportunities for direct contact through school trips and other means.

An attempt to incorporate an integrated conceptualization of *CEFR* intercultural education and language education can be seen in the newly developed 'Learning targets' (provisional version) for Chinese and Korean at senior high school. This is the result of an initiative coordinated by the International Cultural Forum Association, whereby university staff responsible for teacher training and senior high school teachers came together to work on a project funded by MEXT, the Ministry of Education, from 2006 to 2007. As such, there is no connection with the official Courses of Study, and the project has no official authority. However, it was developed with reference to the *CEFR* together with specialists in Japanese language education such as Professor Yasuhiko Tosaku, who was the chairperson of the Japanese section of the *US Standards for Foreign Language Learning in the 21st Century* (ACTFL, 2001) and specialists in English education, and it is now in the process of revision.

The 'Learning Targets' have moved away from the traditional language structure to an activity-based syllabus, and learning objectives are presented as 'communicative competence indices'. The communicative competence indices are divided into the two categories of 'language field' and 'cultural field', which are integrated into units through 'topics'. In contrast to the application of the *CEFR* in English, where language structure through can-do statements is the main focus, and topic content is an afterthought, the 'targets' present the 'cultural field' as a structured 'field of topics of cultural context and phenomena' that high school learners need to know. Korean has 14 areas, ranging from 'language', 'me and the people around me' and 'school' to 'society', while Chinese has 16 topics, including 'myself, friends and family', 'daily life', 'school/education', 'eating habits', 'interacting with people', 'community', 'annual events', 'Chinese and China' and 'Japanese and Japan'. Expressions and vocabulary for each topic are provided. This categorization is similar to that found in the Threshold Level, but is not identical. There are also language activities aimed at encouraging learners to compare and critically reflect on the target language, society and culture and their own language, culture and society as a basis for interaction. Furthermore, it is proposed that language activities should not be restricted to language classes, but should be conducted in coordination with other subjects such as geography and history, and extended beyond the classroom.

The 'communicative competence indices' are divided into four levels, which range from 'ability to transmit basic information' to 'ability to manage to cope in unpredicted situations, and speak and write to some extent in a coherent way'. In Korean, the levels are set as the equivalent of A1 to A2 of the *CEFR*. Each of the 16 topic categories is divided into four levels, with language activity indices, examples of learning activities, language materials and cultural fields. For example, one of the language activities for 'Japanese', which encourages students to discuss their own perspectives on language, is 'Write and present in Chinese the views you have gained of the unique features of Japanese through the process of studying English and Chinese'.

As is evident from this overview, the emphasis in the *CEFR*-influenced 'Targets', within the context of increasing social interest in these languages in Japan, is on continued work to develop an integrated perspective of language and culture learning rather than on can-do statements. Revision work was carried out in 2010 to standardize topic areas across Chinese and Korean, to present four levels in the three modes of 'speaking/writing', 'listening/reading' and 'interaction' and very motivating initiatives are being promoted in a framework of 'cultural field competence indices', comprising: (1) Observation/awareness/discovery; (2) Comparison; (3) Discussion of factors in similarity and difference; and (4) Intercultural negotiation and mediation.

Influence of the *CEFR* – Discussion and Prospects

We have shown that the *CEFR* is exerting an influence in foreign language education circles in Japan, although not yet to any great extent in official government and policy circles. What are its specific features?

The clearest influences of the *CEFR* in foreign language education circles in Japan, especially in universities, are most striking in two areas. In the teaching of English as an international language, there is a move towards transparency and efficiency of learning objectives and assessment systems as common concepts, together with the development of independent can-do statements. The measures to establish an assessment system across different languages at Osaka University of Foreign Studies can be seen as a similar movement. Within this context, initiatives such as that taken within JALT to develop a 'language portfolio' across a range of languages, aiming to encourage learners' independence through 'the development of learning competence' are apparent.

There is a growing realization in many universities that the development of can-do statements requires fundamental debate among teachers and students regarding the aims and assessment of 'English teaching/learning'. At the same time, the significance of retaining foreign language teaching as an element of liberal arts education in higher education is being questioned, as is the relationship between this and specialist education. This issue is thrown into even sharper relief in the case of learning new languages *ab initio*, and can make collaboration between staff difficult. In the process of globalization, as debate develops in the context of requiring higher levels of intercultural competence and citizenship education, there is potential for change in the aims and social status of foreign language education and liberal arts education, which since the Meiji era have centred on European languages mainly as a tool of modernization. For this reason, there is a need to debate how to contextualize the *CEFR* structurally in Japan before thinking about the application of can-do statements.

On the other hand, the *CEFR* is also having an influence on the education of neighbouring languages, Chinese and Korean, in the creation of language communicative competence indices that incorporate intercultural learning factors. Of course, the influence of the experience of the Japanese committee of the US *Standards for Foreign Language Learning in the 21st Century* is also discernible. However, at a time when the *CEFR* is being put to easy use as an assessment tool, especially for English as an international language (Byram, 2009), it is very interesting that it is being used in a learning programme initiative that includes intercultural competence in a systematic way in Chinese and Korean education. There is even the potential here that the development of this learning programme for Chinese and Korean – languages of neighbouring countries taught as second foreign languages – could have an impact on the rethinking of learning methods and assessment in the first foreign language, English.

The development of an integrated learning programme that combines language and intercultural understanding is contributing to the development of a common syllabus for Chinese and Korean for senior high school students. This initiative offers a promising precedent in Japan, where barriers between different language circles have traditionally been high. The path to more coherent, collaborative policy and practice in foreign language education in Japan will not be smooth, but if the *CEFR* becomes an important point of reference in government policy, the Courses of Study and teacher education, it is possible. However long it takes, this is a path that can be forged and, in our view, should be forged, for the sake of future generations of language learners throughout Japan.

Notes

(1) The Japanese version of the *CEFR* was published by Asahi Press, with a second edition being published in 2008.

(2) In national and private foreign language universities, minority Asian and European languages and African languages are also provided.

(3) For example, see the Course of Study for Foreign Languages for junior high school at http://www.mext.go.jp/component/a_menu/education/micro_detail/__icsFiles/afieldfile/2011/04/11/1298356_10.pdf

(4) UK Border Agency Tier 1 Approved English Language Tests (http://www.ukba.homeoffice.gov.uk/sitecontent/documents/partners-other-family/english-tests-partners.pdf). However, the Japanese tests are not included in the stricter revised list published in April 2011 (http://www.ukba.homeoffice.gov.uk/sitecontent/applicationforms/new-approved-english-tests.pdf).

References

Byram, M. (2009) Der Gemeinsame europäische Referenzrahmen in der europäischen Praxis. *Deutschunterricht in Japan* 14, 84–92.

Fukuda, H. (2009) The possibilities of application of the *CEFR* in the field of English in Japan. *Ibaraki University Department of Human Communication Studies Journal* 6, 25–41.

Koike, I. (2008) Pioneering basic research using second language acquisition research to ensure coherent, linked English education from elementary school through junior high and senior high school to university. (Grant-in-Aid for Scientific Research 2004–2007: Scientific Research A) Report on Research Results.

MEXT (undated) Course of Study for Senior High School: Section 8 – Foreign Language. Online at http://www.mext.go.jp/b_menu/shuppan/sonota/990301d/990301i.htm.

Naganuma, N. (2007) The potential of can-do scale to provide better English education *ARCLE Review* 2, 50–77.

Naganuma, N. (2009) Development of module syllabus based on Can-do assessment-learning tasks. *Area and Cultural Studies (Tokyo University of Foreign Studies Journal)* 79, 87–106.

National Center for University Entrance Examinations (2010) Overview of implementation of National University Entrance Examination in 2010. Online at http://www.dnc.ac.jp/modules/center_exam/content0284.html.

Negishi, M. (2006) A general review of validation studies of GTEC for students: Can-do statements. *ARCLE Review* 1, 96–103.

Negishi, M. (2011) The development process of the *CEFR*-J. *ARCLE Review* 5, 38–52.

Majima, J. (ed.) (2006) *Osaka University of Foreign Studies Committee for Educational Improvement Report on Japan-Europe International Symposium 2006: A new Direction in Foreign Language Education: The Potential of the Common European Framework of Reference for Languages*. Osaka: Osaka University.

Sakai, K. (2009) Reception of the *CEFR* and its potential applications in Japan. *ELEC Bulletin* 117, 20–21.

Schmidt, M.G., Naoyuki N., O'Dwyer, F., Imig, A. and Sakai, K. (2010) *Can-do Statements in Language Education in Japan and Beyond: Applications of the CEFR*. Tokyo: Asahi Press.

Takeshita, A. (2008) An initiative to promote the construction of 'my English': Reforming English I and II in the general curriculum from zero. *Eigo Tenbou* 116, 51–61.

The Japan Forum (2007) Learning targets for Chinese and Korean at senior high school *(provisional version)*.

Taiwan

The authors:

Jessica Wu is Program Director of Research & Development Office at the Language Training and Testing Center (LTTC) in Taipei, Taiwan. In 2005, she earned her doctoral degree in language testing and assessment from the University of Surrey, UK. She has been deeply involved in the General English Proficiency Test (GEPT), Taiwan's first countrywide English language proficiency test. In her work on this project, she is responsible for test construction and also for all aspects of research and development and administration subsequently associated with the test. She also serves on the GEPT Examination Committee. Her research interests include oral assessment, language test development and validation. She has published numerous articles and book chapters on various aspects of language testing and assessment. She is currently a member of the Editorial Board of *Language Assessment Quarterly*.

Hintat Cheung is a Professor in the Department of Chinese at the Hong Kong Institute of Education, and was formerly a faculty member of Linguistics at National Taiwan University. He was trained in language sciences and completed his doctoral degree in Child Language at the University of Kansas in 1992. Between 2001 and 2006, he was the director of the Audio-Visual Educational Center of NTU, the predecessor of the Foreign Language Teaching and Resource Center. In that capacity, he led a task force in constructing an English proficiency scale for benchmarking college English education. *CEFR* was introduced to the academics of Taiwan by the task force under this context, and later its six-level proficiency scale was officially adopted by the government of Taiwan.

18 Policy Perspectives from Taiwan

Jessica Wu

Introduction

Influenced by the force of globalization, every country in the world has made the cultivation of human talent a priority in the 21st century. Taiwan is no exception. It has embarked upon a path of education reform, including the implementation of curriculum reforms at various educational stages from preschool to secondary school, and the enhancement of higher education and lifelong learning projects in the past two decades. In particular, as part of its efforts to enhance Taiwan's competitiveness, the government launched the Challenge 2008 National Development Plan in 2002 (MoE, 2005). Under Challenge 2008, some of the tasks aimed to raise the country's overall English language proficiency level. In the interest of establishing a common yardstick of English proficiency in the country, the Ministry of Education (MoE) decided to adopt the *Common European Framework of Reference* (Council of Europe, 2001) in 2005.

The adoption of the *CEFR* has indeed created a new context for English language education in Taiwan, and has had significant impacts, both intended and unintended, on local language teaching and assessment practices (Wu, 2007). To provide background for this evolving context, this chapter begins with a snapshot of current English language teaching (ELT) practices in Taiwan.

Current ELT Practices in Taiwan

The importance of English has become unquestionable in Taiwan. English language education has been classified as a mandatory curriculum or subject area at the secondary level since 1968. Currently, there is a nine-year compulsory period of education in Taiwan, consisting of six years of elementary school and three years of junior high school. English is one of the school subjects for junior high school students, aged 13 to 15, and for senior high school students, aged 16 to 18. Starting in 1997, English learning has even been pushed downward island-wide from the junior high school level to the higher elementary school level (fifth and sixth grades), and further down to the third grade in the school year 2002–2003. Moreover, in some selected metropolitan regions, particularly in Taipei City and Taipei County, English language education has started from first grade since the 2006–07 school year.

The English curriculum adopted the principles of the communicative approach in teaching, and so it places more emphasis on students' ability to communicate in English (MoE, 2005). The current senior high school curriculum also adopts the communicative approach to English instruction and emphasizes the communicative functions of the English language (Chern, 2002). There are no standardized textbooks for either junior or senior high schools. Instead, explicit guidelines for developing teaching materials are provided in the national curriculum standards for textbook writers. Textbooks are now developed by private publishers and reviewed by the National Institute of Compilation and Translation.

As for ELT at the tertiary level, freshman English was a required course until 1993 in all universities. In 1994, however, in response to a strong call for more autonomy, the University Law was amended to allow universities to operate more flexibly based on development plans formulated by the universities themselves. However, recognizing the importance of English, since 1994, many universities have revised their English curricula to offer courses that better meet students' needs. Now, most universities still keep freshman English as a required course, but English curricula vary among the universities. It is common practice for universities to organize committees through which teachers can be involved in giving feedback, reviewing curriculum, selecting textbooks, or writing the material for the mid-term and final exams, and so on.

From the practices described above, we can clearly see that there is a movement away from centralized and standardized English curricula in Taiwan. As a result, the trend has gradually brought more autonomy to schools and teachers at all levels (Chern, 2002). However, as the degree of autonomy in Taiwan's English language education increased, a commonly-agreed standard of English ability expected of learners at all levels was missing, particularly at the tertiary level where no standardized English curricula are imposed. Under these circumstances, the MoE believed that there was a pressing need to establish a common yardstick to help define learners' proficiency in English and to use it to enhance English ability.

CEFR in Taiwan

Given that Taiwan, like many other countries, is an examination-oriented society, examinations and tests are still used as tools to facilitate better teaching and learning of English and to assess the outcome. Therefore, despite the fact that the *CEFR*, as its full title shows, is a framework not only for assessment but also for learning and teaching, it has primarily been used for the purpose of assessment in Taiwan.

In 2005 the MoE decided to use the *CEFR* as a means to establish a common standard of English proficiency. Following that move, the MoE required students, teachers of English and civil servants to demonstrate a level of English proficiency in terms of the *CEFR* framework by taking an external English language test. In the meantime, the MoE required each of the major test providers to calibrate their tests against the *CEFR* levels to assist score users in choosing a test that they considered appropriate for themselves. With governmental support, a score from an external English test has thus become influential in qualifying one for school graduation or for job promotion. As a result, the English language testing population has increased enormously in recent years. Among various English language tests (e.g. Cambridge Main Suite, IELTS, TOEFL, and TOEIC), the locally developed General English Proficiency Test (GEPT) is the most widely used test.

As background to explain the idea of locating different tests in relation to the *CEFR* framework, it is worth noting that Taiwan is a very competitive free-market society and people expect to be offered choices. In addition, the government, for various reasons, does not feel that it is appropriate for it to choose one test or kind of test over another. In fact, the decision by the MoE on the use of *CEFR* as a means to establish a common standard of English can be traced back to an earlier announcement by the Central Personnel Administration (CPA), which encouraged government employees to earn merits for job promotions by passing the GEPT. To ease the pressure from the other test developers, the CPA held two meetings with the aim of producing a conversion scale that would include most of the English proficiency tests in Taiwan. However, the development of a conversion scale was not considered feasible until necessary studies on test comparisons could be conducted. Finally, the *CEFR* was introduced in the meetings as a practical solution to the problem, and the MoE subsequently decided to use the *CEFR* as a common basis on which the comparison between different tests of English could be made. The following are some examples illustrating how GEPT scores and their corresponding *CEFR* levels are required within the new context in Taiwan (the GEPT-*CEFR* Calibration Project and related issues will be covered in the next section).

With the aim of raising the quality of schoolteachers, the MoE urges students who are taking the teacher training programme to demonstrate a minimum proficiency in English. Those who are trained to teach English are expected to achieve a pass at the GEPT-High Intermediate Level, which is equivalent to *CEFR*-B2 (Vantage). Those trained to teach other subject areas are expected to achieve a pass in the GEPT-Intermediate Level, which is equivalent to *CEFR*-B1 (Threshold). The percentage of students who reach the benchmark is taken into account when the training programme applies for funding for Educational Enhancement projects.

Government employees are required to demonstrate a minimum proficiency in English at the GEPT-Elementary Level, equivalent to *CEFR*-A2 (Waystage). Those with a better command of English have a greater chance for promotion.

The MoE expects that university graduates can, at a minimum, achieve a pass in the GEPT-Intermediate Level, equivalent to *CEFR*-B1 (Threshold). For technological and vocational colleges, graduates are expected to demonstrate a minimum proficiency in English at the GEPT-Elementary Level, equivalent to *CEFR*-A2 Level (Waystage). The MoE has further encouraged universities and colleges to establish a regulation requiring their students to pass the GEPT or another external test at an equivalent level prior to graduation. The number of students who pass the test is taken into account when the quality of a college or university is evaluated. Therefore, an increasing number of colleges and universities are now implementing this requirement (Pan, 2007).

The GEPT-CEFR Project

The GEPT, a five-level criterion-referenced EFL testing system, was specially intended for EFL learners in Taiwan. In 1999, the MoE lent its support to the Language Training and Testing Center (LTTC) in its development of the GEPT. The aim of the GEPT is to promote lifelong learning and to encourage the use of the communicative approach to English teaching and learning. The test is administered in five levels, each of which consists of four components of assessment: listening, reading, writing and speaking. According to the GEPT website, the Elementary level is recommended for junior high school graduates in Taiwan, the Intermediate level for senior high school graduates, the High-Intermediate level for university graduates whose majors are not English, the Advanced level for English-major graduates, or those who complete further studies in an English-speaking country, and the Superior level for those who have native-like proficiency. The GEPT is being used by various government institutions and schools for recruitment, classroom achievement and graduation requirements. So far, approximately four million EFL learners in Taiwan have taken the GEPT since its first administration in 2000. (More information about the

GEPT can be found at http://www.lttc.ntu.edu.tw/E_LTTC/gept_eng_main.htm.)

The requirement of mapping the locally developed GEPT against the *CEFR* framework resulted in new challenges for its provider, the LTTC. It is no easy task for a local testing body to demonstrate that its tests conform to an internationally defined proficiency framework. To achieve this, in 2007 the LTTC conducted the mapping project following the 'internal validation' procedure, including familiarization, specification and standardization (judgement session only), presented by the *Manual for Relating Language Examinations to the CEFR* (Council of Europe, 2003). A total of 70 GEPT reading comprehension test questions that exemplify the test constructs of the different levels of the GEPT reading comprehension tests were compiled. A total of 15 EFL teaching professionals were first trained to relate their interpretations of the *CEFR* levels to the calibrated sample items provided by the Council of Europe. During the judgement session, the GEPT tasks and items were presented to the participants who were then asked to determine the minimum *CEFR* level needed by a candidate to successfully answer the item on a given level of the GEPT. The judgement results show that the first four levels of the GEPT, from Elementary Level to Advanced Level, correspond to the *CEFR* A2 to C1 levels, with a generally satisfactory rater agreement of 0.91 (Wu & Wu, in press).

Problems and Issues

The reaction to the use of the *CEFR* in Taiwan is mixed due to the problems that have arisen in its implementation: test comparability, the validity of the alignment with the *CEFR* claimed by a test developer and the use of *CEFR* levels as exiting benchmarks in tertiary education.

Test Comparability

Regretfully, the *CEFR* has been misused as a platform to compare different tests. A number of language testers have addressed concerns about the issue of test comparability. For example, Bachman (1995) remarks that any comparability study needs to take account of more than just score equivalences, and other aspects such as test content and performance must also be investigated. In line with this, Davies *et al.* (1999) and Taylor (2004) also suggest that the concept of test comparison is problematic because each test is designed for a different purpose and a different population. Many Taiwanese test users have focused on the notion of 'score equivalence' only, without paying due attention to test features and constructs when choosing a test.

Claimed Alignment with the CEFR

Subsequent to the problem of test comparability, the validity of the claimed relationship between a test and the *CEFR* is doubtful. The MoE has requested that test developers establish the relationship between their own test and the *CEFR*; however, neither the government itself nor any authorized body has been given responsibility to investigate the validity of the claims. Under such circumstances, as long as a test developer can make a claim for the alignment to the *CEFR*, without providing theoretical and empirical evidence to support such a claim, their test can survive and even prosper in Taiwan's market. Moreover, this situation even allows test users to choose a less challenging test. For example, they may take one that solely assesses receptive language skills rather than taking another that also assesses productive language skills, in order to achieve a *CEFR* level more easily. Therefore, mapping test scores against the *CEFR* framework seems to have become not only a political mandate issue, but also a marketing one. A solution to this problem is desirable.

Exiting Benchmarks in Tertiary Education

As mentioned earlier, an increasing number of colleges and universities now require their students to demonstrate a minimum English proficiency level through taking a test or a course before awarding them a diploma. The model in the appendix depicts how this system is generally practised in Taiwan's tertiary education. Ideally, the model assumes that a student (labelled 'A') who passes certain coursework will be considered as reaching its corresponding *CEFR* level as a student (labelled 'B') who is able to waive the course requirement by presenting a good score in a test of English. This system may sound logical, but it poses a series of questions for policy-makers and curriculum planners, including:

- What is the relationship among the criteria set out in classroom assessment, external tests and the *CEFR*?
- Do these three paths lead to the same product in terms of learners' English language ability?
- To what extent is the curriculum linked with the *CEFR* framework?

The Way Forward

Having noted the problems and issues, however, the introduction of the *CEFR* has stimulated positive developments in Taiwan's EFL education.

To make the *CEFR* better suited to local needs, some measures that may possibly reinforce the positive impact of the *CEFR* on teaching and learning are suggested below.

Bridging the Gap Between the CEFR and Actual Learning and Teaching

It is obvious that only making a decision to adopt the *CEFR* as a common benchmark is insufficient to the overall purpose; rather, the government should play a more active role in bridging the gap between the *CEFR* framework and actual practices of learning and teaching. The GEPT seems to have assumed some responsibility to bridge such a gap. By relating the GEPT to the *CEFR*, GEPT scores are allowed to be interpreted in terms of the can-do criteria specified in the *CEFR*. In other words, both teachers and learners can understand better what a GEPT test-taker with a particular score can accomplish in terms of the communication tasks he/she can perform as specified in both GEPT and *CEFR*-level descriptors. Such understanding can more effectively assist learners and teachers in monitoring learning progress, and in making future learning and teaching plans.

As an example to illustrate how such thinking can be realized, the National Taiwan University (NTU) has now implemented the use of the GEPT-High Intermediate Level (*CEFR*-B2) as the target level of English proficiency for university students in its English curriculum for non-English majors. Unlike other universities that simply use the GEPT as an exit requirement, NTU places sophomores into the Online English Program (OEP) based on their GEPT High-Intermediate test results. Students who attain the passing level of the GEPT-High Intermediate may be exempted from attending the programme. However, students who are below the target level of English proficiency are considered to have an immediate need for the OEP. Moreover, the objectives of the curriculum correspond to the level descriptors of the GEPT-High Intermediate, which also align with those of the *CEFR*-B2 level. According to NTU, more concrete, task-oriented curriculum planning encourages students to study more English. Moreover, it has provided both students and teachers with clearer goals for learning and teaching respectively (Y. M. Ma, personal communications, 10 July 2009). However, according to Professor Hintat Cheung, who organized the core functions of the OEP, whether the students in the OEP reach the proficiency level at *CEFR*-B2 as the expected learning outcome remains merely a claim until necessary empirical studies have been conducted (email communications, 29 April 2010).

Increasing Teachers' Familiarity with the CEFR

Results of a small-scale survey among teachers of English teaching at the tertiary level (Wu & Wu, in press) revealed that the GEPT-*CEFR* linking project has aided in increasing teachers' knowledge of the *CEFR*, the GEPT and the relationship between them. More importantly, it has encouraged teachers to rethink their teaching and assessment practices in their classrooms. However, some of the respondents commented that the *CEFR* is not yet widely known by teaching professionals in Taiwan. A similar finding was reported in another survey investigating teachers' familiarity with the *CEFR* (Cheung *et al.*, 2004). Therefore, it is necessary for the government to be more active in helping teachers to become familiar with the *CEFR* through professional development programmes. For example, by conducting workshops on the scaled *CEFR* descriptors, it would be possible to increase teachers' familiarization with the *CEFR* and assist them in interpreting the *CEFR* framework so that the new input they gain from it can be integrated into their teaching and assessment practices in the classrooms.

The *CEFR*'s influence has recently begun to spread to second foreign language teaching and assessment in Taiwan. In response to global trends, the MoE started encouraging senior high schools to open second foreign language classes in French, German, Japanese and Spanish in 1999. In 2008, to promote further the study of a second foreign language in high schools, the MoE promulgated the 'Trial Program of University Second Language Courses for Senior High School Students' to encourage universities with successful foreign language programmes to open foreign language courses for senior high school students and to recognize the credits awarded to them as part of the basis for university entrance evaluation (MoE, 2009). In this way, the *CEFR* has been used by the MoE as a criterion for the entrance evaluation. High school students who apply for university admission through the programme are required to demonstrate a minimum level at *CEFR*-A2 of the second foreign language that they choose to study at school. Due to this top-down educational policy, teachers and researchers of second foreign languages are urged to familiarize themselves with the *CEFR* levels. Further impact of *CEFR* on second foreign language education is likely to come very quickly. Thus it is essential for teachers, school administrators and government policy-makers to work together to make the *CEFR* serve the intended purposes and avoid the unfortunate outcomes that have been identified in this chapter.

Conclusion

Having noted the problems and issues that have emerged from the adoption of the *CEFR* since 2005, we realize that simply making a decision to adopt the *CEFR* and mandating its use as a policy are absolutely insufficient to serve the overall educational purpose. However, to think in a positive manner, the problems and issues have taught us an important lesson and have pointed a clear direction for us in improving the use of the *CEFR* within Taiwan's educational and cultural contexts. Simply put, to make the *CEFR* better suited to our local contexts, we must recognize the need to take up the *CEFR* as principles that can be applied in local contexts, rather than as a 'one-size-fits-all' package.

References

Bachman, L.F. (1995) *An Investigation into the Comparability of Two Tests of English as a Foreign Language* (Studies in Language Testing Volume 1). Cambridge: Cambridge University Press.

Chern, C.L. (2002) English language teaching in Taiwan. *Asia Pacific Journal of Education* 22 (2), 97–105.

Cheung, H., I.W. Su, S.G. Chou, and M.H.Chen. (2004) Establishing a language framework at tertiary level. Research Report. The Ministry of Education: ROC.

Cheung, H., I.W. Su, S.G. Chou, and M.H.Chen. (2004) Establishing a language framework at tertiary level. Research Report. The Ministry of Education: ROC..

Council of Europe (2001) *Common European Framework of Reference for Languages: Learning, Teaching, Assessment.* Cambridge: Cambridge University Press.

Council of Europe (2003) Relating language examinations to the Common European Framework of Reference for languages: Learning, teaching, assessment. Manual. Preliminary pilot version. Strasbourg, France.

Davis, A., Brown, A., Elder, C. and Hill, K. (1999) *Dictionary of Language Testing* (Studies in Language Testing Volume 7). Cambridge: Cambridge University Press.

Ministry of Education (2005) Challenge 2008: National Development Plan. Online at http://english.moe.gov.tw/ct.asp?xItem=7043&ctNode=784&mp=3. Accessed on 25 January 2010.

Ministry of Education (2005) General guidelines of Grade 1–9 curriculum of elementary and junior high school education. Online at http://english.moe.gov.tw/public/Attachment/66618445071.doc. Accessed on 31 January 2010.

Ministry of Education (2009) The Second Five-Year Plan for Promotion of Second Foreign Language Study in Senior High Schools. Online at http://english.moe.gov.tw/ct.asp?xItem=10730&ctNode=783&mp=1. Accessed on 2 February 2010

National Central University (undated) A general model of requirements for proficiency in English for graduation. Online at http://www.ncu.edu.tw.

Pan, Y.C. (2007) Consequences and evaluation of test use: The washback of exit requirements on tertiary English education in Taiwan. Manuscript in preparation.

Taylor, L. (2004) Issues of test comparability. *Research Notes* 15, 2–5. Online at http://www.cambridgeesol.org/rs_notes/rs_nts15.pdf.

Wu, J (2007) English language assessment in Taiwan: Where do we go from here? Proceedings of 2007 International Conference and Workshop on TEFL & Applied Linguistics, Taipei, 574–586

Wu, J. and Y.F. Wu. (2010). Relating the GEPT reading comprehension tests to the CEFR. In: W. Martyniuk (ed.) *Aligning Tests with the CEFR: Reflections on Using the Council of Europe's Draft Manual*, Studies in Language Testing 33 (pp. 204–224). Cambridge: Cambridge University Press.

Appendix 18.1 A general model of requirements for proficiency in English for graduation (National Central University (n.d.) – my translation)

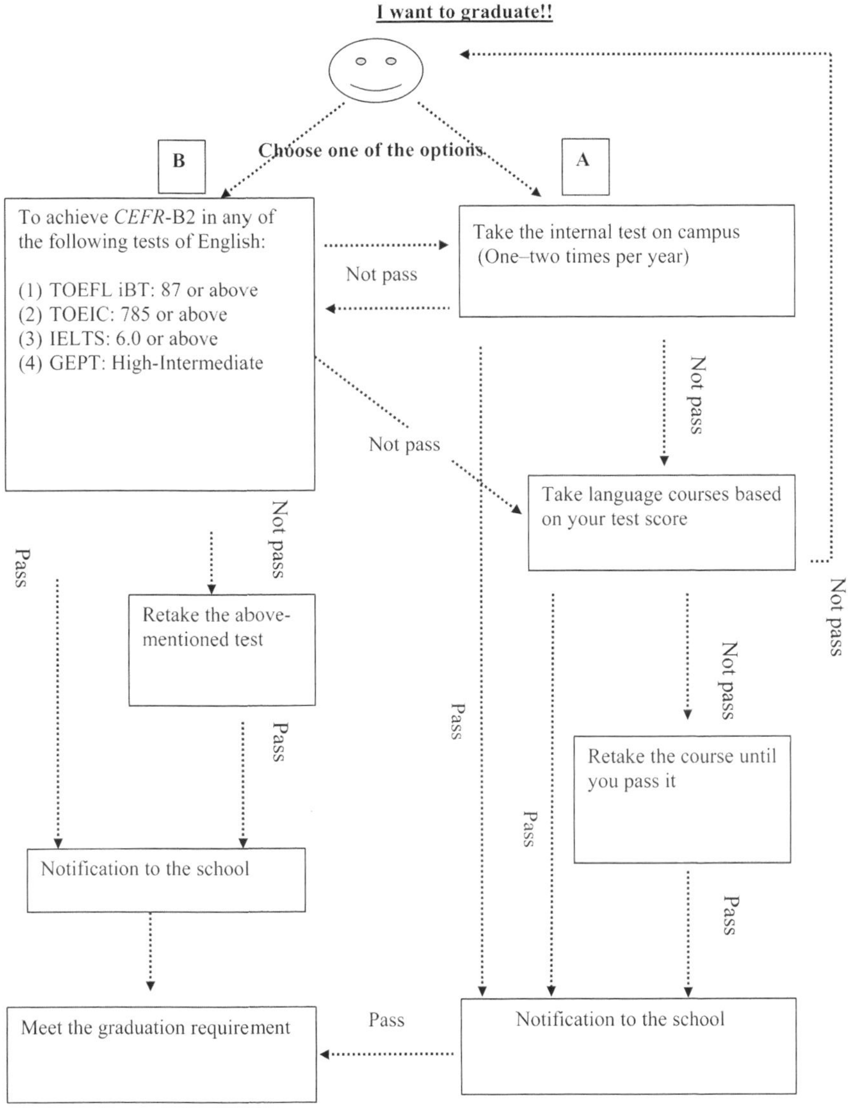

19 Academic Perspectives from Taiwan

Hintat Cheung

Introduction

In 2005, the Ministry of Education of Taiwan officially announced that all institutional polices related to English language proficiency levels should make reference to the Common Reference Levels of the *CEFR*. The former, commonly used proficiency terms such as elementary, intermediate and advanced are now replaced by the six-level scale, from A1 to C2. This de facto official status could easily lead to a misunderstanding that the *CEFR* has been well received in Taiwan, but this is not the case. As pointed out by Wu (this volume), the adoption of the *CEFR* in Taiwan is restricted to the service of a test-equivalent scale, providing an alignment between popular English proficiency tests, such as IELTS, TOEFL and TOEIC. In fact, most English language teachers in Taiwan have never read about the *CEFR* framework and their understanding of the *CEFR* is confined to the notion that the *CEFR* is a six-level proficiency scale. In a study conducted immediately prior to its official adoption, the familiarity of the *CEFR* among university English instructors was surveyed (Cheung *et al.,* 2004). The study found that less than 10% of the respondents indicated that they had a basic understanding of the *CEFR* and the remainder replied that they had never heard of it. Although it is sensible to reason that with its new official status, more people should have a better understanding of the *CEFR*, there is no evidence pointing towards this direction of development. For example, the senior high school English language curriculum of 2010 developed by the Ministry of Education (MOE) taskforce makes no reference to the *CEFR* in the whole document. The *CEFR* appears to be unrelated to the English language curricula of Taiwan.

In this chapter, I will explore the factors that led to the partial adoption of the *CEFR* in Taiwan. My discussion is divided into three parts. The first part concerns the background to the adoption of the *CEFR*, which supplements Wu's account in this volume. The second part examines the mismatch between the *CEFR* and the local ELT practice. In the conclusion I will briefly address the issue of promoting the *CEFR*.

A Possible Solution for a Decentralized System

At the turn of the second millennium, the government of Taiwan released a national development plan in which enhancing English proficiency is explicitly stated as one of the necessary measures in keeping up with the challenges of globalization and internationalization (http://www.gio.gov.tw/taiwan-website/4-oa/20020521/2002052101.html). Many new policies were put forward, including lowering the commencement of English language education in primary school from the fifth grade to the third grade of elementary school. Some municipal and county governments took a bigger step and started teaching English to first grade students. At the upper end of the educational system, many universities introduced new ESL programmes. For example, National Taiwan University was among the first wave in setting up a screening system plus a new remedial English programme for their second-year university students.

With the continuous influx of policies and programmes in enhancing English proficiency, a lack of coordination soon became noticeable. Often no clear objectives were stated in these English enhancement programmes. New practices introduced at one level were not conducive for the next. For example, the high school English curricula were not revised hand in hand with the new English programme in the primary schools. Cheung (2003) pointed out that the MOE should take up a more active role by providing a road map to EFL professionals. This confusing situation, ironically, is largely the consequence of an education reform that took place in 1998, in which the past centralized education system was liberalized and decentralized.

In 1998, the government of Taiwan announced the Twelve Education Reform Mandates, which is an unprecedented, large-scale education reform that has been influential ever since (Li, 1999). The general theme of the reform is to establish a liberalized and pluralistic educational environment. Changes related to English education in this reform include the downward extension of English education from high school to primary school students, the so-called one-principle-multiple-textbook, whereby private publishers are allowed to compile and publish textbooks, and the deregulation of mandatory core courses listed by MOE for higher education. Before this reform, the MOE of Taiwan had absolute control over the curricula of all subjects taught, from primary school to university, and unitary curricula across the whole country were aided by standardized textbooks. Together they constituted an authoritarian and monolithic education system (Tu,

2007). Standardized textbooks were compiled by a government agency and often this was also considered part of the larger censorship. In such a political context, standardized textbooks received more attention from schoolteachers. Official syllabi provided guiding statements that were often too general to be of any practical use. Gradually, the subject curriculum lost its central role in classroom teaching practice and teachers relied heavily on the organization of the standardized textbooks for their understanding of curriculum design.

This wave of reform led to a whole-scale evaluation of the past, underspecified English curriculum. In 2003, a task force for the promotion of English education was appointed by the MOE in providing assistance for coordinating ESL initiatives at all levels. Two projects related to the *CEFR* were conducted by this task force. The first is the development of the Common English Yardstick for English education in Taiwan (Cheung & Su, 2003) and the second is a feasibility study of benchmarking English proficiency of university and college students of Taiwan (Cheung *et al.,* 2004). Both projects made explicit reference to the *CEFR* because of its objective in coordinating educators of different geographical and economical settings and its vision of treating language learning as an activity across the lifespan, as stated clearly in its opening chapter:

> The Common European Framework is intended to overcome the barriers to communication among professionals working in the field of modern languages arising from the different educational systems in Europe. (Council of Europe, 2001: 1)

After a thorough examination of ESL programmes in higher education, the benchmarking project (Cheung *et al.,* 2004) recommended that a new 12-level proficiency scale should be installed. This new scale is a blend of the six-level *CEFR* scale and the ACTFL Young Learners Scale, as most of the issues are related to young learners. It is also suggested that, based on their education orientations, institutes of higher education should postulate their own entry level and exit level requirements for the development of well-defined educational programmes. This proposal pointed toward another round of reform in English education in Taiwan, which, however, was deemed by the MOE as not being as urgent as the re-instalment of self-knowledge in the education system, such as the promotion of heritage culture and languages. The proposal was thus flawed. As a matter of fact, the task force was also dismissed in 2005, the same year as the MOE announced the adoption of the *CEFR*.

In retrospect, the partial adoption of the *CEFR* was indeed a conservative measure that was thought to serve as a safeguard against further commotion amidst the strong tide of education reform. It is understandable that promoting the theoretical framework of the *CEFR* to EFL teachers is a long and demanding task that will take over a decade. Its effectiveness in resolving the confusing situation should undoubtedly be questioned.

Between *CEFR* and the English Curricula in Taiwan

In the development of the Common English Yardstick of Taiwan, the research team had mapped out the similarities and differences between the English curricula in Taiwan (from primary school to senior high school) and the *CEFR*. Major differences lie in two areas: the marginal role of the occupational domain and the skewed distribution of young learners (Cheung, 2005). These differences were, at first, taken as mere technical matters, but they were subsequently found to be telltale signs of the nature of ELT in Taiwan. The issue of occupational domain involves theoretical discussions in defining language competence – whether sociolinguistic and pragmatic skills should be included in the description of language competence. The second issue concerning the predominant interest in young EFL learners also points to the role of sociolinguistics and pragmatics in describing learners' competence.

The Problem of Occupational Domain in CEFR

In the *CEFR*, language domain is one of the key concepts in defining language activities. Four domains of language use (i.e. personal, public, education and occupational) are identified. Yet the focus of ELT in Taiwan is largely on the personal domain, the public domain and the educational domain, which are commonly labelled as 'General English'. Two to three decades ago, the use of English in the occupational domain was classified with the label 'Business English', which was treated as a supplement to mainstream 'General English'. Students were expected to reach a basic level in General English before they could move on to study Business English. Furthermore, only those who participated in international trade and other specific professions should receive training in Business English. Although the current trend of globalization has brought a wider scope of use of English in Taiwan and Business English has now been replaced by ESP, the belief in the logical sequence of a progressive move from general to specific remains unchallenged. The following translation of the description for Basic Listening skills in the 2010 Senior High School Curriculum Guideline is a good illustration (for the Chinese language version, see http://trc.nict.gov.tw/gs/course/sen_ab/A03.pdf):

a. Can comprehend classroom routines.
b. Can have a general understanding of the lesson, as well as questions raised by the teachers, which are delivered in English.
c. Can have a general understanding of everyday conversation.

Most descriptors in this English curriculum guideline are fine-tuned to capture the use of English in a classroom setting as well as certain outward extensions to everyday conversations. Nothing from the occupation domain is included. This seeming neglect is partly due to the fact that English is a foreign language in Taiwan and it has a very limited use in the public domain, let alone in the personal domain. Most students below the age of 18 have neither any immediate and spontaneous need nor any opportunities to use English outside their classroom. Their training in English is therefore mainly in the so-called General English. Although the *CEFR* intends to provide descriptors that are general enough, free from confinement to specific contexts, the range of social roles young students can take in language interactions within a school setting is passive and restricted. Obviously, this is a more basic question on the adequacy of its descriptors when *CEFR* is applied to a population composed of predominantly young language learners. I will further explore this issue in the next section.

Before doing so, it is important to return to the deep-rooted notion of General English in Taiwan, which is related to the Chomskyan competence/performance distinction. Before the 1980s, the teaching of General English mainly took place through grammar translation, which is a good parallel to the generative view of language – a finite set of rules plus a lexicon will generate all possible human sentences. Therefore, instructions on grammar and vocabulary formed the core practice of ELT in Taiwan. Extending the use of English to situations outside the classroom was considered more of a performance concern. Although the grammar-translation practice has now been replaced by communicative language teaching, the generative view persists, but with a much-refined distinction on the differences between competence and performance. Sociolinguistic knowledge is still considered more of a performance factor, so its role in the high school curriculum guideline is minimal and underspecified. Cultural knowledge of English-speaking communities is stated as an expected outcome of the learning process, not as a contributing component in building up the language capacity. Such bias can probably explain why the adoption of *CEFR* is incomplete.

More Young Beginning Learners to be Described

As mentioned earlier, the *CEFR* was once considered a candidate framework for realigning English education programmes in Taiwan. This re-alignment would involve most language learners who are in formal schooling, from young children in primary schools to young adults in universities, and their ages range from nine to 21. According to the Common Reference Levels of *CEFR*, A1 is the level assigned to beginning learners. Besides, in Taiwan, B2 is the ideal level of English proficiency for non-English major university graduates. In other words, a total span of 12 years of formal English education will be covered by four levels, from A1 to B2. Simple arithmetic shows that each level has to describe approximately three years of learning outcome. The coverage is definitely too sparse. A quick answer to this problem is to include more and finer descriptions in each level.

Although the *CEFR* has indicated that finer levels can be branched off from the basic six-level scales (2001: 32) and instructions are provided in the framework for this purpose (2001: 205), it is not a very promising option. On the practical side, it is difficult to estimate the time and effort that will be required for doing so. It might require intensive work for a period of three years or more.

A short excursion into current ELT practice in Taiwan reveals that the expansion task is not a simple one. For a young learner between nine to 12 years of age, very few of their social actions involve the use of English and often they are very different from those of adults. For example, young learners at A1/A2 level in Taiwan have little experience with English TV news. The social and cognitive demands of viewing English TV channels such as CNN and the BBC are far beyond their mental capacity. Another example is about receptive skill as a live audience. In Taiwan, it is quite common for primary schools to run interclass English single act play contests, and these young learners therefore have the chance of viewing drama live. However, in the *CEFR* nothing is stated in A1 and A2 for this kind of activity in the area of receptive activities and strategies. The predominance of young EFL learners in Taiwan poses a big challenge to the plan for the full-fledged adoption of the *CEFR*.

Conclusion

The *CEFR* is being developed in a socio-economic context within which language learners are considered social agents that participate in a wide spectrum of social activities where language learning and language use take place. This action-oriented approach, however, does not fully fit in with the ELT context of Taiwan. The socially immature young learners, who do not receive special attention in the *CEFR*, are now in the centre stage. Fine-grained modifications addressing the social and cognitive characteristics of young learners have to be completed if the *CEFR* is to be adopted as a full-fledged framework in Taiwan in the future. Workshops and training programmes for the purpose of familiarizing teachers, publishers and related professionals with the *CEFR* are needed. These training activities should pay special attention to the theoretical assumptions underlying the action-oriented approach because it is quite a foreign notion to many locally trained EFL teachers. Without a wide understanding and support from stakeholders, the implementation of the *CEFR* will continue to be uneven.

References

Cheung, H. (2003) What can we learn from *CEFR*¿ Invited speech presented in a seminar on the future of English education in Taiwan. Taipei: Taiwan University (in Chinese).

Cheung, H. (2005) The adoption of *CEFR* in Taiwan. Invited speech presented at English Teaching/Learning Resources Center in Southern Taiwan. KaoHsiung: Wenzao Ursuline College of Languages.

Cheung, H. and Su, I. (2003) Common English Yardstick for English Education in Taiwan (written in Chinese). Taiwan: MOE technical report. Online at http://ejee.ncu.edu.tw/committe/hintatntu.pdf.

Cheung, H., Su, I., Jau, S. and Chen, M. (2004) Towards a Proficiency Scale for College English Education in Taiwan (written in Chinese). Taiwan: MOE technical report. Online at http://ejee.ncu.edu.tw/committe/ejee02.pdf.

Council of Europe (2001) *Common European Framework of Reference: Learning, teaching, Assessment*. Cambridge: Cambridge University Press.

Council of Europe (2006) *Reference level descriptions (RLD) for national and regional languages*. Online at http://www.coe.int/t/dg4/linguistic/dnr_EN.asp. Accessed on 1 August 2006.

Li, C-C. (1999) Sweeping educational reform in Taiwan: From primary education to lifelong and global learning. *Educational Policy Forum* 2, 1–32.

Tu, C-S. (2007) Taiwan's educational reform and the future of Taiwan. Invited speech presented at London School of Economics and Political Sciences. Online at http://www.lse.ac.uk/collections/taiwanProgramme/TaiwanEducationalReform_English.pdf.

New Zealand

The authors:

Glenda Koefoed's language journey began at high school with French and Latin, with German and Spanish added later. Two years at a United World College in Wales encouraged her to study Japanese at university on her return home. Qualifying as a teacher of Japanese, French and English, she taught languages in state and private high schools for 11 years. This was followed by four years working in advisory services funded by the Ministry of Education and as Senior Adviser Languages at the ministry.

Over the last decade she has managed contracts for the Ministry of Education and has had extensive involvement in professional development for teachers, especially that relating to the ongoing implementation of the National Certificate of Educational Achievement (NCEA) in languages. She has been a National Examiner at different levels of NCEA Japanese and has both participated in and led examination marking panels. Other projects have included the development of internal assessment activities and exemplars for NCEA Japanese. She is now Deputy Principal of Tangaroa College, in a low-decile area of South Auckland where heritage language maintenance is a priority.

Adèle Scott is a senior lecturer in language teacher education (languages other than English) in the College of Education of Massey University, Palmerston North, New Zealand. Adèle's language teaching experience (Japanese and French) spans schools in both New Zealand and Australia. For the last 17 years, however, Adèle has been a teacher educator at Massey University. She principally teaches on the pre-service secondary programme, but also has input into the teaching of the languages component of a new four-year primary degree. She is the President of the New Zealand Association of Language Teachers (NZALT) and has long been involved in curriculum and assessment development for languages in New Zealand. She was one of five writers contracted by the Ministry of Education to write the *Learning Languages* learning area for the New Zealand Curriculum released in 2007. Adèle is completing a PhD on the professional identity of teachers of languages in New Zealand.

Martin East is coordinator for language teacher education (languages other than English and Māori) in the Faculty of Education of The University of Auckland, New Zealand. He teaches principally on a pre-service secondary programme, with special responsibility for a generic language teaching methodology course, and oversight of language specialist courses in a range of languages. An experienced teacher of French and German, his past experience has included head of department responsibility and work with both pre-service and in-service teachers of languages. He is an active member of several professional associations, including the New Zealand Association of Language Teachers (NZALT) and the Applied Linguistics Association of New Zealand (ALANZ). Martin's research and teaching interests focus on two broad areas: second language acquisition and assessment, and the development of policies to support the teaching and learning of languages other than English in contexts where English is the predominant language.

20 Policy Perspectives from New Zealand

Glenda Koefoed

'We need to emphasise multiplicity, diversity and connectivity, not linearity, uniformity and autonomy. We need an education system that develops peoples' ability to connect with one another, work across their differences and add value to each other.' (Gilbert, 2005: 68)

The development of curriculum policy for additional languages in New Zealand schools resembles more closely the disparate nature of the development of various elements of the New Zealand constitution than it resembles a comprehensive and cohesive policy direction for language teaching. As with developments in our constitutional legal framework, policy developments in languages in this country gain traction through a combination of the legacy of history, external policy, legal, academic and economic influences, changing population demographics, internal stakeholder pressure and overall government policy directions. James (2008) used the term 'incremental pragmatism' to describe the way that he expected New Zealand's constitution to continue to evolve over the subsequent 25 years. New Zealand is one of only three countries in the world – together with the United Kingdom and Israel – that do not have a constitution that is written or 'codified' in a single document. Similarly, the lack of a single overarching policy framework can be observed in the language teaching landscape and its evolution in New Zealand. However, the gradual steps taken towards the new direction set by Learning Languages in *The New Zealand Curriculum* (Ministry of Education, 2007b) may yet, with time, manifest such a framework.

Language Policy Developments, 1987–1993

In New Zealand, the 1980s saw a flurry of legislative activity to create a context for extensive economic and administrative change (Boston *et al.*, 1996; Kelsey, 1993). Over the course of the decade education became an increasingly important political issue (Shearer, 2000). Significant legislation from this period includes a statute giving official language status to te reo Māori, (*The Māori Language Act*, 1987). This legislation was of significance to the whole of the language sector in New Zealand as English has never been recognised in statute as an official language of New Zealand. Indeed, Waite (1992a) observed the impact as widespread:

> ...renewed calls from the Maori world for their language to be recognised in the wider New Zealand context have brought the question of language diversity to the attention of a larger number of New Zealanders. (1992a: 9)

Despite a change of government after the announcement in August 1990 of the commissioning of a report to consider the development of a languages policy for New Zealand, the impetus was maintained. The report that later emerged, Waite's *Aotearoa* (1992a, 1992b), was a discussion document for a comprehensive languages policy for New Zealand in which six priority areas were identified:

- Revitalisation of the Maori language.
- Second-chance adult literacy.
- Children's learning of English as a second language and first language maintenance.
- Adult learning of English as a second language.
- National capabilities in international languages.
- Provision of services in languages other than English.

The report remains relevant in the New Zealand of today, and work done in 2007 on the development of the Ministry of Education's report, *A Draft Strategy for Languages in Schooling* (Ministry of Education, 2007c), was greatly influenced by Waite's discussion.

Aotearoa was, however, never developed beyond a discussion document after being circulated for consultation, and this is attributable to three issues, of which two were to largely replicate themselves 15 years later. The first was concern about language teacher supply (Spence, 2004). The second was the small number of responses received to the request for feedback (Benton, 1996). The third was the '*turbulent*' (Shearer, 2000: 1) broader educational context of 1987–1993, where the Ministry of Education, established by the Education Act (Education Act, 1989) to replace the Department of Education, was working towards further development of work begun during the 1980s to produce a national curriculum framework and seeking to manage the fiscal implications of this process.

In the midst of major policy developments, it is not difficult to see how wider language issues were largely submerged and the report's recommendation on the inclusion of another language in the curriculum for students aged 13 to 15 was not put into practice. Similarly, in 2007, it was competition for resources and continuing concerns about teacher supply that saw the ministry's Strategy for Languages in Schooling not even reach the point of external consultation. These factors also contributed to the decision not to mandate offering opportunities for language learning in years 7–10 in the 2007 New Zealand Curriculum.

The New Zealand Curriculum Framework/Te Anga Marautanga o Aotearoa, 1993

'Language and Languages' was one of seven learning areas outlined in the NZCF. Although slim in itself, the NZCF provided for the subsequent development of specific curriculum guidelines for the seven different learning areas, with eight levels in each:

> Each level would have achievement objectives against which student outcomes could be assessed. (Shearer, 2000: 11)

Although the learning of additional languages was not included as a stand-alone essential learning area in the core curriculum, budget appropriations were secured and a series of initiatives begun (Spence, 2004). Among these, specific language curriculum guidelines were produced. Supporting resources to enable generalist teachers of years seven and eight to begin to teach a language also began to appear by the end of the century, and this is an initiative that continues today. Languages thus supported include European, Asian, Pasifika and official languages (Te reo Māori and New Zealand sign language). Ministry-funded research and evaluation in the languages sphere have also continued (Ellis, 2005; Gibbs & Holt, 2003; Peddie, 1999; Scott & Butler, 2007; Harvey *et al.*, 2009; Newton *et al.*, 2010; Harvey *et al.*, 2011). In addition, the Ministry of Education released a guide for language learning in New Zealand schools, linking echoes of *Aoteareo's* priority areas to emerging domestic and international languages research (Ministry of Education, 2002d).

Need for a Generic Framework for Additional Languages

The development of individual essential learning area curriculum guidelines throughout the 1990s was a complex and lengthy process for all learning areas, but especially so within the realm of additional languages. In addition to historic relationships and languages already offered over the previous decades, dominated by French, Japanese and German, there were also new and emerging trade and diplomatic ties. Hence, driven by developing relationships with countries such as Spain and China, the government was keen to see an increase in learners of Spanish and Chinese. Advocacy by domestic lobbyists and community groups had also seen Samoan begin to be offered in schools. Advocates of the teaching of other Pasifika languages were watching this development closely.

The first sets of curriculum guidelines for additional languages to be developed were therefore two publications to support Chinese and Spanish (Ministry of Education, 1995a, 1995b), followed by curriculum guidelines for Samoan, in 1996 (Ministry of Education, 1996). Six years after the appearance of the first curriculum guidelines, the influence of the process of development of the *Common European Framework of Reference* (*CEFR*) could be seen to be informing the proficiency levels of the 2001 drafts for French and German (Spence, 2004).

Common features of all of the guidelines were the eight levels of learning as required by the NZCF (Ministry of Education, 1993). However, there were considerable variations in other aspects:

> The curriculum statements for each language differ in identification of strands; the extent to which the achievement objectives are related to text types; the ways of expressing the achievement objectives; the presence or absence of proficiency statements; and the nature, extent and importance of the socio-cultural aspects. (Spence, 2004: 398).

During the 1990s and early 2000s, New Zealand was radically overhauling its system of assessment for qualifications. Series of standards for each subject to be assessed were established as the model for senior secondary assessment for the National Certificate of Educational Achievement (NCEA). The question of how to assess languages was a contentious one (Spence, 2004). Influenced by the Council of Europe's work towards development of an overarching framework of linguistic progression, New Zealand education officials convened a discussion on the possibility of a generic matrix for assessment of languages as early as 1998. This was eventually acceded to, and the draft matrix promulgated in New Zealand in 2002 for language assessments was a generic skills-based one, providing for assessment of single skills. (See Appendix 20.1)

The Curriculum Stocktake Report (2002)

A curriculum stocktake process was begun in 2001 to review the developments of the previous decade and their implications for teaching and learning, and to consider what they indicated for future curriculum development. This culminated in the *Curriculum Stocktake report to Minister of Education, September 2002* (Ministry of Education, 2002a). In sources used for the report, international critiques (ACER, 2002; Le Métais, 2002) noted that poor provision for second language learning was a shortcoming in the curriculum. Ongoing attention to overseas practice and research (initially a recommendation of the 1964 Currie Report, cited in Shearer, 2000) was also apparent in the Reference Group's report. Le Métais (2002) identified the English-speaking context as one of the challenges for the teaching of additional languages in New Zealand. This is a theme that Byram *et al.* (2010) have also addressed in an overview of Language teaching in Anglophone countries.

Among other things, the Curriculum Stocktake recommended that:

> Schools should be required to provide instruction in an additional language for students in years 7 to 10 (except for Māori immersion settings), but it should not be mandatory for all year 7–10 students to learn another language. Generic outcomes for Languages should be developed and included in the revised New Zealand Curriculum Framework and Te Anga Marautanga o Aotearoa. (Ministry of Education, 2002a: 52–53)

Development of a New Learning Area in the New Zealand Curriculum (NZC) (2007)

The process of development of the learning area statement, proficiency descriptors and achievement objectives for Learning Languages spanned five years. It involved a large reference group of approximately fifty teachers, advisers, pre-service educators and academics. They represented a wide spectrum of languages. In addition, a reference group was established, comprising five academics plus representatives of the primary and secondary teachers' unions (New Zealand Educational Institute and the Post-Primary Teachers' Association). This group continued to meet until mid-2007.

Key to the process was a group of five writers. Between them, they represented three universities, an intermediate school and a secondary school. They were led by Gail Spence, who at the time was the Ministry of Education's senior adviser on languages. Professional, capable, widely read and visionary in equal measures, Gail met with the writers on many occasions between 2002 and 2007. She adroitly managed the challenge of being both a public official, and therefore constrained within the government's executive, and also a passionate advocate for language learning in New Zealand.

In the early years of this century, two domains of research and publication were of particular interest to her. The first was the *CEFR* (Spence, 2004). Discussion papers had circulated during the 1990s to provide information about its development. Following publication of the *CEFR* in 2001, Gail familiarised herself with the dimensions of the document, including the communicative basis of the analysis of language use that supported the development of the descriptive scheme presented. She circulated the online synopsis of the *CEFR* to the writers' group. Subsequently, as a group, the writers and Gail agreed on four possible banded proficiency levels for LL (to comply with New Zealand's requirement for eight levels of proficiency in curriculum development). These were adapted from the *CEFR* proficiency descriptors, and the summary developed was one of the references used by the five curriculum writers and circulated to the members of the two reference groups.

A second major influence on the development of the learning area statement for learning languages was academic work in progress in Australia on developing the intercultural dimension of language teaching (Liddicoat *et al.,* 2003). Angela Scarino of the University of South Australia provided two critiques of the draft learning area that were to inform its final shape (Scarino, 2004, 2005; the Curriculum Project).

The process of development of the NZC was a hugely consultative one. There was a large reference group, and the stakeholders consulted were as varied as boards of trustees, principals/school leaders, principals' unions, teachers, business groups, parents and organisations within the wider community. The process was open and transparent in a way not often seen in other parts of the world or indeed in New Zealand (Mary Chamberlain, personal communication, October 2007). Criticism had been levelled at the ministry for the perceived paucity of consultation during the development of the NZCF (Carpenter, 2000). This process instead saw over 10,000 responses received, as questionnaires, short submissions and long submissions.

Learning Languages in the New Zealand Curriculum

Reflecting the influences from overseas research and literature, Learning Languages is characterised in its essence as concerning the development of (intercultural) communicative competence (Ministry of Education, 2007a, 2007b):

> In learning languages, students learn to communicate in an additional language, develop their capacity to learn further languages, and explore different world views in relation to their own.

There are therefore four key dimensions to the learning area:

- the development of skills for communicating in another language;
- the development of metalinguistic understanding of languages as systems;
- exposure to and exploration of different perspectives on the world;
- through active reflection about these perspectives in comparison with their own, iterative development of personal identity.

The key shifts in Language Learning in the NZC are also implicit in this statement: the shift to intercultural communicative competence, a dynamic process (Newton *et al.*, 2010) beyond knowledge about socio-cultural contexts; the new emphasis on communication as the strand to be assessed; and generic statements of outcomes for learning languages.

These concepts resonate strongly with another dimension of the NZC. This is the inclusion of five key competencies to support lifelong learning:

- thinking;
- using language, symbols and texts;
- managing self;
- relating to others;
- participating and contributing.

The inclusion of these competencies, which are not explicitly connected to outcomes, is problematic in some areas (Doig, 2007), but there is a natural fit between them and the development of proficiency in Learning Languages. Begg (2006) characterised the connections between notions of education as including cognitive, social and personal domains, and the key competencies of the draft NZC as below:

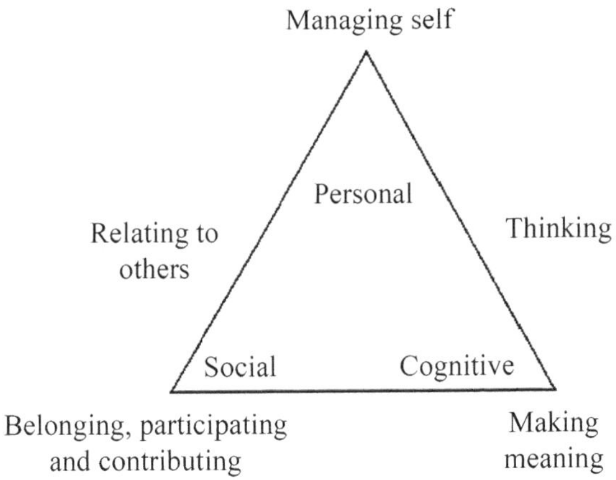

Figure 20.1 Five competencies, three domains (Begg, 2006)

The Learning Languages learning area statement as published in the NZC includes extensive reference to the intercultural dimension of language teaching. For example, 'their ability to interact appropriately with other speakers', 'Interaction in a new language…introduces them to new ways of thinking about, questioning, and interpreting the world and their place in it' (24).

The proficiency descriptors developed for Learning Languages in the NZC for each pair of banded levels were adapted from the *CEFR*-level descriptors. A minimal number of underlying communication achievement objectives act in some sense as *indicators* of what students will be able to do in a communicative context that illustrates their attainment of the proficiency outlined. Although there are also achievement objectives for language knowledge and cultural knowledge, it is the achievement objectives in the communication strand that 'provide the basis for assessment' (Ministry of Education, 2007b: 25).

This approach allowed the learning area to avoid capture by a new series of atomised achievement objectives that would cut across the intended flexibility of the NZC (Aitken, 2007) and of the learning area, and would have later had unfortunate implications when it came time in 2008 to begin to align the achievement standards of the national qualification, the NCEA, to the NZC. The final matrix agreed for the new Level 1 standards is outlined in Appendix 20.2. This is especially significant in the NZ context, where ERO's comment (ERO, 2001: 4) remains apposite today:

> In the senior secondary school, the content of teaching programmes is determined more by qualifications requirements than the curriculum statements.

During development of the learning area, note was also taken of the *savoirs* in the *CEFR* (Council of Europe, 2001: 101–105) and although a framework for the progression of intercultural communicative competence is not yet part of the *CEFR*, this aspect might be reviewed in the future. The Learning Languages wallchart (Ministry of Education, 2007a) developed to support teacher planning for additional languages programmes includes the 10 principles for instructed second language acquisition developed by Ellis (Ellis, 2005), the proficiency descriptors and achievement objectives for Learning Languages (Ministry of Education, 2007b) and also three quotes relating to the development of intercultural communicative competence (Byram, 1995; Kramsch, 1993; Scarino, 2000). The wallchart therefore contains information about both process and levels, as is the case with the NZC itself (Aitken, 2007).

By 2007, when the wallchart was designed and printed, the Ministry of Education had already contracted a team (Newton *et al.*, 2010) to carry out a literature review and develop a framework for teachers of additional languages in the New Zealand context to support the development of intercultural communicative competence. The six iCLT principles have now been developed (Newton *et al.*, 2010) and have already attracted overseas commentary (Byram, 2012).

Constructivist concepts of learning are evident throughout the NZC (Le Métais, 2002). Lifelong learning is a major emphasis in the vision of the curriculum: 'Confident, connected, actively involved lifelong learners' (Ministry of Education, 2007b: 8). Development of the Key Competencies (KCs) in young people is supported by language learning with an emphasis on intercultural communicative competence.

There is no question that the numbers of students in years 7–10 who are now learning languages has grown over the last 15 years (Education Counts, 2009 statistics). We have built access, but there is more to do to build quality and sustainability. Concerns remain regarding the implementation of the curriculum, with debate still apparent in some fora about the move to a generic languages framework and the primacy of the communication strand. We are just beginning to explore the implications for intercultural language teaching in New Zealand schools and the coming years will see more written on this new feature of our language learning landscape. Undoubtedly they will also see further discussion of the NZC-aligned achievement standards for NCEA and their implementation, which begins with year 11 in 2011.

Conclusion

Regardless of the absence of a comprehensive languages policy, change in language teaching is occurring: driven by lobbyists; by a new curriculum;

by the ministry's range of research, publications, evaluations; by professional development support for schools; by influences from overseas jurisdictions; and in some cases by local community demand. However, wider educational policy still seems focussed on only some of the priority areas identified by Waite (1992a, 1992b), and we face the challenge of many Anglophone countries. Byram (2010) challenges the notion that communicative language teaching alone will suffice to increase language learning in such a context. In Aotearoa, Waite's work has stood the test of time and remains relevant almost two decades later. Advocates for the teaching of additional languages have been informed by his recommendations and have pushed on despite the lack of overarching policy. Hence incremental pragmatism has brought us to the brink of seeing opportunities for language learning mandated in schools as part of the core curriculum. Of constitutional matters, James (2008) wrote:

> Formal change to the constitution will be most durable when it recognises and codifies organic change and at most takes it a careful step or two further.

In terms of language policy, we do now need that careful step or two further and this would be consistent with ERO's (2001) suggestion of incremental curriculum updates, and with the principle of sustainability. In this process, further reference to the *CEFR* seems likely.

References

Aitken, G. (2007) *Commentary for MoE Reference Group Meeting, 1–2 March 2007 on reports analysing submissions to the New Zealand curriculum draft for consultation, 2006.* Auckland: University of Auckland.

Australian Council for Educational Research (ACER) (2002) *Report on the New Zealand National Curriculum.* Melbourne: ACER.

Begg, A.J.C. (2006) Emerging Curriculum. PhD thesis. Milton Keynes, UK: Open University.

Benton, R. (1996) Language policy in New Zealand: Defining the ineffable. In M. Herriman and B. Burnaby (eds) *Language Policies in English-Dominant Countries: Six case studies* (pp. 62–98). Clevedon: Multilingual Matters.

Boston, J., Martin, J., Pallot, J. and Walsh, P. (1996) *Public Management; The New Zealand Model.* Auckland: Oxford University Press.

Byram, M. (1995) Intercultural competence and mobility in multinational contexts: A European view. In M.L. Tickoo (ed.) *Language and Culture in Multilingual Societies* (pp. 21–36). Singapore: SEAMO Regional Language Centre.

Byram, M., Lapkin, S., LoBianco, J., Met, M. and Scott, A. (2010) Fremdsprachen didaktik in Englischsprachigen Ländern. In W. Hallet /F.G. Königs (Hrsg.) *Handbuch Fremdsprachendidaktik.* Seelze-Velber: Klett/Kallmeyer.

Byram, M. (forthcoming) Reflecting on teaching 'culture' in foreign language education. In D. Newby (ed.) *Insights into the European Portfolio for Student Teachers of Languages*. Newcastle: Cambridge Scholars Publishing.
Doig, C. (2007) The New Zealand curriculum: Draft for consultation 2006-Impact of the feedback on the final curriculum. Paper prepared for the Ministry of Education's Curriculum Marautanga Project.
Education Review Office (2001) *The New Zealand Curriculum: An ERO Perspective*. Wellington: Education Review Office.
Ellis, R. (2005) *Instructed Second Language Acquisition: A Literature Review*. Wellington: Ministry of Education.
Gibbs, C. and Holt, R. (2003) *The Teaching of International Languages in New Zealand Schools in Years 7 and 8. An Evaluation Study: Report to the Ministry of Education*. Wellington: Ministry of Education.
Gilbert, J. (2005) *Catching the Knowledge Wave? The Knowledge Society and the Future of Education*. Wellington: NZCER Press.
Harvey, S., Conway, C., Richards, H. and Roskvist, A. (2009) *Evaluation of Teacher Professional Development Languages (TPDL) in Years 7–10 and the Impact on Language Learning Opportunities and Outcomes for Students*. Wellington: Ministry of Education.
Harvey, S., Roskvist, A., Corder, D. and Stacey, K. (2011) *An Evaluation of the Language and Culture Immersion Experiences (LCIE) for Teachers Programmes: Their Impact on Teachers and their Contribution to Effective Second Language Learning*. Auckland: AUT University.
James, C. (2008) *Take me to your leaders: the constitution in 2033*. Online at http://www.colinjames.co.nz/speeches_briefings/IPS_constitution_08Sep.09.html. Accessed on 19 June 2010.
Kelsey, J. (1993) *Rolling Back the State: Privatisation of Power in Aotearoa/New Zealand*. Wellington: Bridget Williams Books.
Kramsch, C. (1993) Language study as border study: Experiencing difference. *European Journal of Education* 28 (3), 349–358.
Le Métais, J. (2002) *New Zealand Stocktake: an International Critique*. Foundation for Educational Research, United Kingdom. Contract Research for the New Zealand Ministry of Education.
Liddicoat, A.J.,Papademetre, L., Scarino, A. and Kohler, M. (2003) *Report on Intercultural Language Learning*. Canberra: Australian Department of Education, Science and Training.
Ministry of Education (1987) *The Māori Language Act*. Wellington, New Zealand: Government Printer.
Ministry of Education (1989) *Education Act 1989*. Wellington, New Zealand: Government Printer.
Ministry of Education (1993) *The New Zealand Curriculum Framework*. Wellington, NZ: Learning Media, Ministry of Education.
Ministry of Education (1995a) *Chinese in the New Zealand Curriculum*. Wellington: Learning Media.
Ministry of Education (1995b) *Spanish in the New Zealand Curriculum*. Wellington: Learning Media.
Ministry of Education (1996) *Samoan in the New Zealand Curriculum*. Wellington: Learning Media.
Ministry of Education (1998) *Japanese in the New Zealand Curriculum*. Wellington: Learning Media.

Ministry of Education (2002a) *Curriculum Stocktake Report to Minister of Education, September 2002*. Wellington.
Ministry of Education (2002b) *French in the New Zealand Curriculum*. Wellington: Learning Media.
Ministry of Education (2002c) *German in the New Zealand Curriculum*. Wellington: Learning Media.
Ministry of Education (2002d) *Learning Languages: A guide for New Zealand Schools*. Wellington: Learning Media.
Ministry of Education (2007a) The generic framework for teaching and learning languages in English-medium schools. Online at http://nzcurriculum.tki.org.nz/Curriculum-resources/NZC-resource-bank/Learning-languages/Key-resources. Accessed on 26 April 2010.
Ministry of Education (2007b) *The New Zealand Curriculum for English-Medium Teaching and Learning in Years 1–13*. Wellington, NZ: Learning Media, Ministry of Education.
Ministry of Education (2007c) Education report to the Minister of Education: *A Draft* Strategy for Languages in Schooling. Unpublished.
Ministry of Education (2007) The Curriculum Project, References. Wellington, New Zealand: Ministry of Education. Online at http://nzcurriculum.tki.org.nz/Archives/Curriculum-project-archives/References.
Ministry of Education (2008) *Te Marautanga o Aotearoa*. Wellington, NZ: Learning Media, Ministry of Education.
Ministry of Education (2009) *Ta 'iala mo le Gagana Sāmoa: The Gagana Sāmoa Guidelines*. Wellington: Learning Media. Online at http://pasifika.tki.org.nz/Pasifika-languages/Gagana-Samoa. Accessed on 23 January 2011.
Newton, J., Yates, E., Shearn, S. and Nowitzki, W. (2010) *Intercultural Communicative Language Teaching: Implications for Effective Teaching and Learning*. Wellington: Ministry of Education.
Peddie, R.A. (1999) *Starting Younger: The Second Language Learning Project Evaluation: Final Report*. Wellington: Auckland Uniservices Limited.
Scarino, A. (2000) The Neglected Goals of Language Learning. *Babel* 34 (3) (Summer 1999–2000), 4–11.
Scarino, A. (2004) Response to draft essence statement learning languages. Paper prepared for the Ministry of Education.
Scarino, A. (2005) Learning languages in the New Zealand curriculum. Paper commissioned by the New Zealand Ministry of Education for The New Zealand Curriculum Marautanga Project.
Scott, A. and Butler, P. (2007) *Evaluation of Pilot Programmes for Effective Teaching in Languages, Years 7 and 8: Final Evaluation Report*. Palmerston North: Massey University.
Shearer, R. (2000) *The New Zealand Curriculum Framework: A new paradigm in curriculum policy development*. ACE papers online. Online at http://www.education.auckland.ac.nz/uoa/ace-issue7. Accessed on 26 June 2010.
Spence, G. (2004) The practice of policy in New Zealand. *Current Issues in Language Planning* 5 (4), 389–406.
Waite, J. (1992a) *Aoteareo: Speaking for Ourselves. Part A: The Overview*. Wellington: Ministry of Education.
Waite, J. (1992b) *Aoteareo: Speaking for Ourselves. Part B: The Issues*. Wellington: Ministry of Education.

Appendix 20.1

LANGUAGES: GENERIC ACHIEVEMENT STANDARDS - DRAFT MATRIX – April 2002

		Listening	*Speaking*	*Conversation*	*Reading*	*Writing*	*International Languages Writing*	*Pacific Languages Visual*
		External	*Internal*	*Internal*	*External*	*External*	*Internal*	*Internal*
		6	3	3	6	3	3	3
1	Curric L 6	1.1 Listen to and understand spoken language in (selected second language) in familiar contexts	1.2 Give a prepared talk in (selected second language) on a familiar topic	1.3 Converse in (selected second language) in a familiar context	1.4 Read and understand written language in (selected second language) in familiar contexts	1.5 Write text in (selected second language) on a familiar topic	1.6 Write text in (selected second language) on familiar topics with the support of resources	1.Participate in cultural situations using visual and specialised language
2	Curric L 7	2.1 Listen to and understand spoken language (selected second language) in less familiar contexts	2.2 Give a prepared spoken presentation in (selected second language) on a less familiar topic	2.3 Converse in (selected second language) in a less familiar context	2.4 Read and understand written language in (selected second language), in less familiar contexts	2.5 Write text in (selected second language) on a less familiar topic	2.6 Produce crafted writing in (selected second language) on a less familiar topic, with the support of resources	2.7 Participate in less familiar cultural situations using visual and specialised language
3	Curric L 8	3.1 Listen to and understand complex spoken (selected second language) in less familiar contexts	3.2 Give a prepared speech in (selected second language) using complex language, in a formal situation	3.3 Exchange and support ideas and opinions in an extended conversation in (selected second language) using complex language	3.4 Read and understand written (selected second language) containing complex language, in less familiar contexts	3.5 Write text in (selected second language) using complex language on a less familiar topic	3.6 Write crafted text in (selected second language) using complex language on a less familiar topic, with the support of resources	3.7 Participate in less familiar cultural situations using and responding to complex visual and specialised language

Appendix 20.2

Generic Languages Matrix 2011

Note: Expiring Level 1 internal achievement standards can also be used for assessment in 2011. All registered and expiring achievement standards can be accessed at NZQA.

Level 1				
Listen and Respond	**Speak, Present**	**Interact**	**View and Respond**	**Write**
1.1 Demonstrate understanding of a variety of spoken TARGET LANGUAGE texts on areas of most immediate relevance. 5 credits External	**1.2** Give a spoken presentation in TARGET LANGUAGE that communicates a personal response. 4 credits Internal	**1.3** Interact using spoken TARGET LANGUAGE to communicate personal information, ideas and opinions in different situations. 5 credits Internal	**1.4** Demonstrate understanding of a variety of TARGET LANGUAGE texts on areas of most immediate relevance. 5 credits External	**1.5** Write a variety of text types in TARGET LANGUAGE on areas of most immediate relevance. 5 credits Internal

	Listening	**Speaking**	***Conversation***	**Reading**	**Writing**	**International Languages Writing**	**Pacific Languages Visual**
Level 2	**2.1** Listen to and understand spoken language in (selected second language) in less familiar contexts 6 credits External	**2.2** Give a prepared spoken presentation in (selected second language) on a less familiar topic 3 credits Internal	**2.3** Converse in (selected second language) in a less familiar context 3 credits Internal	**2.4** Read and understand written language in (selected second language), in less familiar contexts 6 credits External	**2.5** Write text in (selected second language) on a less familiar topic 3 credits External	**2.6** Produce crafted writing in (selected second language) on a less familiar topic, with the support of resources 3 credits Internal	**2.7** Participate in less familiar cultural situations using visual and specialised (selected second language) language 3 credits Internal
Level 3	**3.1** Listen to and understand complex spoken (selected second language) in less familiar contexts 6 credits External	**3.2** Give a prepared speech in (selected second language) using complex language 3 credits Internal	**3.3** Converse in (selected second language) using complex language in less familiar contexts 3 credits Internal	**3.4** Read and understand written (selected second language) containing complex language, in less familiar contexts 6 credits External	**3.5** Write text in (selected second language) using complex language on a less familiar topic 3 credits External	**3.6** Write crafted text in (selected second language) using complex language, with the support of resources 3 credits Internal	**3.7** Engage in a less familiar cultural situations using complex visual and specialised (selected second language) language 3 credits Internal

21 Academic Perspectives from New Zealand

Adèle Scott and Martin East

Introduction

The idea that an island country located some 18,000 km from Europe should be influenced by the *Common European Framework of Reference for Languages* might appear to be quite bizarre. This country has no national policy for languages education and no compulsion for its children to learn a language additional to the one through which they are educated. Why would New Zealand consider a framework for language learning, developed a world away for a completely different context, in the creation of its own learning area for languages in its national curriculum? In order to answer this question it is necessary to consider the language teaching traditions of New Zealand leading up to the consideration of the *CEFR* as a framework for planners and curriculum developers.

Innovation Without Change

Since the early 1990s, the favoured approach to L2 teaching at the level of policy in New Zealand's schools has been 'communicative', informed by the theoretical models of communicative competence that have been articulated and developed in various ways since the early 1970s (Bachman, 1990; Canale, 1983; Canale & Swain, 1980; Hymes, 1972; Savignon, 1983, 1997; Widdowson, 1978). This was signalled by the introduction of the *New Zealand Curriculum Framework* (NZCF) of 1993 (Ministry of Education, 1993).

The NZCF was the first attempt since the 1940s to provide a government-endorsed national 'foundation policy' and 'coherent framework' for teaching, learning and assessment in New Zealand's schools (Ministry of Education, 1993: 1). With reference to the 'essential learning area' of 'Language and Languages', the document stated:

> All students benefit from learning another language from the earliest practicable age. Such learning broadens students' general language abilities and brings their own language into sharper focus. It enriches them intellectually, socially and culturally, offers an understanding of the ways in which other people think and behave, and furthers international relations and trade.
>
> (Ministry of Education, 1993: 10)

Essentially, the message to schools at this time was that L2 teaching and learning practices should move away from viewing language as a purely academic study, which might be operationalised through a more traditional grammar-focused pedagogy. Rather, it was expected that schools should be providing programmes for students who were learning languages because they needed to make practical use of them in an ever-shrinking world (Benson & Voller, 1997). Subsequently, government-funded initiatives were created to extend the teaching of languages from secondary schools (from year nine onwards), where they had been traditionally located, into the pre-secondary (primary/intermediate school) sector (years seven and eight). Years 7 to 10 therefore became the principal target age range for language learning programmes alongside examinable courses available in years 11 to 13 (Gibbs & Holt, 2003).

The new focus was therefore on *language in actual use* – rather than language as a purely academic pursuit – and following the publication of the NZCF, language-specific curriculum guidelines were published (Ministry of Education, 1995a, 1995b, 1996, 1998, 2002a, 2002b), where the typical guidance offered was that teachers should adopt a 'communicative approach' to their teaching in a way that 'encourages learners to engage in meaningful communication in the target language – communication that has a function over and above that of language learning itself' (Ministry of Education, 2002a: 16), as described in more detail by Koefoed in the previous chapter.

Unlike the NZCF, the guidelines were not mandatory, but were framed as 'suggestions'. Having guidelines in print, however, meant that many teachers came to adopt them as a kind of 'prescribed syllabus' which followed what Klapper (2003: 35) calls 'conventional L2 curricula' – prescriptions which 'divide the language into lexis, structures, notions or functions, which are then selected and sequenced for students to learn in a uniform and incremental way'. In this type of 'synthetic' syllabus '[d]ifferent parts of the language are taught separately and step-by-step so that acquisition is a process of gradual accumulation of parts until the whole structure of language has been built up' (Wilkins, 1976: 2).

This 'conventional' or 'traditional' way of structuring a teaching programme, which found expression in the curriculum guidelines, reflects what Nunan (2004) claims is 'the common-sense belief that the central role of instruction is to simplify the learning challenge for the student'. However, this traditional structure reinforced three negative tendencies:

- The guidelines led to a teacher-led approach to language learning in the sense that, despite the encouragement to create partnership between the teacher and the learner, the teacher 'controlled' the language that the learners could or could not use, and made the decisions about when topics, language and structures were to be introduced.
- The guidelines failed to take into consideration that samples of authentic language inevitably contain both language and structures that students may not have encountered in a step-by-step incremental model of teaching and learning, and that, by implication, would have to be adapted or abandoned.
- The effect of constraining what was taught and when it was taught was not in accord with second language acquisition theory.

Alongside these developments was the change to the National Qualifications system from a norm-referenced system to a standards-based assessment system that focused on students' knowledge and skills for the three senior levels of the curriculum (levels six to eight). The process that was followed for languages was to bring them all together in order to develop one generic set of Assessment Standards through which students gain credits towards the new qualification called the National Certificate of Educational Achievement (NCEA). This was the beginning of the genericisation of languages – including genericisation of proficiency levels – and laid the foundation for a similar process to be followed in the development of a new learning area in the curriculum.

In short, there was both change and stasis in the post-1993 situation, with emphasis on language learning for and through use and, at the same time, guidelines that allowed the continuation of tradition and convention (East & Scott, 2011).

Innovation and the *CEFR*

The need to reconceptualise language teaching and learning in a more open-ended and less prescriptive way was signalled in 2007 by a revision of the national curriculum and the subsequent development of a new learning area. A major emphasis of the revised *New Zealand Curriculum* (Ministry of

Education, 2007a) is the further encouragement of a learner-centred and experiential approach where the teacher and the learner will be engaged in a co-construction of knowledge (Ministry of Education, 2007a, 2009). The curriculum is therefore not to be seen as teacher-directed, with the teacher representing the authority figure (Weimer, 2002), and the new learning area 'Learning Languages' has been conceptualised with this shift from the teacher to the learner in mind. In fact, in some cases, the teacher is *also* the learner, working alongside students to ensure that languages can be offered even when they themselves may only have beginning knowledge of the language they are teaching (Daly, 2010; Ministry of Education, 2009; Scott & Butler, 2007).

The significance of this is that although the new learning area does not appear to be advocating anything philosophically different to the CLT approach encouraged earlier, in this move to foreground the learner, and in contrast to what happened earlier, there has been no attempt to define the language and structures that students should acquire as they progress in their learning, or to constrain the language that students may use to complete any tasks or activities, or any attempt to limit or prescribe the topics or themes students can explore.

To facilitate this, teachers are being dissuaded from using the former language-specific guidelines and, instead, to use new web-based more open-ended guidelines (Ministry of Education, 2008). These guidelines suggest tasks and activities, but are not prescriptive in terms of content, and the learning area statement for languages (Ministry of Education, 2007a: 24) and its supporting wallchart (Ministry of Education, 2007b) advocate using new language to 'make meaning' and encourage application of a set of ten principles brought together in a report by Ellis (2005a) that 'draw on a variety of theoretical perspectives and are offered as 'provisional specifications' for a learning-centred language pedagogy'(Ellis, 2005b: 209). It is clear, then, that the emphasis for curriculum and assessment and the new guidelines, has now been placed more firmly on what a Council of Europe author earlier described as 'what the learner will have to be able to *do* in the foreign language' at each stage of learning (van Ek, 1977: 5, emphasis in original). There were parallel modes of thinking about language learning developing in the *CEFR* and in emerging curricula and practices in New Zealand.

There is, however, still a requirement within the revised curriculum to retain eight progressive levels of attainment in all subject areas, and therefore still a requirement to provide meaningful differentiation in languages across eight levels. The five writers appointed to write the new learning area (see the previous chapter by Koefoed) decided that proficiency levels in languages would be aligned with, and adapted from, the *CEFR* (Council of Europe, 2001). This decision was made after considering curriculum documents from a number of English-speaking countries (Australia, England, Wales, Northern Ireland, the United States) alongside the mandates that were in place for writing groups of all learning areas in the New Zealand Curriculum. These mandates included the requirement for an outcomes-focused curriculum alongside an acknowledgement of a common set of future-focussed themes, key competencies and values. The writing group for 'Learning Languages' regularly accessed the competency framework of the *CEFR* as they grappled with appropriate descriptors to define outcomes for what students *can do* at each of the eight levels of the curriculum. The global scales in particular provided a meaningful framework, which, with some adaptation, could be lined up with the eight curriculum levels (see Appendix 21.1).

The motivation for incorporating aspects of the *CEFR* into education policy and practice in New Zealand was therefore to have benchmarking that would enable the eight levels of the curriculum to be understood, but not to require specifications of topics, vocabulary and structures at each level of the curriculum.[1] Indeed, although the *CEFR* has been critiqued for lack of detail about what learners should know and be able to do at different levels, it is commensurate with a 'learner-centred action-oriented approach' to language learning (Martyniuk & Noijons, 2007: 6) and is therefore in accord with the aims and philosophy of the 2007 curriculum. Furthermore, open-endedness and lack of prescription is, in our view, a particular strength of the *CEFR* in the New Zealand context because, as Crombie and Whaanga (2006) point out, the *CEFR* aims not to 'define what should be taught' but rather 'to stimulate reflection and discussion' (North, 2004). Lack of definition about what should be taught is, we argue, commensurate with the open-ended and non-prescriptive nature of the new 'Learning Languages' learning area.

One aspect of the *CEFR* that has not been considered directly in the New Zealand context is the benchmarking of assessment standards for National Certificate of Educational Achievement against the *CEFR* framework. When, however, these assessment standards were aligned to the senior levels of the new curriculum (levels five to eight), the New Zealand Association of Language Teachers (NZALT), who were contracted to do this work, did refer to the scales of the communicative language activities and strategies of the *CEFR* in the development of the assessment criteria.

At the lower levels of the curriculum (levels 1–4) the CEFR has been used in the development of some learning progressions for interpersonal speaking. These progressions, although currently draft and not available for use (N. Hill, personal communication, 31st January, 2012), are intended to:

- describe the way learners develop their use of language through the communicative strand of the achievement objectives for learning languages in *The New Zealand Curriculum;*
- give sufficiently clear descriptions so that teachers can design properly focused instructional activities;
- support teachers to chart student achievement in communicative, intercultural communication and to inform the next steps in teaching and learning;
- assist in articulating a common language of progression to monitor and chart communicative language learning; and
- allow teachers to gather and analyse data of evidence of student achievement (Ministry of Education, in press).

While these progressions account for progress through a series of levels and acknowledge that learners may not achieve native-speaker competence (Newton *et al.,* 2010), they do address the concept of plurilingualism and pluriculturalism considering that in the New Zealand context the intercultural dimension of communicative proficiency is important. This, as Byram (2008) suggests, allows for the fact that the principal focus of the *CEFR* is on levels of *linguistic* competence rather than on levels of *socio-cultural* competence.

Having said all this, a restraint that limits the influence of the *CEFR* in educational policy and practice in New Zealand and, more particularly, the influence of an open-ended curriculum like the 2007 curriculum, is the washback effect of the examination system mentioned earlier. The perceived pressure that externally assessed components of the aforementioned NCEA put on teachers and their programmes means that there is a constant call for lists of vocabulary and grammatical structures that will limit what examiners can use in examination questions, and which teachers can incorporate into units of work.

Referring to a wide range of international literature about standards-based assessment reform, Rawlins *et al.* (2005: 112) found that such reform 'has a positive impact on teacher pedagogy, student achievement and programme adaptation to better meet the needs of an increasingly diverse range of students'. Perhaps in the case of languages teachers, as discussed elsewhere by the authors (East & Scott, 2011), engaging with a new learning area as well as ongoing revisions to a relatively new assessment system may need more time to benefit from this positive impact. Indeed, when the NZALT surveyed its members about their readiness to implement the revised *New Zealand Curriculum* (Ministry of Education, 2007b), it was found that, in response to a question seeking to determine the extent of teachers' awareness about the links between the Achievement Objectives and the *CEFR*, fewer than half of the respondents said they were even aware of this connection. Key to interpreting such a response is that, as indicated earlier, there have been numerous curriculum and assessment changes in the past decade which have not been conducive to teachers taking on board the detail of the frameworks and thinking behind those changes.

Conclusion

In line with the removal of specified vocabulary and structures and an understanding that communicative competence is relative and never complete, the emphasis of the new learning area is no longer on stating or prescribing the language required to achieve the communicative outcomes. In this sense, 'incremental language learning' is no longer part of the conceptualisation of 'best practice' with regard to language teaching pedagogy. There is, however, still a requirement within the revised curriculum to retain eight progressive levels of attainment in all subject areas, and therefore still a requirement to provide meaningful differentiation in languages across eight levels. In this sense, 'incremental language learning' is still a necessity, and in this respect the *CEFR* has been of considerable practical help. The impact of a philosophy of teaching and learning that is learner-centred and task-based is yet to be seen in practice.

Notes

(1) It is interesting to note, however, that this was not the first time that the *CEFR* had been drawn on to inform curriculum development in New Zealand. Crombie and Whaanga (2006: 51) report on their engagement with the *CEFR* in the process of drafting the curriculum for te reo Māori as part of a Ministry of Education contract. The authors consulted the *CEFR* as 'a useful starting point for those involved in language curriculum design, particularly where there is a need to benchmark students' performance against accepted achievement standards'. Crombie and Whaanga critiqued the *CEFR*, however, in that, in their view, it was insufficiently prescriptive to facilitate meaningful operationalisation within curricula for foreign languages. They argued that '[t]here is no guidance on the construction of specific achievement objectives ... no indication of how topics, text-types and socio-cultural aspects might be accommodated' (Crombie & Whaanga, 2006: 51).

References

Bachman, L.F. (1990) *Fundamental Considerations in Language Testing*. Oxford: Oxford University Press.

Benson, P. and Voller, P. (eds) (1997) *Autonomy and Independence in Language Learning*. London: Longman.
Byram, M. (2008) *From Foreign Language Education to Education for Intercultural Citizenship* (pp. 57–73). Clevedon: Multilingual Matters.
Canale, M. (1983) On some dimensions of language proficiency. In J.W.J. Oller (ed.) *Issues in Language Testing Research* (pp. 333–342). Rowley, MA: Newbury House.
Canale, M. and Swain, M. (1980) Theoretical bases of communicative approaches to second language teaching and testing. *Applied Linguistics* 1, 1–47.
Crombie, W. and Whaanga, H. (2006) The te reo Maori curriculum: Design, review, rewrite. Paper presented at the New Zealand Association of Language Teachers International Biennial Conference, 'Building bridges, reaching heights', Auckland, NZ, 2–5 July.
Daly, N. (2010) An evolving picture: First-year primary language teachers describe their work and the relevance of their language teacher education after six months. *New Zealand Language Teacher* 36, 39–46.
East, M. (2012) *Task-Based Language Teaching from the Teachers' Perspective: Insights from New Zealand*. Amsterdam / Philadelphia, PA: John Benjamins.
East, M. and Scott, A. (2011) Assessing the foreign language proficiency of high school students in New Zealand: From the traditional to the innovative. *Language Assessment Quarterly* 8 (2), 179–189.
Ellis, R. (2005a) *Instructed Second Language Acquisition: A Literature Review*. Wellington: Ministry of Education.
Ellis, R. (2005b) Principles of instructed language learning. *System* 33 (2), 209–224.
Gibbs, C. and Holt, R. (2003) *The Teaching of International Languages in New Zealand Schools in Years 7 and 8: An Evaluation Study*. Wellington, NZ: Ministry of Education.
Hymes, D. (1972) On communicative competence. In J.B. Pride and J. Holmes (eds) *Sociolinguistics* (pp. 269–293). Harmondsworth, UK: Penguin.
Klapper, J. (2003) Taking communication to task? A critical review of recent trends in language teaching. *Language Learning Journal* 27, 33–42.
Martyniuk, W. and Noijons, J. (2007) *The use of the CEFR at national level in the Council of Europe Member States: Executive summary of results of a survey*. Strasbourg: Council of Europe.
Ministry of Education (1993) *The New Zealand Curriculum Framework*. Wellington, NZ: Learning Media, Ministry of Education.
Ministry of Education (1995a) *Chinese in the New Zealand Curriculum*. Wellington: Learning Media.
Ministry of Education (1995b) *Spanish in the New Zealand Curriculum*. Wellington: Learning Media.
Ministry of Education (1996) *Samoan in the New Zealand curriculum*. Wellington: Learning Media.
Ministry of Education (1998) *Japanese in the New Zealand Curriculum*. Wellington: Learning Media.
Ministry of Education (2002a) *French in the New Zealand Curriculum*. Wellington: Learning Media.
Ministry of Education (2002b) *German in the New Zealand Curriculum*. Wellington: Learning Media.
Ministry of Education (2002c) *Learning Languages: A Guide for New Zealand's Schools*. Wellington, NZ: Learning Media.

Ministry of Education (2007a) *The New Zealand Curriculum for English-Medium Teaching and Learning in Years 1–13*. Wellington, NZ: Learning Media, Ministry of Education.

Ministry of Education (2007b) The generic framework for teaching and learning languages in English-medium schools. Online at http://nzcurriculum.tki.org.nz/Curriculum-resources/NZC-resource-bank/Learning-languages/Key-resources. Accessed on 26 April 2010.

Ministry of Education (2008) Learning Languages - second-tier guidelines. Online at http://seniorsecondary.tki.org.nz/Learning-Languages. Accessed on 8 February 2010.

Ministry of Education (2009) *Te aho arataki marau mō te ako i te reo Māori – Kura Auraki: Curriculum Guidelines for Teaching and Learning te reo Māori in English-Medium Schools: Years 1–13*. Wellington, NZ: Learning Media, Ministry of Education.

Ministry of Education. (in press) Draft Learning Progressions for Interpersonal Speaking in Learning Languages.

Newton, J., Yates, E., Shearn, S. and Nowitzki, W. (2010) *Intercultural Communicative Language Teaching: Implications for Effective Teaching and Learning* (Report to the Ministry of Education). Wellington: Victoria University of Wellington

North, B. (2004) Europe's framework promotes language discussion, not directives. *Guardian Weekly,* 1 April.

Nunan, D. (2004) *Task-Based Language Teaching*. Cambridge, UK: Cambridge University Press.

Rawlins, P.L.C., Brandon, J.B., Chapman, J.E., Leach, L.J., Neutze, G.G., Scott, A.J. and Zepke, N. (2005) Standards-based assessment in the senior secondary school: A review of the literature. *New Zealand Journal of Teachers' Work* 2 (2), 107–115.

Savignon, S. (1983) *Communicative Competence*. Reading, MA: Addison-Wesley.

Savignon, S. (1997) *Communicative Competence: Theory and Classroom Practice* (2nd edn). New York: McGraw-Hill.

Scott, A. and Butler, P. (2007) 'My teacher is learning like us': Teachers and students as language learners. *The New Zealand Language Teacher* 33, 11–16.

van Ek, J. (1977) *The Threshold Level for Modern Language Learning in Schools*. London: Longman.

Weimer, M. (2002) *Learner-Centered Teaching Five Key Changes to Practice*. San Francisco, CA: Jossey-Bass.

Widdowson, H.G. (1978) *Teaching Language as Communication*. Oxford: Oxford University Press.

Wilkins, D. (1976) *Notional Syllabuses*. Oxford: Oxford University Press.

Appendix 21.1 Benchmarking the *CEFR* against the New Zealand curriculum (taken from East (2012))

Common European Framework (2001)	
Level	Level descriptor: Users can …
A1	1. understand and use familiar everyday expressions and very basic phrases aimed at the satisfaction of needs of a concrete type; 2. introduce self and others; 3. ask and answer questions about personal details such as where he/she lives, people he/she knows and things he/she has; 4. interact in a simple way provided the other person talks slowly and clearly and is prepared to help.
A2	1. understand sentences and frequently used expressions related to areas of most immediate relevance (e.g. very basic personal and family information, shopping, local geography, employment); 2. communicate in simple and routine tasks requiring a simple and direct exchange of information on familiar and routine matters; 3. describe in simple terms aspects of background, immediate environment and matters in areas of immediate need.
B1	1. understand the main points of clear standard input on familiar matters regularly encountered in work, school, leisure, etc.; 2. deal with most situations likely to arise whilst travelling in an area where the language is spoken; 3. produce simple connected text on topics which are familiar or of personal interest; 4. describe experiences and events, dreams, hopes and ambitions; 5. briefly give reasons and explanations for opinions and plans.

New Zealand Curriculum (2007)	
Level	Proficiency statement: Students can …
1 - 2	1. understand and use familiar expressions and everyday vocabulary; 2. interact in a simple way in supported situations.
3 - 4	1. understand and construct simple texts using their knowledge of the target language; 2. describe aspects of their own background and immediate environment.
5 - 6	1. understand and produce more complex language; 2. communicate beyond the immediate context, for example, past and future events; 3. understand and produce a variety of text types.
7 - 8	1. use language variably and effectively to express and justify their own ideas and opinions, and support or challenge those of others; 2. use and identify the linguistic and cultural forms that guide interpretation and enable them to respond critically to texts.

Note: Commensurate with the desire not to constrain the language that students can use, articulating levels should not be interpreted as limiting the progression that students can make. It is easy to envisage that when some students reach the end of year 13 (level eight) they may well reach a level beyond *CEFR* level B1. Instead, the levels should be seen in the context of the curriculum requirement to specify eight levels of proficiency, balanced with the desire not to specify specific language, structures and topics for each level.

Commentary on Cases beyond Europe

Lynne Parmenter and Michael Byram

An area classified as 'beyond Europe' clearly encompasses huge diversity, and the chapters in Part 2 exemplify this. What is possibly more surprising is the degree of commonality among these cases, and between these and the European cases.

Firstly, the issue of 'chronological coincidence' that was discussed in the commentary on European cases is also apparent in all seven cases in Part 2. Whether in policy or academic discourse, the *CEFR* responds to an identified need or lack in current policy or practice at the time of education reform. The actual perceived need or lack varies from situation to situation, of course, but perceptions of the *CEFR* as a bridge to facilitate change are constant. This is seen in the United States, where the *CEFR* provided a form of self-assessment in a positive mode, in contrast to the deficit model of the Proficiency Guidelines. The same is true in Japan, if only at the academic level, where the *CEFR* is seen as a key to something that is proclaimed but not achieved in language education, be this a 'can-do' attitude or real classroom practice that focuses on language use rather than language knowledge.

Simultaneously, the cases from beyond Europe all demonstrate that the *CEFR* could not be referenced or used if it was too distant or unfamiliar, and it is usually the familiar that is appropriated first. Thus work on appropriating the scales could progress more quickly in the United States and New Zealand because the concept of such a scale was already familiar. Perhaps this accounts for another commonality in the cases beyond as well as within Europe, namely the use of the levels as an entry point, accompanied by a bias toward assessment rather than the learning and teaching aspects of the *CEFR*.

The key issue that countries beyond Europe have to tackle to an even greater extent than countries within Europe is how to situate the *CEFR* in relation to national/regional/local policy and systems. All seven cases in Part 2 grapple with this issue, having to create arguments and solutions much more complex than the appeal to European recommendations available to

European states. In this debate, issues of globalization, localization, acceptance, resistance, external authority and foreignness come into play. In almost all cases, there is reference to language education reform responding to globalization, although the point is made explicitly in the Argentinean contribution that this is globalization on the global periphery. Reference to international standards such as PISA is an example of the impact of global pressure. At the same time, all contributors highlight the processes and importance of localization, and it is clear from the examples that use of the *CEFR* diverges from country to country, as indeed does the selection and prioritization of aspects of the *CEFR* to be used.

This is true in European contexts too, of course, but in the cases beyond Europe, debates over globalization and localization are compounded by the 'alien' origins of what is explicitly a 'European' frame of reference. In some cases, such as in Colombia, this may be cast in a positive light, with the *CEFR* portrayed as an 'external authority', based on extensive research, which will facilitate Colombia's alignment with international standards in language education. In the United States, the appeal is less to the generalized 'international' other and more to the specific 'European' nature of the *CEFR*, or what Byrnes describes as the 'multilingual exuberance of the imaginary construct "Europe" with its strong tradition of language education in schools'. This is one of the few examples of discussion of direct 'borrowing' from a specific geographical other. In most cases, the fact that the *CEFR* is 'international' seems to be more significant than the fact that it is European.

Yet the international status of the *CEFR* also means that it is seen as 'foreign' or 'alien' in what may be a threatening way. In Colombia, whilst perceived as an 'authority', the origin of the document, together with its mode of policy implementation, has also been perceived as threatening. The tension of positive and negative seems here to be quite open. In Japan in contrast, the proposed solution to the foreignness, in some quarters at least, is to rewrite the *CEFR* as a specifically national document and rename it as such, thus concealing its 'foreign' origins. It is quite ironic that 'foreignness' should sometimes be perceived as negative, even among academics and policy-makers whose careers have been devoted to foreign language and culture education. Nonetheless, whatever the case, all contributors show awareness that the issue of situating the *CEFR* within a national/regional discourse and system of language education is complex but central in the adoption of the *CEFR* at all levels.

As well as commonalities among all seven cases beyond Europe, there are identifiable regional or cluster aspects, as is to be expected given the huge reach of the area. The first of these is linked to socioeconomic and political context. On the Human Development Index (United Nations Development Programme, undated) on measurements of education, health and income, the seven cases beyond Europe span positions ranging from 3 to 89 on the index of 169 countries. What this means in practice is that policy-makers, teachers and students have different perspectives on education, including language education, and may be facing challenges which are common to some of the cases but not to all. For example, barriers listed in the Argentina policy chapter, such as high drop-out rates in primary and secondary schools, crisis of teacher recruitment and retention, poorly qualified teachers, low salaries and problems with absenteeism, are likely to be familiar to people working in many other countries too, but are not challenges commonly faced in Japan or New Zealand, for example. The reality of everyday education cannot but impact on planning, implementation and negotiation of policy.

Another interesting regional aspect is the ideological and philosophical context. For Latin America, this is brought up explicitly in the Argentinean case, when the concept of 'ideological coherence' in the region is introduced, and again in the Colombian case, where appeal is made to the regional validity of the *CEFR* in that it is being used 'in a similar context' in Chile and Mexico. For the East Asian contributions from China, Japan and Taiwan, there is no explicit reference to a shared regional ideological or philosophical context. However, the issue of how the *CEFR* might be reconciled with the Confucian tradition of 'mastery' learning is raised in all three case studies, and this is a question that merits further investigation.

Turning from geographical to linguistic boundaries, one of the clearest commonalities among contributions from the cluster of countries in which the dominant language is not English is the emphasis on English. Even if the centrality of plurilingualism to the *CEFR* is recognized and understood in theory, the reality is that the *CEFR* is being widely seen as a tool of English education. To some extent, this is inevitable, given the dominance of English in the curriculum of most of the countries in Part 2, and its importance in determining the life chances of individuals. For example, in Taiwan, China and Japan, all countries where ability to use English in everyday life is rarely required, but ability to pass examinations in English determines education and employment prospects, the greatest impact of the *CEFR* has been on English language testing regimes. Efforts are being made to use the *CEFR* in other languages, to be sure, and this is well illustrated in the Japan chapter, but the fact is that in many countries, English has become so predominant that other languages hardly even register on the radar of many policy-makers and employers, and the *CEFR* can only have any effect if it impacts English language education.

As with the European cases, there are also many differences in influence and use of the *CEFR* in the seven cases beyond Europe. The state of multilingualism and multiculturalism in a society, the degree to which it is recognized, and the status accorded to this recognition, influence whether and to what extent plurilingual aspects of the *CEFR* are picked up and highlighted. In Colombia and New Zealand, therefore, plurilingualism and pluriculturalism are concepts that affirm the official multilingual and multicultural imaginary, and they can be highlighted. In Japan, on the contrary, where government still clings to the myth of homogeneity, a document promoting plurilingualism and pluriculturalism could be seen as destabilizing, and these aspects are generally not emphasized in academic discourse.

Connected to this is the degree of centralization of the control of education. The seven cases in Part 2 cover almost the entire range, from highly centralized to highly decentralized, and this leads to different concerns and issues in discussions of the appropriation of the *CEFR*. In countries with a highly centralized system, a decision at the top to adopt the *CEFR* would in principle mean that regional and local boards of education, materials developers, schools and teachers would have no choice, although the actual degree of compliance depends on the efficiency of the system and the degree of acceptance or resistance from all those involved. An example is the Ministry of Education in Colombia, which decreed that all educational institutions must align their programmes with the pre-established levels in the *CEFR*. Other highly centralized countries may use textbook authorization systems or detailed, obligatory syllabi. At the other end of the spectrum, more variety of approach is required in a highly decentralized system, and this is evident in the US case, where a whole range of dissemination methods is used, including the filming and distribution to language associations of a 30-minute interview with the director of the European Association of Quality Language Services. While the degree of centralization may not directly affect the adoption or rejection of the *CEFR*, it does have a significant impact on the way in which the *CEFR* is appropriated, used and disseminated.

Reference

United Nations Development Programme (undated) Human Development Reports. Online at http://hdr.undp.org/en/. Accessed on 20 March 2011.

Conclusion

Lynne Parmenter and Michael Byram

The aim of this chapter is to identify the main themes emerging from the contributions to this book, exploring how they reflect and contribute to theories concerning the globalization of education. The contributions from countries in and beyond Europe provide rich detail but they also go further than illustrating the process or stages of educational 'borrowing' or 'migration', providing new insights into the often messy business of motivations, structures and relationships involved in education policy change. The major themes discussed in this chapter are the increasing importance of global frames of reference for education, mobilities and communications, networks, policy-academic relationships, negotiation of discourse and happenstance.

Global Frames of Reference

The increasing prominence of global frames of reference for education is a relatively new phenomenon, relating to extra-national rather than international influence. This is where the term 'borrowing', in its literal meaning of using something that belongs to another, can be misleading. Traditionally, the Ministry of Education of a particular country may have 'borrowed' and adapted the policy of another specific country, where the policy is closely identified as belonging to the country of origin. Recent policy developments such as the *CEFR* are quite different, in that they never specifically 'belong' to a particular country. They may be associated with a particular entity, in the way that the *CEFR* is associated with the Council of Europe, or the Millennium Development Goals are associated with the United Nations, but they transcend the restraints of ownership and are available to all. In the area of education policy, where there is often a strong emphasis on national interests and the maintenance of national identity and cultural traditions, this issue of ownership can be a sensitive one, and deterritorialization can be a major advantage, as is evident in several of the contributions, in quite different ways. The Bulgarian case shows how an extra-national policy can be appropriated as a symbol of Europeanization and as a link to transnationalism, but it is significant that the *CEFR* is not seen as being 'borrowed', but belongs to Bulgaria as much as any other country. Outside Europe, too, the fact that *CEFR* is an extra-national rather than national policy seems to favour its adoption, with Argentina being a good example of the way in which national or regional ideologies and policies can be aligned with an extra-national framework to further national interests in a global context. In these and other cases, the appropriation of the *CEFR* as an extra-national frame of reference, in whatever form, is used to legitimate or validate national or regional language education policy, a use which is often less politically acceptable in the case of 'borrowing' from another national education system.

A second way in which global frames of reference seem to be linked to the appropriation of the *CEFR* is through international assessment and comparison regimes. Several contributions mention the perceived gap between national and international language competence as a push factor in incorporating elements of the *CEFR* into national policy. Goullier's description of 'the vague feeling of inadequate performance' leading to international comparisons, a 'proven' gap in competence and subsequent recourse to the *CEFR*, especially to its levels of competence, is not unique to France. The creation of national education inadequacy complexes, heated by the fires of PISA, TIMMS, TOEIC and TOEFL comparative statistics, lead to a global frame of reference in which catching up with 'international standards' can become an obsession at worst, and a lever for education funding at best. Hu's description of the PISA shock in Germany provides an excellent example of the logic of this process.

Within this context of the global playing field of education competition, the *CEFR* has two major attractions. The first is that it offers a 'common language' that can be shared by language educators across national boundaries. The second is that it provides clear goals and measurable achievement by reference to the levels. Like the PISA results tables, the Millennium Development Goals or TOEIC international statistics, the capacity of the *CEFR* to provide a clear, easily comprehensible, international overview of achievement in a particular aspect of education or competence means that it can take its place as a global frame of reference, thus becoming more available and attractive for appropriation by national, regional and local organizations and systems.

A third way in which the contributions prove that global frames of reference are relevant to the spread of the *CEFR* is through the way in which policy-makers and academics, faced with specific challenges in their own contexts, 'shop around' globally for answers to their problems, especially in the cases beyond Europe. This phenomenon of 'policy shopping', which in itself is an example of 'the institutionalization of the policies of marketisation' (Furedi, 2011: 1) is most explicit in the policy contribution from Colombia, where Peña Dix and de Mejia describe the process of reviewing international standards from Australia, Britain, the United States, Ireland, Canada and Spain, and outline the advantages of the *CEFR* as being its richness, lack of curriculum specificity, contextualized, integral vision of languages, and the fact that most of the supporting documentation and analysis is free. In other countries, too, the *CEFR* was compared and selected from a range of possibilities, or sometimes used in conjunction with other standards, such as the ACTFL Young Learners Scale in Taiwan. Further empirical research is necessary to investigate why the *CEFR* is selected or not selected in specific contexts, but contributions to this volume seem to support the point made in the Introduction that the influence of the *CEFR* is due in part at least to its inherent quality in the global education marketplace.

Mobilities and Communications

One of the classic definitions of globalization is time-space compression. Compression of time and space has led to increased mobility on the part of individuals, and also to many more opportunities for direct and indirect communication across cultures and national boundaries. It seems reasonable to assume that this has also been a major factor in the use of the *CEFR* not only within, but also way beyond, Europe. Part of this is very deliberate, an example being teams of Japanese researchers visiting the Council of Europe Language Policy Division in person, then holding conferences, publishing and perhaps introducing elements of the *CEFR* to their own universities in Japan. The same phenomenon is described in relation to the United States in the chapter by van Houten. This would have been much less likely to happen 30 years ago, when air fares were prohibitively expensive, conferences were much more local, and publications were not internet-searchable but often lingered unread in a departmental library. The latter scenario is indeed still closer to reality in many places and helps to explain the imbalance of knowledge production and dissemination. In most places where the *CEFR* has been influential, though, the influence of increased mobility and communications is evident, albeit in a less planned way than in the Japanese and US cases.

In general, the easy availability of information about systems and policies to anyone with access to the internet and some knowledge of English is crucial, although the latter is becoming less important with the creation and constant updates of Google Translate. While it was quite difficult to obtain first-hand information about education policies in most countries only 20 years ago, many ministries of education and equivalent bodies now not only have multilingual websites, but provide full policy and curriculum documents for any interested party to read. The same is true for extra-national documents such as the *CEFR*, and its accessibility and searchability (it comes top on most search engines under the search terms '*CEFR*' or '*CECR*'), together with the fact that it has been translated into almost 40 languages, increases its visibility and availability worldwide.

As a shared resource made possible by mobilities and communications, therefore, the wide availability of the *CEFR* can be seen in a positive light, as it serves to mirror, highlight and explain issues that are important to people in very different contexts. In this respect, as Tonkin (2003: 331) suggests:

> A greater understanding of the issues involved... may help ultimately to move our collective strategy towards a linguistic order that is fairer, more equitable and more effective.

As several authors in this volume point out, this does not mean that the *CEFR* requires conformity to a predetermined vision of what a global linguistic order should be, but rather that it provides 'a common language' to talk about language education. Within and across countries and regions, this is perhaps one of the most valuable contributions of the *CEFR* to global communication regarding language education.

Networks

Comparative analysis of policy networks is still relatively rare (Nagel, 2010: 200). One key theme that seems to emerge across a whole range of national and regional contexts in this book is the significant role played by networks in the spread of the *CEFR* within and, possibly even more so, beyond Europe. An interesting example of this is the way in which bodies closely associated with specific national governments and languages take a leading role in the promotion of the *CEFR* before it becomes the subject of governmental policy. One example, described by van Houten, is the sponsoring of workshops and seminars for German teachers in the United States by the Goethe-Institut, and a similar role was played by the British Council in Colombia. It would be very interesting to find out how widespread this phenomenon is, and the extent to which it is promulgated as a deliberate policy to introduce European education ideas to other parts of the world, or whether it is merely a function of familiarity. Whichever it is, there is certainly scope for investigation of the role of such organizations in the globalizing of educational and cultural policy.

Teacher associations seem to be important networks all over the world. One example is the role of the American Association of Teachers of German in promoting the *CEFR* in the United States. Another example, which is interesting in terms of its border-crossing role, is the influence of the Association of Japanese Teachers in Europe on debates on the *CEFR* within Japan.

Teacher associations coexist with a wide range of other networks, at a number of levels. In his analysis of awareness of the *CEFR* in Poland, Poszytek mentions teacher training centres, publishers, private training institutions, universities and central institutions affiliated to the ministry. Many teachers and teacher educators are involved with one or more of these sources of information and training, but networks can also cover the spectrum from colleagues within an institution to an internet-based SIG to the other network mentioned by Poszytek, which is the network of people directly involved with the Council of Europe Language Policy Division. Increasingly, networks also include informal contacts among policy-makers and academics internationally, as there are so many more opportunities than ever before for face-to-face interaction through conferences, visits and other events, backed up by the possibility of face-to-face interaction through technology. All these networks serve a function in spreading information and ideas, and in influencing change in thinking and policy, and our question in the introduction as to whether Steiner-Khamsi's 'epidemic' metaphor would find some empirical support in this book has been answered positively.

What is interesting about networks in relation to the influence of the *CEFR* is how they reflect the way that, even if the world is not yet as 'flat' as Friedman (2005) claims, more 'horizontal' flows of information and influence are beginning to affect international education policy migration. The role of international language teacher professionals in language education policy change, in particular, is one that would merit further research. The phenomenon serves as a pertinent illustration of Castells's claims about the network society:

> Thus, while there are still power relationships in society, the bypassing of centres by flows of information circulating in networks creates a new, fundamental hierarchy: the power of flows takes precedence over the flows of power. (Castells, 2000: 20)

Policy-Academic Relationships

One way in which there are quite significant differences between the cases in this book is in the relationships between policy-makers and academics as determined by the educational structure in each country or region. In some cases, such as New Zealand and Argentina, there is a high degree of fluidity, so that academics can be directly involved in policy-making, and policy-makers are quite likely to transfer out of policy-making into universities or schools. This fluidity, combined with commissioned research to inform policy and substantial policy consultation processes in New Zealand, makes for a situation where there is a close fit between policy and research, to the extent at least that even if individuals or groups do not agree, they know what the other is talking about.

In other countries, such as Japan and to some extent Germany, there is a sharp distinction between policy-makers, who are career civil servants, usually rotated between departments and job roles, and academics, who have much more freedom to research and have opinions about language education, but much less power to actually implement policy. In Japan, committees of academics, professionals and business people are appointed by the Ministry of Education to advise policy-makers during the process of drawing up reforms, but these committees have varying degrees of influence and anyone advocating radical change is extremely unlikely to be appointed to a committee, so policy change tends to be slow and heavily influenced by more conservative academics.

New Zealand and Japan are probably the two extremes in terms of policy-academic relations in the cases in this book, but it is interesting to consider the impact of such relations on the influence of the *CEFR* and other extra-national policies, and this is another area which would be fascinating to research in greater depth.

Negotiation of Discourse

The way that contributors create and negotiate discourses around the *CEFR* is another theme worthy of attention. At one level, there is a discernible gap here between the European and beyond-European cases. Discourses in Europe tend to focus on which aspects of the *CEFR* have been accepted, rejected and ignored. As Komorowska points out in discussion of the reaction to the *CEFR* in Poland, resistance or rejection of the *CEFR* at this specific point in Polish history ran the risk of being seen as outdated or anti-European, so lack of response was the most reliable indicator of resistance. Beyond Europe, in contrast, there is no statutory requirement or political pressure to use the *CEFR*, so the discourse here is centred on adoption or appropriation, with the emphasis on justification for reference to a 'foreign' policy.

This difference is significant, but even more striking is the way in which all cases make some reference to the conflicting discourses of the 'instrumental' (neo-liberal/ functional/ competitive) aims of language education and the 'educational' (traditional/ sociocultural/noble) aims of language education. Maguire (2010: 59) claims that, 'dominant discourses emphasizing the economic aims of education currently seem to have displaced alternative discourses'.

The advantage of the *CEFR* is that it responds to both. Through the scales and applications in assessment, it provides a way of aligning individual achievement to global standards, and this is very often the entry point for policy-makers keen to join the global race to be recognized as achieving high standards. At the same time, as emphasized in the introduction, the *CEFR* is a value-laden document, and its view of the aims of language education accords with what Porto and Barboni describe as 'the discovery of what unites human beings, with a focus on commonalities and bonds, in an attempt to be as much at ease as possible with each others' languages, cultures, and individualities'. Porto goes on to claim that foreign language education reform has been propelled in Argentina by the realization that 'educational purposes can coexist with functional-pragmatic goals'. This is a sentiment echoed by many other contributors, and the success of the *CEFR* internationally may well be due in part to the fact that it answers the needs of educators to work within both discourses.

Happenstance

Finally, a totally unexpected theme that emerged from the cases in the book is happenstance. It was quite surprising for us as editors to read how often the adoption of aspects of the *CEFR* occurred through sheer chance – a particular person in a particular place at a particular time. Two examples that stand out are China and New Zealand. In the Chinese case, one of Zou's interviewees happened to come across the *CEFR* in some research on testing and mentioned it to one of the chief advisors to a policy-maker in the Ministry of Education, who then presumably thought the information worthy of being passed on. In New Zealand, happenstance was even more dependent on the individual, in that the one of the lead members of the group designing and writing curriculum for the new 'learning languages' area was knowledgeable and enthusiastic about the *CEFR*, and this led to significant influence. Such individual happenstance, together with the 'chronological coincidence' described by Goullier and echoed in almost every chapter, suggests that the globalization of education is a much less systematic process than is often assumed. Again, it would be interesting to know whether these are isolated examples, or whether happenstance is actually quite common. Whether, using John Trim's citation from Goethe, there are more examples of the 'the lamp [that] awaits the flame that will ignite it'.

Conclusion

In our introduction we said that our hope is to interest at least two kinds of reader: those interested in the impact of the *CEFR* and those concerned with comparative education and the globalization and borrowing of education policy. In many ways the chapters speak for themselves, particularly on the question of the impact of the *CEFR*, but it has also become clear from our comparative reading of the chapters that the phenomenon of the globalization of education policy is well exemplified here. Perhaps it might be expected that those responsible for foreign language education would pay attention to developments in other countries and continents and that the influence of the *CEFR* might be greater than comparable documents in other areas of the curriculum. We have seen some evidence that this is the case, that for example the ability to read documents in a foreign language is important, that cultural institutions and teachers' organizations can be significant catalysts. We have also seen some indication of national bias in the reception of the *CEFR*, contrary perhaps to the internationalist openness to other ways of thinking that language educators see as one of their purposes in educating their learners.

As always, a project such as this begins to answer some questions and opens up others. We have argued that the cases presented here – cases which we chose in a focused rather than random way – suggest that globalization of policy is an empirically observable phenomenon. We can, however, only speculate about the comparable openness of other areas of the curriculum to policy globalization. There is a need to pursue the analysis of the power of networks. There is a need to theorize the 'happenstance' that appears contrary to systematic dissemination and to the concept of theorization itself. Further case studies would help to clarify some of these issues, but in the meantime we hope that this book will satisfy but also stimulate our readers, whether their focus is on language teaching or comparative studies or both.

References

Castells, M. (2000) *The Rise of the Network Society* (2nd edn). Oxford: Blackwell.
Friedman, T. (2005) *The World is Flat: A Brief History of the Twenty-First Century*. New York: Picador.

Furedi, F. (2011) Introduction. In M. Molesworth, R. Scullion and E. Nixon (eds) *The Marketisation of Higher Education and the Student as Consumer.* Abingdon: Routledge.
Maguire, M. (2010) Towards a sociology of the global teacher. In M. Apple, S. Ball and L. Gandin (eds) *The Routledge International Handbook of the Sociology of Education.* Abingdon: Routledge.
Nagel, A-K. (2010) Comparing education policy networks. In K. Martens, A-K Nagel, M. Windzio and A. Weymann (eds) *Transformation of Education Policy.* Basingstoke: Palgrave Macmillan.
Tonkin, H. (2003) The search for a global linguistic strategy. In J. Maurais and M. Morris (eds) *Languages in a Globalising World.* Cambridge: Cambridge University Press.